D0329237

Religion

282
7
09

# CATHOLIC BELIEFS AND TRADITIONS

## *Ancient and Ever New*

### Rev. John F. O'Grady

**PAULIST PRESS**
New York • Mahwah, N.J.

Nyack College Library

Scripture quotations are either the author's own translation or are taken from the Revised Standard Version of the Bible, Old Testament copyright © 1952, New Testament copyright © 1946 by Division of Christian Education of the National Council of Churches of Christ in the United States of America. Used by permission. All rights reserved. Excerpts from the English translation of *The Roman Missal,* copyright © 1973, International Committee on English in the Liturgy, Inc. (ICEL); excerpts from the English translation of *Rite of Penance,* copyright© 1974, ICEL; excerpts from the English translation of *Rite of Confirmation,* 2nd edition, copyright © 1975, ICEL. All rights reserved. Excerpts from the English translation of the *Catechism of the Catholic Church* for use in the United States of America, copyright © 1994, United States Catholic Conference, Inc.–Libreria Editrice Vaticana. Used with permission. Excerpts from *The Documents of Vatican II,* edited by Walter M. Abbott, S.J., copyright © 1966, America Press. All rights reserved. Reprinted with permission of America Press, Inc. Four-line excerpt from "Talk" by Yvgeny Yevtushenko, from *Selected Poems: Yevtushenko,* translated by Robin Milner-Gulland and Peter Levi (Penguin Books, 1962), copyright © 1962 Robin Milner-Gulland and Peter Levi. Used with permission of the Penguin Group, UK. Three-line excerpt from "Do Not Go Gentle Into That Good Night" by Dylan Thomas, from *The Poems of Dylan Thomas,* copyright © 1952 by Dylan Thomas. Reprinted by permission of New Directions Publishing Company. Excerpt from "We Remember" by Mary Haugen, copyright © 1980 GIA Productions, Inc., Chicago, Illinois. All rights reserved. Used with permission.

NIHIL OBSTAT:
The Reverend John Roos, J.C.D.
*Censor Librorum*

IMPRIMATUR:
The Most Reverend Howard J. Hubbard, D.D.
*Bishop of Albany*
July 5, 2001

The Nihil Obstat and Imprimatur are official declarations that a book or pamphlet is free of doctrinal or moral error. No implication is contained therein that those who have granted the Nihil Obstat or Imprimatur agree with the contents, opinions or statements expressed.

COVER DESIGN BY A. MICHAEL VELTHAUS

BOOK DESIGN BY JOSEPH E. PETTA

Copyright © 2001 by John F. O'Grady

All rights reserved. No part of this book may be reproduced or transmitted in any form or by any means, electronic or mechanical, including photocopying, recording or by any information storage and retrieval system without permission in writing from the Publisher.

Library of Congress Cataloging-in-Publication Data

O'Grady, John F.
    Catholic beliefs and traditions : ancient and ever new / John F. O'Grady.
        p.   cm.
    Includes bibliographical references and index.
    ISBN 0-8091-4047-0 (alk. paper)
    1. Catholic Church–Doctrines. 2. Catholic Church–Customs and practices. I. Title.

BX1751.3 .O36 2001
282–dc21

                                                                        2001051026

Published by Paulist Press
997 Macarthur Boulevard
Mahwah, New Jersey 07430

www.paulistpress.com

Printed and bound in the
United States of America

# 48003300

# TABLE OF CONTENTS

For the religious women and men who taught me the traditions:

*Sisters, Servants of the Immaculate Heart of Mary of Westchester*
*Congregation of the Mission (Vincentian Fathers)*
*Order of St. Benedict (Benedictine Fathers)*
*Order of Preachers (Dominican Fathers)*
*Society of Jesus (Jesuit Fathers)*

# PREFACE

I have deliberately used the plural in the title of this work: beliefs and traditions. The Catholic Church has many beliefs and traditions. Most think of the Catholic Church as the Roman Catholic Church but, in fact, along with the Roman rite, the Catholic Church has the Maronite rite, the Chaldean rite and a host of other Eastern churches, all of which form part of the Catholic heritage. The classic definition of the Catholic Church—people with the same faith and the same sacraments under the authority of the bishop of Rome—join all of these beliefs and traditions together. The Eastern Catholic churches share these three characteristics but differ from the Roman Catholic Church in regard to liturgy, spirituality, theology and law.

Even within the Roman Catholic Church there exist a variety of beliefs and traditions. Compare the *Catechism of the Council of Trent* to the *Baltimore Catechism* and then to the present *Catechism of the Catholic Church* to see how many traditions not only exist but also seem to come and go. To be Catholic is to be one with plurality and diversity. Different theologies, different liturgies, different spiritualities, different laws and discipline characterize the Catholic Church more than any uniformity. Belief and tradition narrow. Beliefs and traditions broaden.

A church that has been in existence for two thousand years must have different beliefs and traditions. A church universal, alive in every country and in every language and culture also multiplies traditions. As people change in their understanding of themselves, they also change in their understanding of God. Yet, in the midst of discontinuity, some continuity always remains.

Studying Catholic beliefs and traditions liberates and gives security and roots. No one can claim an exclusive right to any one belief or tradition or even to a collection of beliefs and traditions. The plurality itself enriches and distinguishes. Catholics are not Baptists or Methodists or Anglicans. Catholics are also not Orthodox, whether Greek or Russian. Catholics are Catholics precisely because of their varied beliefs and traditions. The present crisis among some Catholics may lie in the failure to appreciate the diversity of the beliefs and traditions.

Writing a book about Catholic beliefs and traditions should bring an uneasiness to any writer, even one privileged not only to have grown up in the Catholic Church but to have lived through the turmoil of the past thirty years. Who can know the history of an international institution of two thousand years? Who can know the many theologies and practices of this same institution of two thousand years?

History and theology humble their students. No one can ever know it all. The phenomenon looms too large in the foreground hiding the background of centuries. Even the interpreter of the traditions must suffer, and will never overcome, the limitations of being an individual in a given time and place. But if beliefs and traditions truly liberate, then Catholics, and especially American Catholics, will benefit.

Each section of every chapter of this book deserves a book on its own. That, of course, would defeat the very purpose of this writing. What makes a Catholic a Catholic rather than a member of some other Christian denomination? What beliefs and traditions form the foundation for this Christian institution of almost two thousand years? How do American Catholics differ from other Catholics and how are they the same? What new interpretations of age-old beliefs and traditions have taken place in recent years? Where is the continuity and where is the discontinuity?

This book arose from a need to teach a course on Catholicism. I wanted to use a book heavily grounded in Scripture and also one that would respond to the questions of young American Catholics. I also wanted to include some of the beliefs and traditions with which their parents and grandparents could identify.

While developing the different chapters I continued to grow in my realization of just how complicated some of these so called "simple beliefs" really were. Images of God and of Jesus, models of the Church and the problem of evil and sin, death, judgment, heaven and hell and the ever elusive understanding of grace in Catholic theology—all are part of the Catholic heritage and each one seems to offer more questions than easy answers.

All of these Catholic beliefs and traditions fall under the general rubric of mystery, not in the sense that no one can understand anything about them, but rather that no one can ever *fully* understand. Mystery involves inexhaustible intelligibility. This book offers some light for the paths of those who are interested in continuing the centuries-old effort of faith seeking understanding.

The Bible forms the heart of everything I have written. Centuries of traditions and human efforts to understand create a kind of "body" that surrounds the "heart" of faith. As in the analogy of Paul, each part of this body needs the other and each contributes to what makes a Catholic a Catholic. Some parts receive more attention than others. Sometimes this unequal distribution reflects my own understanding or lack thereof. At other times I have decided that complex issues need more reflection or that some beliefs and traditions need more emphasis for an American Catholic audience at the beginning of the third millennium.

This book is written for the ordinary believer, not the expert. In my opinion the latter have too many books and the former have too few. I want to help the confused college student who questions his or her Catholic heritage as well as the frequently disillusioned Sunday churchgoer who often feels in the dark about what has happened to the Catholic Church in the past thirty years. The bibliography included at the end, along with the references within the text, offer to the interested reader ample opportunities for further study.

Giving credit where it is due, I am grateful to the help of Dr. Edward R. Sunshine in dealing with moral issues. Judge Lurana Snow, while a graduate student at Barry, devoted much time to the study of conscience in the Catholic tradition. She helped me with that particular chapter. Dr. Mark E. Wedig, O.P., offered many helpful suggestions regarding the chapter on liturgy and sacraments. Dr. Pedro B. Gonzalez helped with the chapter on the philosophical notions of God. The Rev. Maurice Hogan of Maynooth Seminary in Dublin read the entire manuscript and offered many insightful and clarifying suggestions concerning my use of Scripture. Finally, Dr. Mary Ann Jungbauer performed the marvelous and accurate service of proofreading the entire text, including checking every biblical reference. I live grateful to each one.

I continue to write in the summers in Voorheesville, New York, and the rest of the year in the sunshine of Florida. Summer and sunshine always give hope to a sometimes dark world. In a similar way the Catholic Church has had its dark side but also continues to give much light to those who look. "The light shines in the darkness and the darkness has not overcome it" (John 1:5).

Feast of St. Monica
August 27, 2001
Miami, Florida

# INTRODUCTION: CATHOLIC TRADITIONS, AMERICAN TRADITIONS

Traditions are beliefs, practices, events and rituals that are passed from one generation to another. The New Testament has two words for tradition, *parathaekae* and *paradosis*. The first word means that whatever is passed on does not change in the process, while the second implies that the tradition is affected, modified, adapted. Something remains but something changes. Both the Catholic Church and the United States possess each of these two kinds of traditions.

A Bible can be passed on from one generation to another and over the years the pages are affected by the oil of the hands that have turned the pages. Light may discolor the paper, and some pages may even become torn. The Bible remains part of the family but changes in its appearance as one generation slides into another. On the other hand, the Bible can be passed on while remaining in its unopened box, never shedding its transparent protective cover. In each instance the Bible is passed on, the tradition continues, but the process and the end result could not be more dissimilar.

The Catholic Church has many traditions, as do Americans. One generation of Catholics hands on their Catholic faith to the next, as one American family hands on the meaning of being an American to its children. Most American Catholics, whether they belong to the Roman rite or to one of the many other rites within the Catholic tradition, are Catholic because they were born

1

Catholic. The Catholic traditions come from parents and take root within a family. They also come from Catholic schools and the actual experience of living as a Catholic, a member of a particular Catholic community. Some people freely choose this particular expression of Christianity, but for most, being "Catholic" is in the bones. Even when these same Catholics become "fallen away," they still retain their fundamental Catholic outlook on life. Like genetic characteristics, being a Catholic seems to determine a person forever. The traditions do not die easily.

Some nationalities seem to be identified with being Catholic. The Irish and the Poles, the Italians and the French, the Spanish and the Austrians—all are more likely to be Catholic than to adhere to any of the other religious traditions in their respective countries. For some, being a Catholic becomes joined to nationalism. "Irish Catholic" seems to go together as does "Polish Catholic." While each of these nationalities has a different outlook on what it means to be Catholic, at the same time they share much in common. The traditions are the same and yet are expressed differently. Throw in the adjective "American Catholic" along with those other nationalities and the matter becomes ever more complicated.

Americans are freedom-loving people, fiercely independent, generous in forgiving yet often intolerant of anyone who wants to limit their horizon. Americans are generous and fair, like to think for themselves, try new things and never fear new possibilities. Americans do not like any human interference from above, especially in their personal lives. Americans like the underdog and support and cheer as the lesser takes over and conquers the greater. They readily accept a belief in God, whom they regard as the ultimate source of their being and promise for the future, but are suspicious of anyone who claims to act in the name of God. Yet, one out of four or five Americans is Roman Catholic. Why?

The answer that they were born Catholics does not suffice. Some other reason must exist as to why the Roman Catholic Church has taken root so deeply in this country. Even the majority of Americans who are not Roman Catholic tend to admire this Church, and yearly tens of thousands of Americans from other religious traditions make a profession of faith as Roman Catholics. What is it in this Church that is so compatible with the American experience? Certain characteristics of the Roman Catholic traditions show some correspondence to the historical experience of being an American. Perhaps that explains some of the reasons why so many Americans are Catholic.

## The Goodness of Creation

The United States is a beautiful country from sea to shining sea. Mountains, lakes, oceans, prairies, deserts, wetlands, filled with charming towns, picturesque villages and dominating cities mix and match through a country extending three thousand by fifteen hundred miles. Of course in this same expanse polluted rivers, hovels and shacks, teeming tenements and dirty streets interact to form a contrast that shames and embarrasses. Still, there is goodness in creation and in the country in spite of all that is bad and evil. Nothing can ever destroy the goodness that God has bestowed in creation: "And God looked on everything he had made, and behold it was very good" (Gen 1:31). Americans believe in the goodness and beauty of their country.

Catholics believe in the goodness of creation in spite of the presence of evil. Great cities are good even if sometimes dirty and crime-laden. Towns and villages are good even if controlled by corrupt politicians. Rivers and mountains and lakes and oceans are beautiful even if not appreciated and abused. God has made a wonderful world and no amount of evil and sin and corruption can ever destroy the goodness that God has implanted in the universe. Good will win out. Evil will never completely destroy goodness. A dark, cloudy night tries to obscure the moon, but the moon always wins. So goodness will always win, even if it is not so evident at one moment of time. Americans and Catholics agree on the goodness of creation.

# People Are Good

> Then God said, "Let us make man in our image, after our likeness; and let them have dominion over the fish of the sea, and over the birds of the air, and over the cattle, and over all the wild animals of the earth, and over every creeping thing that creeps on the earth." So God created man in his own image, in the image of God he created them, male and female he created them. (Gen 1:26–27)

God created the human family to act as vice-regents in creation. Both male and female take the place of God in creation. They are to follow the example of God in acting responsibly in creation. They are to be creative not only in producing other human beings but in making this world a better place for all. The phrase "created in the image of God" *(selem)* emphasizes the role of people in taking the place of God. "Created in the likeness of God" *(demut)* emphasizes the creative aspect of every individual, especially the procreative activity (Vogels: 3–7). Since man and woman are created in the image of God, the possibility of a relationship with God exists. The responsibility in creation for the human race flows from how people are created. God said it was good, and God created men and women to act in God's place and be creative. Nothing can destroy this fundamental goodness of the human person. Individuals may try to destroy how they have been created but nothing can take away what God has given. Perhaps this explains the love of Americans for the underdog. Both Americans and Catholics readily accept the basic goodness of all people, and especially the disadvantaged.

# Faith and Reason

The Enlightenment affected the founding fathers of the United States. As a movement it rejected external authority in favor of the authority of reason. People accept the truth, not on account of the proclamation of some office holder but because good reasons exist for believing it to be true. The Enlightenment sounded a call for freedom of inquiry, freedom in decision making and freedom in action. Each of these had its effect on the Constitution of the United States.

At first glance the concept of the authority of reason may appear to be contrary to the authority of the Roman Catholic Church. In fact, the Catholic Church has always celebrated human reason. No contradiction can exist between what the human mind can perceive and what the human person can believe:

> The fundamental harmony between the knowledge of faith and the knowledge of philosophy is once again confirmed. Faith asks that its object be understood with the help of reason; and at the summit of its searching, reason acknowledges that it cannot do without what faith presents.
>
> (John Paul II, *Fides et Ratio,* no. 42)

Theology in its traditional definition has always been faith seeking understanding. Human reason has always been used by the great thinkers of the Catholic tradition from Augustine to Aquinas to Newman to Rahner. Certainly in times past some individual members of the Catholic tradition attempted to impose the authority of office over human reason, but such has never been the continuous tradition of the Roman Catholic Church. People have to think. People have to question. People have to reason and draw conclusions in an atmosphere of freedom.

The Roman Catholic approach to Christian theology draws upon not one tradition but many traditions. The thoughts of Aristotle and Plato found expression in medieval theology. Kant, Hegel, Marcel, Heidegger, Maritain, Gilson, Lonergan—all have influenced contemporary theology. The thinking of history's finest minds supports faith even as faith can go beyond their reasoning. Limitations exist, but no one can ever exclude any aspect of human knowledge from influencing the endless effort of faith seeking understanding. Anthropology, psychology, sociology, linguistics and science have made their contribution to understanding faith. For as the human person understands more about being human, so this understanding must of necessity affect how a person perceives God. Even the slightest change in knowledge brings about a shift, slight or considerable, in the understanding of God. Reason, as a continuing gift, never reaches the point of fulfillment. Knowledge, like love, is infinite in its expressions and in its potential. The Catholic celebrates human reason, and the American experience rests upon the ability of reason to accomplish anything in freedom.

## Sacramentality

The flag rises and the "Star-Spangled Banner" begins. People stand with their hands over their hearts and celebrate an Olympic medal, the opening of a sports event, a graduation from college. The ritual, the symbols, the music touch the hearts of the participants, filling them with pride. Americans love their symbols and their rituals. The spiritual finds expression in the physical, the natural and the earthly. Some cloth with red and white stripes and a galaxy of stars on a field of blue remains in one sense only cloth and color and arrangement but is in another sense so much more. No wonder some people want to burn the flag while others want to have a constitutional amendment outlawing such flag burning. Americans are caught between the love of their country symbolized in the flag and their love of an individual freedom ensuring any American the right to burn the very symbol of the country that gives them freedom.

True symbols contain the reality they express even if never completely. The Roman Catholic Church loves symbols and rituals. In Catholic belief, water is more than water. It not only gives life naturally, but the waters of Baptism provide a new and spiritual life. Bread and wine are more than a meal but a sacred banquet in which the believers experience the presence of the Lord Jesus. Oil has a healing quality and a strengthening power. In the context of Baptism, Confirmation, Orders and the Anointing of the Sick, people of faith become empowered and blessed. Roman Catholics use symbols frequently to express contact with the nonmaterial world, the spiritual reality existing everywhere and at all times.

Ritual entices and fascinates. When President John F. Kennedy died, his sorrowing widow offered to a grief-stricken country and world a ritual that glued millions to television sets.

The lying-in-repose at the Capitol, the kissing of the casket, the procession from the White House to the cathedral, the ceremonies at Arlington—each movement expressed a solemn grief and a solemn respect for the slain president. Symbols filled the ritual: the riderless horse with the boots in reverse, the flag-draped casket and, finally, the eternal flame. The ritual remains burned into the consciousness of everyone who watched.

The Roman Catholic Church celebrates the presence of God in the Lord Jesus through ritual and symbol. Carefully orchestrated movement, the repetition of a patterned behavior in daily and Sunday Mass, the prayers and actions associated with each of the sacraments, the centuries-old rituals of pope, bishop, priest and people, all contribute to an awareness of the sacred. Even the presence of stained glass, organ and choir music, the smell of incense, singing of hymns and prayers combined with movement contribute to an acute awareness of some contact with the divine. Symbols and ritual contribute to the soul of the Roman Catholic traditions and nourish the spirit of everyone who participates.

## Catholic and Universal

The Catholic Church, as distinguished from the Protestant, Orthodox or Anglican Churches, has always had a worldwide and universal vision. The principal reason the pope travels each year to many parts of the world is to meet the Catholics living in each place, even if he also meets other Christians and people from other or no religious traditions. "Catholic" stretches beyond national boundaries. The Catholic Church is one of the truly international organizations in the world today: not just European or Western but also Latino, African and Asian. Every race and culture find welcome within the arms of the Catholic Church.

Of course, other churches also claim a universality embracing all cultures and races, but no other church exhibits a universality to compare with that of the Catholic Church. Catholic rituals and sacraments are celebrated in every known language and in every country of this world. Many races and countries bring their own distinctive elements to their observance of these Catholic traditions, but all are united in the same faith, the same sacraments and under the same authority of the bishop of Rome. The one universal Church becomes multiple in time and space, and the multiplicity contributes to the strengthening of the unity of the Church of Jesus Christ.

The United States experiences its own kind of universality. Its residents include members of every race and ethnic origin and nationality. Like the Catholic Church, the United States is both one and diverse. The diversity of its population has always strengthened this country, adding new life. Americans pride themselves on assimilation, making everyone feel at home and allowing all people to make their own contribution. They may retain some elements from former countries or traditions, but soon, and especially through their children, they become part of the encompassing American culture. The same principle exists in the Catholic Church.

## Mediation

If objects can represent something other than what they are, then people can also represent otherness. God remains God. But if God wishes to communicate with humans, then God must use humans. God has communicated to the human race through Abraham and Moses, through the prophets and John the Baptist and Jesus and Mary, his mother, and all the men and women saints of thousands of years. A mediator can bring two individuals together. People mediate God to other people. Since everyone is created in the image of God, then everyone can speak the Word of God to others. Certain individuals have heard this Word, made it their own and were gifted sufficiently to speak this same Word to other people. Historically the Church calls these holy men and women saints. In the Christian tradition the one principal mediator is Jesus himself: the divine Son of God and the human son of Mary. In Jesus the divine has entered into human history in a historical person, and the historical person has become the mediator between God and other human beings.

In American history many individuals have been mediators. Certainly priests, ministers and rabbis have always acted in a role of bringing people to God and God to people. But American spirituality has never been limited to official priests and ministers. Many men and women who were not officially ordained have acted as mediators between God and people. Thomas Jefferson has been characterized as a deist, and perhaps he was. But Jefferson also mediated a profound spirituality to the people of his own day and continues to do so for the people of our own time. Abraham Lincoln was mediator between North and South and black and white. Although this mediation involved a bloody war of fratricide, it concluded with people of color and the white population living together freely. In more recent American history, Martin Luther King, Jr., was a mediator in bringing black and white together under the fatherhood of the one God. Clara Barton mediated between the healthy and sick, and Susan B. Anthony mediated the political rights of women. Of course, some will say that every one of these mediators was a sinner. Both Jefferson and Washington owned slaves, and Martin Luther King failed in marriage fidelity. Apart from the Lord Jesus and, in the Catholic tradition, Mary his mother, no mediator lives without sin. The sin, however, never effaces the goodness.

People need mediators in daily life and in their relationship to God. No one lives or dies totally isolated from others. Human beings live socially, and in all their relationships they require a social dimension. Spirituality in most cases becomes part of a person's life only because of the presence of other spiritual people. Religion depends on one generation passing on to another its religious traditions and faith. Being an American also depends upon one generation passing on its heritage to another or the same generation welcoming into the American tradition people who were once outside it. Social isolation destroys the individual. Being part of a history of good and holy men and women nourishes each generation and prepares for the next. In the Catholic tradition mediation joins the present generation to the many preceding generations and promises a handing-on to those generations yet to come.

# History

The Catholic Church has been around for almost twenty centuries. This is four or five times longer than the oldest Protestant tradition and ten times the age of the United States. A church with such a broad historical perspective gives its members a profound sense of history. In this long history the Catholic Church has lived under despotic emperors and kings, in dictatorships and democracies, under feudalism, capitalism and communism. Different political systems and differing economic systems have affected the Catholic Church but have not essentially changed its purpose and meaning. The Catholic perspective demonstrates that no political or economic system can ever destroy the human spirit or suppress the drive for some relationship to God.

The gospel of Jesus as expressed in the Catholic tradition can live and flourish in any time or place, under any conditions. The strong sense of roots and continuity augurs well for the future. Just knowing that hundreds of years ago people visited the same holy places, said the same or similar prayers to the same Lord, offered the same eucharistic sacrifice, listened to the same scriptures and acknowledged the same traditions gives a sense of security to anyone who bears the name *Catholic.*

In this same history the Catholic Church has been guilty of many sins: the suppression of people, the Inquisition, the Crusades, the abuse of authority and power. But since it is a historical church, one generation can atone for the sins of a previous generation. One pope can ask pardon for the failings of an earlier pope. Pope John Paul II personally demonstrated his concern for the sins of the past in his call to repentance and acknowledgment of sins in the Jubilee celebration of the Day of Pardon on March 12, 2000.

> One of the characteristic elements of the Great Jubilee is what I described as the "purification of memory" [Bull *Incarnationis Mysterium,* no. 11]. As the Successor of Peter, I asked that "in this year of mercy the Church, strong in the holiness she receives from the Lord, should kneel before

God and implore forgiveness for the past and present sins of
her sons and daughters"
(John Paul II, Homily, Day of Pardon, no. 3)

History relativizes all. History makes the playing ground level,
even if it takes generations. A church of two millennia surely will
have its dark side, which can never obliterate the bright side.

Americans have a limited history of only two hundred years.
But for most Americans this limited history provides much to
admire. The founders of this country were good people. No
American need ever feel ashamed to see the pictures of Washington or Jefferson or Lincoln on currency. "In God We Trust"
appears on all American currency, even coins. And in God this
country did trust, through wars and depression, through civil disturbance and national celebrations of liberty. Americans cherish
their history, brief as it is in comparison to other nations, and
joyfully celebrate their country's heritage. On Memorial Day the
country recalls those who died for freedom. On July Fourth, the
birthday of the country, people still affirm their belief that "all
men are created equal, that they are endowed by their Creator
with certain unalienable rights" such as "life, liberty and the pursuit of happiness." Labor day celebrates the contribution of the
laboring class to the building of this country, and Thanksgiving,
the most American of all the historical celebrations, gathers family and friends to enjoy the gift of life with much food and drink
and unity in the act of thanking God. The Catholic Church
extols history, and the American seeks every opportunity to
express the history of this country.

Like that of the Catholic Church, American history has its
dark side. Slavery and racial discrimination, the oppression of
certain groups, the failure to appreciate the place and role of
women, the exploitation of the poor by the rich, the poverty and
waste of human life and potential, the abuse of freedom and lack
of honesty—all can be found in the two-hundred-year history of
the United States. But again, like the Catholic Church, the positive contributions of this country to its citizens and to the world
far outweigh the failures. Both Catholics and Americans can
look back on their history with gratitude and pride.

# Catholic Theology and Protestant Theology

Theology never offers the last word on anything. People pursue theology in their efforts to understand faith. Christians have come to know and love God through Jesus Christ. Because people are curious, they continually want to understand more and more about this relationship to God and to each other in light of the Word of God in Jesus. Because theology arises from the human effort to understand faith, theology remains forever incomplete and imperfect since no individual or group ever creates anything perfect and complete. Theology needs a continual updating and rethinking based on the new knowledge and insights that become evident each day.

Protestants and Catholics share the same faith but differ in their understanding of Christian faith. Clear distinctions exist between Catholic theology and Protestant theology. The basic faith certainly remains the same: the acceptance of Jesus as the revelation of God. But people can regard this faith from different perspectives. One Lord, one faith and one baptism do not mean one theology.

# Protestant Theology

Protestant theology concentrates on the life of the individual believer and his or her faith based on the Word of God in Scripture. For these reasons Protestant theology has always been more individualistic and more dedicated to the Bible than its Catholic counterpart. This does not mean that Protestant theology does not include a community dimension, nor that in Catholicism the individual is swallowed up in a collectivity. It is just that the perspective and emphasis differs.

Utilitarianism has also figured prominently in American Protestant theology. The general American experience has contributed to this influence. Americans want things to work. Abstract thinking and metaphysical analysis add little to a utilitarian understanding of life. Protestant thought has developed within this distinctive American framework.

# Catholic Theology

Catholic theology stresses the community. The individual lives in relationship to the group, even while remaining an individual. The church community with its structure, its teaching function and its communal life forms the basis for its theology. A priority for the common good has always characterized Catholic beliefs and traditions. Individual theologians must take into consideration what the Church has taught and what the Church believes.

In Catholic traditions the Church interprets the Word of God. The Church teaches its faithful disciples how to understand the Word of God for them as manifest in their own history. Unfortunately, while this principle has generated much good, it also has tended to separate the Catholic from the Bible. Catholics do not read the Bible as much as their Protestant friends. They have the Church to interpret for them and use the past traditions and beliefs of the Church to give guidance in their daily efforts to live a Christian life. The ecumenical movement, however, and the return to sources from the Vatican Council have encouraged Catholics to pay more attention to the Word of God in Scripture.

Tradition binds Catholics more than Protestants. Catholics tend to pay more attention to the thinking and beliefs of the entire community and its historical past. They have a consciousness of a relationship to those who preceded them, both saints and sinners, and especially church leaders (popes and bishops). All these form part of the many traditions upon which Catholics rest their personal faith. The various councils, the teachings of the popes, the thoughts of theologians of the past or their counterparts today, saints who lived exemplary lives, whether from the Middles Ages or the present century—all form part of the Church's traditions and all affect Catholic beliefs.

Catholic thinking loves the metaphorical. Sacramental systems depend on the imagination and the use of metaphors. Life cannot be explained merely scientifically. What might appear to be useless in fact adds a hidden and much needed dimension to life. Art, music and poetry transcend the utilitarian, and the Catholic Church loves them all. Silence and sound, movement and stillness find welcome in Catholic theology and Catholic life. Metaphors abound. God is silence and God dances.

The Catholic principle in theology, however, does not mean that contemporary American Catholics have not been affected by the Protestant elements of individualism and utilitarianism. In an age of ecumenism Catholic theology has begun to pay more attention to individual faith and stresses the need for frequent Bible reading and praying on the part of the individual. With regard to utilitarianism, the American bishops' greatest contribution in the Second Vatican Council came in the discussions on religious liberty, ecumenism and liturgy. All include the utilitarian.

On the other hand, Protestant theologians today pay more attention to the traditions and to the community aspect of faith. The common good has influenced some of contemporary Protestant theology, and the continual contact with Catholic traditions has begun to bring a greater appreciation of metaphor in addition to utilitarianism. While significant differences remain, a greater possibility of unity among Christians and their different churches grows as each tradition learns to appreciate the values of the others.

Many of the ideas presented here need further explanation and development. The Catholic Church does not come from nor does it maintain only one tradition. Many traditions flow together to create contemporary American Catholicism. Many beliefs also characterize the worldwide Catholic Church, just as many theologies have flourished in the almost two millennia that form its past.

Although the United States has a limited history compared to the Catholic Church, many of the values and traditions that Americans hold dear have also been part of the Catholic heritage. At the same time the American experience has influenced the Catholic Church in this country, and the American Catholic Church has influenced the universal Church. Catholic beliefs and traditions have taken deep root within American history and practice. Understanding these beliefs and traditions helps American Catholics understand just who they are.

## TOPICS FOR DISCUSSION AND STUDY

1. What American values do you find similar to Catholic values?
2. Do some Catholic values appeal to you more than others? Which?
3. Myths, ritual and symbols are important in life. How do they fit into your life?
4. Mediators are all imperfect except Jesus and Mary. Who are the mediators in your life? How are you a mediator for others?
5. How do you deal with the evil and sin in the history of the Church and in American history?
6. How do values relate to virtues and vice versa?
7. *Catholic* means both true and universal. What does *Catholic* mean to you?
8. What are your thoughts on being both American and Catholic? Can you be American on the outside and Catholic on the inside, or vice versa?

# Works Consulted

Bellah, Robert. "Religion and the Shape of National Culture." *America* 181, no. 3 (1999): 9–14.

Ellis, John Tracy. *American Catholics and the Intellectual Life.* Chicago: Heritage Foundation, 1956.

Fogarty, Gerald P. "The American Catholic Tradition of Dialogue." *America* 175, no. 12 (1996): 9–14.

Grabner-Haider, Anton. "God-Talk in a Multireligious Society." *Theology Digest* 45 (1998): 51–58.

Happel, Stephen, and David Tracy. *A Catholic Vision.* Philadelphia: Fortress, 1984.

———. *Fides et Ratio.* October 15, 1998.

O'Grady, John F. *Models of Jesus Revisited.* Mahwah, N.J.: Paulist Press, 1994.

———. *The Roman Catholic Church: Its Origin and Nature.* Mahwah, N.J.: Paulist Press, 1997.

Rahner, Karl. "The Theology of the Symbol." *Theological Investigations.* Baltimore: Helicon, 1961, vol. 4, 221–52.

Shelley, Thomas. "Lessons from Early Maryland Catholics." *America* 174, no. 20 (1996): 9–16.

Tripole, Martin R. "The American Church in Jeopardy." *America* 175, no. 8 (1996): 9–15.

United States Bishops. *The American Catholic Heritage.* Washington, D.C.: United States Catholic Conference, 1992.

Vogels, Walter. "The Human Person in the Image of God." *Theology Digest* 43 (1996): 3–7.

# SECTION I:
# GOD IN CATHOLIC TRADITIONS

# CHAPTER 1:
# THE PROBLEM OF GOD

Catholics believe in one God: Father, Son and Holy Spirit. They believe like other Christians that this one God has spoken through Abraham and Moses and the prophets, and finally through God's only Son Jesus Christ. Catholics, like other Christians, also believe that both Father and Son have sent the Holy Spirit to dwell in the Church and in the members of the Church.

Most Americans believe in God, but all must admit that a large part of the world's population is atheistic or at least indifferent to the God question. Does God really exist? Does God care about this world and its people? Does life make any sense? Even if Americans believe in God, no one can live in the contemporary world and not be affected by the cultural influences embodied in these disturbing questions. A certain skepticism about God has always been present in the human mind.

Today the existence of God does not seem as evident as it was in the past, when the common understanding of the universe seemed compatible with Christian faith. Contemporary science and its analysis of the universe do not immediately suggest a God, as did medieval cosmology. Some even see the idea of God as useless to modern people, since scientists can attribute most if not everything to the natural forces in the universe. Today believers and nonbelievers alike give scientific explanations for things as they occur. The vast and fantastic universe dwarfs the human race, and so many find it hard to believe that the universe is made for humanity. Galaxies exist of which science has no knowledge. Many may well include elements dangerous to earth and the human race such as asteroids, viruses and bacteria. Introducing the idea of God into this understanding of the world brings God from outside without any apparent need. And yet, Catholic faith does just that. The Catholic faith professes that the God and Father of the Lord Jesus Christ lives within and beyond the universe and within each individual since all are created in the image and likeness of God. God is "without," and "within" as totally "other" and yet within both the universe and the individual, especially in Jesus of Nazareth.

Some believe that the idea of God has limited the human race in its development. God and theology (and in particular Catholic theology), in the opinion of certain philosophers and scientists, have alienated people from their true human vocation. Being completely human involves realizing oneself as a person, fulfilling one's possibilities. Every individual has a right to do just that. Alienation forcefully prevents people from this realization, and God, and theology, for some contemporaries, have been such an alienating force. Believing in God in the past has encouraged people to pay no attention to the things of earth. Hegel, the nineteenth-century German philosopher, asked what new forces humanity could use to build the universe and a New World. He saw the need to disconnect from religion, which focused its attention on another world, heaven. Marx, the philosophical father of communism, claimed that religion alienates people from the real world. Communism denied that it was antireligion but asserted that both religion and theology have hindered the development of the New World. Any student of history must admit some truth in these opinions. God and theology did in fact often focus primarily on the future life rather than the present life. Certain individuals used God and theology to control people instead of freeing them to become whole. Dom Helder Pessoa Camara, former archbishop of Recife, Brazil, once remarked: "The Church must overcome that magic and fatalistic Christianity that she has transmitted to the Latin masses; a religion preached to men without freedom easily becomes a fatalistic one; there should be real hope on earth, not only an other-worldly reward."[1]

For the true atheist, the denial of God should never be seen as only negative. Atheism has its positive side as well. People have the responsibility to build the earth, and the idea of God has not always helped to realize this goal. For example, in underdeveloped countries a fatalism often paralyzes development. Large numbers of people in these countries are deeply religious, with many of them Catholic. Theology and their clergy have told them that God has the world in God's hands and people have to accept things as they are. God, religion and theology then become an alibi for laziness or neglect or a passive acceptance of present conditions. This bothers not only atheists, but also many believing Christians. Focusing on the future can distract from needed attention to the present.

The current denial of or indifference to God has many precedents in history, but today the extent of its impact seems far wider. In the last century Friedrich Nietzsche, another German philosopher, proclaimed the death of God, and succeeding generations have produced an orchestra of trumpeters. With a visionary power, Nietzsche asked what this would mean to future humanity. He foresaw a future in which people would no longer strive for the moral good, since morality has always been closely connected with God. Nietzsche mocked the atheists who thought you could deny God and maintain morality. He believed that with the death of God the will to destroy would be as essential to life as the will to create. Secondly, Nietzsche believed that in the future people would lose interest in the search for truth. With no eternal truth, people would no longer see any truth in things. Deceit will then control much of life. Finally, because of God's death, human life will become a senseless martyrdom. The human being of the future becomes his or her own torturer and executioner. Nothing remains to humanity except to say no to all things. This view, called nihilism, holds that all values are nothing but bait through which life's comedy endeavors to prolong itself without ever coming nearer to a solution.

While these ideas appear in the philosophy of Nietzsche, whether he personally ascribed to the inevitability of nihilism and anarchy remains unclear. The impact of many of these thoughts on contemporary reality, however, no one will deny.

The decline in morality, the increase of deceit in every aspect of life, the vigorous stance of self–destruction and violence against others, alarm most people. In eliminating God from the picture, the human race in the past century seems to have moved along the path foretold by Nietzsche. Believing in nothing has led the human race to believe in all things, except of course, God.

In the middle of this century Jean Paul Sartre and Albert Camus, both French philosophers, dominated existential atheism. Sartre says that humanity must face up to the fact that God does not exist. Sartre finds it distressing that God does not exist since people are then condemned to be free in a world that, without any reason, is absurd. Everything is born without reason, prolongs itself out of weakness and dies by chance. Human consciousness makes a human being a useless passion. Sartre emphasized that the person as absolutely free is also absolutely responsible for the absurdity of human life. Whatever the person does becomes personal property and can neither be excused nor justified. Whatever the person is, the person has made it so, and whatever the faults of others, the individual freely accepted them when he or she freely chose to live with others. Hell is other people. Values exist not as a given but as something invented. Sartre tried to avoid the nihilism of Nietzsche, but in his process he allows no place for the existence of God. Life begins and ends in absurdity.

Albert Camus was also influenced by an absurdity resulting from the meeting of the universe with the human mind. The mind desires that the world should be explicable. It isn't. A person unconsciously drifts on the monotonous current of life until one day he or she asks "why" of this tedious, boring, mechanical existence. At this moment life gives birth to absurdity with a sickening jolt. There is no why. The true thinkers have embarked on a metaphysical rebellion. No reason exists for why things are. In his later writings Camus does not remain the total pessimist. He has some hope in the future, but this hope is limited to humankind perfecting itself in the light of potentialities. Camus the rebel rejects divinity in order to share in the struggles and destiny of ordinary people. In *The Plague,* Tarrou asks the critical question for Camus: "In short, what interests me is to know how to become a saint." "But you do not believe in God." "Exactly, can one be a saint without God? This is the sole problem I know today."[2] Camus died without the opportunity to resolve his problem. Ironically at forty-six, his life was snuffed out in a senseless automobile accident. He was not the driver of the car. He was a victim of the absurd, in the form of a chance mishap.

## Catholics and the God Question

Catholics do not ascribe to any of these theories on the death of God. Catholic beliefs and traditions preach a need to take God into consideration in every aspect of life, even that which appears absurd. Most Americans do not ascribe to these theories. But anyone living in this scientific and ever postmodern age is bound to be influenced by them. Does God exist? What does life mean? Can moments of absurdity give way to total absurdity? Are all truths relative? Can people just do whatever they want provided they do not hurt anyone else? Why is there so much violence if God truly exists? Does anyone really care? Has believing in God made this a better world or a worse one?

The Protestant theologians of the past century and some of the Catholic theologians of this century tended to forget that the central affirmation of theology is God and not the human race. The Jewish theologians have not as yet succumbed to this desire to view theology as first the study of humanity and history and only then of God. Important as humanity and history remain, today theologians are returning to the notion that theology first and most fundamentally tries to say something about God, however limited, before it can say anything about the human race. The theologian and the minister of religion must face fundamental questions about God when confronted with wholesale indifference to, if not rejection of, God. This position of indifference includes the apparent acceptance that God does not fit into the world picture at the moment. Many, especially the young, feel no need for God. Yet millions still claim to believe in God, and millions identify themselves as Catholic even while somewhat indifferent to the whole question. The present situation of thinking about God, religion and theology demands an examination of the understanding of the notions of God in the past and how these same notions of God are present or absent in the thinking and lives of people today.

## The Traditional Proofs for the Existence of God

Certain paths have traditionally led people to posit the existence of God. Conscious that the universe as they know it is somehow incomplete, many people point beyond themselves to an ever more encompassing One. They call this One by a host of names like God or *Dios* or *Dieu* or *Adonai* or *Allah* or the Great Spirit or the Eternal Energy. They use the term *God* to describe that oneness in which and by which the parts have their existence. This explanation for the dependence and incompleteness of the universe may lead people to worship and commit themselves to the One called God or *Allah* or *Adonai*. This forms the foundation for religions such as Christianity, Islam or Judaism.

Others are driven to seek a unified explanation for the order within things and think in terms of a cosmic mind or intelligent will. They are likely to see in this coherent pattern something of supreme worth. They may call this cosmic mind or will "God," or any of the other titles listed above. People want to know where things come from. This also influences the three great Western religions.

Others see themselves in dependence on another for their existence. People experience themselves as creatures and are led to posit a ground of being or power of being. They understand God to be the reason and cause of all contingent being. God is the only necessary being; all others are contingent. They accept this God as a personal being on whom they depend.

Still others see the need for an absolute value as rooted in the individual conscience. In their moral experience they confront a reality that expects them to live in a certain way. Some, of course, explain this in terms of the superego of Freud or the demands of society and thus have no need to use God as the explanation. But others find that this "ought," this fundamental obligation present in conscience, has an ultimacy and authority that cannot be explained by culture or psychology. They call this God. The "oughtness" or duty to abide by rules and conscience thus forms the bases for religious obligations.

Finally, some speak of God in relationship to religious experience. "The numinous" of Rudolph Otto or the characteristics of religious experience of William James: the ineffable, the noetic content, the transiency and the passivity of the individual make a person think of something beyond the self and the material world. This religious or mystical experience brings contact with the transcendent One and then demands worship and commitment. Thus the idea of the sacred develops with its myth, ritual and symbol, each of which contributes to an actual contact with the Other beyond the human and material realms.

To these can be added the other traditional ways of perfection in the universe, the theory of the unmoved mover of Aristotle or the five proofs of Thomas Aquinas: the argument from motion, the nature of efficient cause, possibility and necessity, gradation in things and the governance of the world. Each of these approaches presents a different notion of God. But perhaps it would be better to see these approaches as not mutually exclusive but all intimately related and dependent. Some have tried to update these approaches to the modern problem of God and many good advances have been made. However, all seem insufficient today.

## Reasons against the Existence of God

1. These traditional ways of thinking about God have only a tenuous hold in contemporary experience. The notion of the whole is so vast and so remote that a person finds it difficult to experience self as part of the whole in a way that develops into religious fervor. The laws of science and human control increase daily and can explain the notion of order. The sense of dependence is limited today to the individual's need for others and stops there, with many people very comfortable without going further. In the area of morals, the sense of what ought to be frequently

relates to sex, and today questions of sexual morality appear time-conditioned. Society often screens out the question of religious experience or becomes suspicious of anyone claiming to have it. Finally, the proofs from philosophy are much too involved and abstract and offer little to the modern imaginative mind.

2. The second difficulty concerns the problem of evil. If God exists and is all good and powerful, why is there so much evil in the world? Why do children suffer? Most efforts to explain evil do not satisfy. The realities of the human situation just do not fit with the traditional belief in the God who is omnipotent and a good Creator. In theology after Auschwitz, many Jewish theologians say that they can no longer believe in a God of history. Believers claim that in every historical calamity God has a secret design. If the murder of six million Jews and millions of others—Catholics, gypsies and other non-Jews—contains a secret design of God, then many moderns reject this kind of God.

3. The third objection is based on the claim that faith in God actually operates against attainment of full humanity. The Jewish and Christian images of God as Father, Creator, Lord of history, Lawgiver, Judge and the One who alone is Holy have caused more problems than solutions. People have suffered considerably under these images of God, which were supposed to liberate.

Feminists reject the notion of God as Father since historically this has limited women's development and offered oppression in its place. Children who experienced abuse from their fathers cannot think positively of the image of "father" as descriptive of God. The understanding of God as Creator, Source of order and Ground of being suggests that people are powerless in God's presence, since they depend on God for all. Modern life contradicts this. Or if God did create all, God has done a poor job, leaving it up to humanity to make it better. The names *Creator* and *Lord of history* evoke the response of awe, obeisant self-abnegation and resignation, which can create a tension with the notions of human dignity and worth. It goes against the contemporary conviction that individuals are responsible for themselves and must work to overcome injustice and oppression and make this world a better place for all people. The idea that God has expectations translates into an image of God as Lawgiver and Judge.

People must obey God or be punished. Then God functions in the modern consciousness as the enemy of the human effort to become whole and free by making mistakes and learning from them. A punishing God, someone who gets even with weak human beings, the Grand Inquisitor, mitigates any sense of a good God loving people in spite of human failure and sin.

Finally, the idea that God alone is holy robs the human person of proper meaning. This concept stresses the transcendence of God and the separation of God from all creation, thus concentrating the meaning of reality on God and away from humanity. Many just do not accept this today. People consider themselves as holy and full of value and meaning, and are distrustful of anything, even God, that will rob them of worth. Modern people tied up with progress and development will not accept a God who denies them the right and interest to continue this development and, as a result, many people become indifferent to God. Many contemporary people reject most of the traditional notions of God even if they all claim to believe in God and however much they fill up churches and synagogues and mosques on the weekends.

4. Science does rather well without God. The Big Bang theory, the evolution of the species, natural selection, contemporary physics and modern biology all contribute to understanding the universe without God. In the past, ignorant of many of the laws of the universe, the immature human race needed God to explain the "how" of things. As scientific knowledge develops and expands, it leaves less room for ignorance regarding the how of things. The further convergance of physics, biology and mathematics will continue to narrow the need for explanations outside the laws of science. Even as the behavioral sciences continue to develop, people will feel less of a need to turn to God for an explanation of how things are.

## Contemporary Hopes

Many people, especially the young, live their lives content with the notion that they must first develop the talents that they have.

They must continue to perfect themselves and the world and be content to let the whole question of the possibility of God and the afterlife remain unanswered. *Now* is the only reality for them as humanity works for the future, seeking the betterment of society. All else is left over from the age when humanity was immature and unable to find the right place in the universe. Religion, like the oxcart, must bow to the superiority of evolutionary forces and human progress. People just do not need God, religion or theology.

Americans, including Catholics, find themselves principally in the realm of the material: economics, propagation and family, health, sport, recreation, food, technology and organization. And also in the realm of the not quite spiritual: education, research, fine arts and beauty, social order and philosophy. In these areas the human race can make progress without any need for a God. Or can it? Science may well offer sufficient explanations for the "how" of things but can science offer explanations for the "why" of things?

## The Universe Desacralized

The way in which many view contemporary society and culture could be called the desacalization of the universe, the separation of the profane from the sacred. The advent of Christianity actually accelerated this movement, although the origins of Judaism foreshadowed the separation of God from the universe. Both religions saw the separation as good. The magic and mystery had been broken in the Judaic tradition, but this desacralization of the universe did not stop here. Christianity taught that God had entered into the human race through Jesus. God was not an abstract force committed to controlling and then punishing and rewarding people. People would find God in a person, a person who loved them. The universe became regarded as the place for people to grow and develop rather than the place for the gods to play with human life. God gave the earth to people and endowed them with their own value and dignity and rights.

The present desacralization of the universe, however, went far beyond Judaism and Christianity. The advent of modern science saw a further retreat of the sacred from the cosmos, with humanity finding no need for the positioning of God involved in the world. If God did create, God gave to the human race the vocation to develop. The next step saw no need for a Creator and considered the whole world as eternal and having within itself the possibilities of development and perfection. A further desacralization of the universe arose from space exploration. The Russian cosmonauts remarked that they did not find any trace of God in the universe. Such a changed worldview does not leave much place for the Creator and Ruler of the universe. Yet Catholicism professes the need for such a Creator, even while it also maintains the importance of encouraging personal development and human worth and the unlocking of the secrets of the universe through science and exploration.

The Catholic tradition emphasizes that the individual person finds true emancipation in the light of the renewed view of the world. Persons have the possibility to perfect and develop both themselves and their environment. The universe centers on the human race not in any biological sense but in a dynamic sense. The human race can do wonderful things with the will and mind to do so. In the same light, the individual sees himself or herself as developing and becoming a person in interaction with people, *now* and not just in the future. People do not want to wait for some future date for salvation. Salvation, if it exists, must be *now*. All of these hopes and expectations remain a valued part of Catholic beliefs and traditions even if many Catholics live their lives unaware of their heritage.

Hundreds of thousands of American Catholics hold on to the idea of the God of their fathers and mothers, but these are increasingly older people. Many younger people turn the whole process off on a large scale. If the young do not accept the reality of God or are indifferent, then who will replace the older believers? Will religion, like so many other institutions, wither and die?

Catholicism, through its beliefs and traditions, says no to all of the negative elements in contemporary society, even while it admits the influence of these forces on the Church, especially in the younger generation. Somehow what had been passed on must continue to be passed on not just for the sake of the individual but for the sake of the race. Certain traditions will fade and certain beliefs will be reinterpreted. The valuable will last. The useful will continue. The outdated and harmful will be forgotten. Theology must speak of God in a way which makes sense to the younger generation as well as the older.

## TOPICS FOR DISCUSSION AND STUDY

1. Can people believe in God and yet be indifferent to God? How? Why?
2. "With no eternal truth, people will lose interest in any truth." Thus wrote Nietzsche. What are your thoughts?
3. Do you have absurdity in your life? How do you deal with it?
4. "Hell is other people." Thus wrote Sartre. Was he right?
5. Can anyone prove that God exists? Do any traditional proofs appeal to you?
6. Do all people experience transcendence? Do all people have religious experiences? Can they be the same?
7. How can belief in God include accepting evil in the world?
8. What images do you have of God?

# Works Consulted

Armstrong, Karen. *A History of God.* New York: Knopf, 1994.

Eliade, Mircea. *Images and Symbols.* New York: Sheed and Ward, 1969.

Fantino, Jacques. "Whence the Teaching Creation *ex nihilo?*" *Theology Digest* 46 (1999): 133–40.

Fortman, Edmund. *The Triune God.* Philadelphia: Westminster, 1972.

Gleason, Philip. *The Search for God.* New York: Sheed and Ward, 1964.

Grant, Robert M. *Gods and the One God.* Philadelphia: Westminster, 1986.

James, William. *The Varieties of Religious Experience.* New York: Random House, 1929.

Otto, Rudolph. *The Idea of the Holy.* New York: Oxford University Press, 1958.

Robinson, John A. T. *Honest to God.* Philadelphia: Westminster, 1963.

# CHAPTER 2:
# IMAGES OF GOD

Contemporary Christian ideas of God borrow heavily from earlier notions of God, even if these ideas have been superseded by the understanding of the one Christian God—Father, Son and Holy Spirit. People today often include in their understanding of God some notions that come from the earliest understanding of gods and goddesses of thousands of years ago. They also include in their personal image of God the experiences of childhood and the initial ideas implanted by family and teachers.

Earlier peoples first encountered God in nature. By examining the world around them, people of thousands of years ago realized the presence of a power outside the human race, something that no one could control. People faced nature and were at a loss to explain it. And so they developed stories that expressed in language others could understand just how the individual and the race, as well as the cycles of nature, fit into the cosmic picture. These stories became the myths of ancient peoples.

## Myths

Earliest stories about God and people first looked at God in a cosmic and nature-based sense. God was lightning and thunder, rain and snow. God was a waterfall or a great mountain or a great tree, or at least God was responsible for all of these and present in them. With time, people recognized more intriguing things in the universe. Individuals became aware of order in the midst of chaos. And so the gods became the order-makers. Gods became the subjects of myths concerning the conquest over the chaos. These early thinkers, however, were not content merely to look at the elements of the world. When they had, at least to personal satisfaction, answered the very basic questions of life and God, they then turned to look at themselves. In looking at themselves, they found a more complex reality and again turned to the reality beyond themselves to explain human nature.

A person could stand back from the things of nature and observe them. But often the individual was not at one with self and was unable to obtain objectivity about personal existence. The difficulty lay in trying to explain the reality seen within the human person. The person experienced severe emotions, which could not always be understood. Thus gods and goddesses became representative of those emotions. Ancient peoples had gods and goddesses of love and fear and war and death and happiness and joy and strength and fortitude.

## Gods and Goddesses

These same people could not control that which they did not understand and could not understand that which they could not control. What could not be controlled nor understood became the realm of gods and goddesses. The gods and goddesses of fertility (human and animal and plant) had a role to play in the everyday life of the human race, and they had to be appeased. If not, all life would cease. These gods and goddesses of myth took on human characteristics even while they remained divine. They were like human beings, perhaps distant, perhaps in control, but like men and women. Earlier peoples regarded gods and goddesses in a fashion similar to their view of human hierarchy and people of importance. Yet despite the increasingly human characteristics of the gods and goddesses and despite the humans who assumed attributes like those of the gods, there was no thought of the divine becoming totally human.

In advancing beyond a study of primitive understandings of gods and goddesses, one must appreciate that the development of a concept of God proceeds along two lines. One is a purely natural, rational, logical explanation of a power that is beyond. The other develops along the lines of faith, in an encounter with a Divine Person. The best example of the purely rational progression toward a conception of God can be found in Greek thought. The gods were seen as superhumans who, although eternal, had at some point in time come into being. The Greek concept, especially in its early stages, was neither monotheistic nor polytheistic. Rather it was an ordered totality of male and female gods. The gods were not creators. They brought order out of existing chaos. Their many human qualities even included a gamut of emotions, and their customs were markedly mortal. They were aware of humanity's fate, but powerless to change it. Often the male gods represented the static principles and the female goddesses personified the creative and dynamic principles.

## Greek Philosophers

The early Greek philosophers presented no sharp break from the natural theologies, which viewed gods through the dominant myths and in the forces of nature. They represent, rather, a gradual change in the explanation of physical phenomena. Greek philosophers believed that the elements of nature are the bases of all things or that all things are full of gods. Thales, for example, explains that water is the principle of all things. Later Xenophanes and Heraclitus and others began to criticize the earlier anthropomorphic gods. The philosophers became disgusted with the drunken, brawling gods of mythology and spoke of gods in a more abstract fashion.

Perhaps the greatest degree of development of Greek thought about God came with the philosophies of Socrates, Plato and Aristotle. Socrates accepted the conventional belief in a plurality of gods but also refers to "God" or "The God." Plato clearly delineates the nature and role of this one God as a being with a nature developed to a supreme degree, but not to be confused with ideas, however eternal. Plato's God does not appear to be the cause of the ideas, but is described as bringing order out of chaos. Plato had a great reverence for the divine and an exalted notion of it, but even this is more implicit than explicit.

In Aristotle, God becomes the Prime Mover. Each of the heavenly spheres necessarily requires its own unmoved mover to account for its particular motion. What relationship exists between this Prime Mover and the other unmoved movers remains unclear. Aristotle also shows traces of approaching God on a personal level, but his main emphasis is on God as a cosmic principle, removed from any preoccupation with the universe or the human race. God, for Aristotle, is the final necessary and adequate condition of a world order. But God does not will anything because God is beyond the world.

The idea of God becoming human was always alien to Greek thinking. The Greeks thought that humans could become like God. This idea continued to exert an influence into the Christian era. Christians influenced by Greek philosophy tried to reconcile their earlier understandings of God with a strictly monotheistic, creationism theology. But however progressive this refinement becomes, a strictly Greek philosophy rejects a personal monotheistic view of God as the creator of heaven and earth. God is a power or essence, which assures permanence.

## Hebrew Faith

Israel offers a much different development. Israel, too, begins with particular beliefs and religious practices. Before achieving their own political-religious identity, Israel shared the gods of other nations. Monotheism developed gradually. In the meantime other gods and goddesses existed side by side with the God of Israel. The male gods represented the static principles and the female gods signified the creative, dynamic and spontaneous principles. This distinction will form the foundation for the development of Yahweh, the one God of the people and of Wisdom, Word, Spirit and Torah as the ways by which God interacts in the human world.

Perhaps the oldest name found for God in this tradition is *El.* Found in all ancient Semitic languages, the exact meaning of the term eludes complete evaluation and explanation. The term relates more to species rather than person. The name could perhaps best be translated as "power," specifically power that humans cannot master. The use of the term is shared, with slight philological differences, with the Arabic and Akkadian. Outside of Israel *El* was the father of the gods and the lord of heaven. But in Israel's tradition, *El* is never clearly associated with a pantheon, although the name was used with modifiers. These modifiers are found in such expressions as *El Elyon,* the "God of the Most High," or *El Shaddai,* the "God of Power."

In a culture where names were most significant, *El* had no proper name. *El* was the God of Abraham, Isaac and Jacob. God entered into a personal relationship with Abraham. For no apparent reason God called Abraham forth to become the leader of a mighty nation and a great people. *El* became the God of history, and the God of faith, for by faith Abraham responded. Belief in one God, however inchoate, seems to have been present since Abraham.

In the patriarchal periods, the concept of God underwent greater development. The God of the patriarchs was one, personal, almighty, transcendent, eternal and deeply interested in Israel. The people of Israel, however, did not speculate about God's metaphysical nature. The actions of God in their history told them about God. It was in all likelihood during this period that Israel clearly developed into a monotheistic religion. *El* became the one true God of Abraham, Isaac and Jacob, and Spirit, Word, Wisdom and Torah expressed the presence of God in life. Even the ancient creed of Israel, "Hear O Israel the Lord your God is one," might not refer to an exclusive monotheism at first but to the belief that their God is the God alone for them.

## Moses and God

The true founder of Israel's religion was Moses. To Moses God revealed the name, *ehyeh asher ehyeh,* which has come into English as "I am who am" or simply Yahweh. Since Hebrew has no developed number of tenses but is mainly characterized by actions completed or not completed, the phrase could be translated as "I will be what I will be," or "you will learn who I am by what I do." The expression could also have been an attempt to articulate an experience of divine presence in such a way as to express the presence with humans of a substantially hidden and transcendent God. The God of the ancient fathers and mothers and of Moses is ever present, active and powerful. This Yahweh cared about Israel gratuitously. Yahweh's effects were not limited to the nation of origin like the gods of other peoples. Yahweh was the only God. No other gods existed before this one God. Moses and other religious leaders may have recognized monotheism, but the attitude was slow in filtering down to the rest of the people. They were not so ready to see Yahweh as the only God. Monotheism developed slowly over many centuries. They learned the existence of one God through God's presence in history.

## The Prophets

The idea of God in Israel became increasingly clearer during the prophetic period. Israel was a tiny nation living among the giants of the Middle East. The lure of the gods of these other more powerful nations often enticed and seduced the people of Israel. The prophets, responding to these evil influences on Israelitic religion, did little to create a new image of Yahweh; rather they called the nation back to the old one. The prophets constantly told the people of Israel that worshiping false gods would only bring destruction. Their words often went unheeded but their prophecy came true. Worshiping false gods brings problems for all.

Monotheism, the hallmark of Jewish religion, ironically came to its fullness after the exile, when the nation was disbanded and the cultic places lay in ruin. Then the Jewish mind turned inward. The anthropomorphism of God became less and less. The one God of the past overcame all other rivals.

In spite of Israel's eyes of faith, the Israelites' developing images of their God were often influenced by their particular needs. When they were in need of deliverance, God became the deliverer and even the Lord of armies. When they were in need of a moral principle, God became the Lawmaker and Judge. When Israel was threatened, God became the Avenger. Still over and above these necessities, their God called them to be a people and to this one God Israel was required to answer in faith. Judaism offered to the world the belief in one God responding to human needs.

## God the Creator

Like the Greek gods, the God of Israel also brought order out of chaos. The first verse of Genesis makes this clear. The Hebrew word *bara* (created) does not necessarily mean creation from nothing but ordering what is there. This God created man and woman in his image *(selem)* and likeness *(demut)*. They would be the vice-regents of God in creation continuing to overcome chaos by their own creativity.

Entering into a covenant with Moses God promises to be the God of Israel:

> Now therefore if you obey my voice and keep my covenant, you shall be my own possession among all peoples; for all the earth is mine and you shall be to me a kingdom of priests and a holy nation. (Exod 19:5–6)

God accepts the responsibility to remain faithful to Israel even if Israel does not remain faithful to God. God will show the virtues of compassion, kindness and mercy *(hesed)* and fidelity *(emeth)*. He will give the people of Israel guidance and instruction through Torah, continue to create them into a holy people through the Word *(dabar)*, offer helpful hints for living through Wisdom *(hokmah)* and remain present through the Spirit *(ruah)*.

## New Testament

The New Testament continues Israel's greatest contribution, monotheism. God expects in the New Testament to be the center of all human life and activity. Idolatry will not be tolerated. One God alone exists, but now this one God is the Father of Jesus Christ. Some New Testament passages will give human characteristics or feelings to God, such as goodness and kindness, or even wrath, with references to patience and long-suffering. Fundamentally, however, the New Testament related God to Jesus of Nazareth. The anthropomorphisms of the Old Testament can be found fulfilled in the incarnation itself: God became human in Jesus. While the Old Testament applied the title "Father" to God very cautiously and never in the sense of being father to all, the New Testament sees all people not only as children of God, but as able to speak to God without ceremony. All people can call God "Abba."

Universal love characterizes God in the New Testament. God is love. In the Old Testament, love was never universal. God's love for all humanity and not just some special people explains the mystery of Jesus in the New Testament. God in the New Testament is transcendent and, most importantly, triune. God the Father sends the Son to redeem the world. The Son dies for all and, once ascended to the Father, with the Father sends the Spirit to teach all truth. God exists and God loves all people, giving the Word human form in Jesus of Nazareth. Jesus is the Word of God become flesh, the incarnation of the wisdom of God, the one who gives instruction through his teaching and gives his spirit to his followers.

## Early Christian Thought

Early patristic literature seemed content to use general attributes in describing God: omnipotence, goodness and mercy. A wider investigation into the nature of God by the fourth century saw God as existence. St. Hilary, an early church theologian, said that no property belongs to God as exclusively as does existence. For Augustine, the name of God is best translated by the abstract term *essence*. Perhaps all the ideas of this development are best summed up in the dogmatic statement of the Fourth Lateran Council in 1215:

> We firmly believe and profess, without qualification, that there is only one true God, eternal, immense, unchangeable, incomprehensible, omnipotent and indescribable, the Father, the Son and the Holy Spirit, three persons but one essence, substance or nature that is wholly simple.[3]

Thomas Aquinas taught that while a person can, by reason alone, know THAT God exists, human reason cannot grasp WHAT God is. Thomas maintains that the nature of God is a matter of supernatural faith. God, for Thomas, is absolute necessary being. God is therefore an act of existing of such a kind that this existence is necessary. To describe God in this way affirms an act of existence that has no cause of its own existence.

Vatican I's Dogmatic Constitution on the Catholic Faith sums up the Catholic thinking on God:

> The Holy, Catholic, Apostolic, Roman Church believes and confesses that there is one true, loving God, creator and Lord of the universe, almighty, eternal, immense, incomprehensible, infinite in intelligence, will and in all perfection, who as being one, sole, absolutely simple and immutable spiritual substance, is to be declared as really and essentially distinct from the world, a supreme beatitude in and from Himself and ineffably exalted above all things beside Himself, which exist or are conceivable.[4]

For the American Catholic all of the previous images of God pale in the one image of Jesus of Nazareth. Jesus is God's human face. Everyone can learn from the past. Certain images of God from ancient times persist. Yet for one to know something of God demands knowing something of Jesus. Knowing who Jesus of Nazareth is and how he relates both to God and people will not solve all of the world's problems but surely will contribute to our understanding more answers to such age-old questions as: Does God exist? Does God care? What does life mean? Is everything useless since in the end all dies? Does truth exist? What is the best way to live? Is love that rare? Does nothing remain?

## TOPICS FOR DISCUSSION AND STUDY

1. Do some people still have vestiges of gods and goddesses in their ideas about God? Do you?
2. What value do myths offer to contemporary believers?
3. What do you know about the God presented in Greek philosophy?
4. The Hebrew God battles *tohu we bohu* (chaos). How can people in our own day do likewise?
5. *Selem* and *demut* are important Hebrew words. Why?
6. *Dabar, ruah, hokma* and Torah are creative aspects of God. How do these ideas affect your understanding of God?
7. Does the Old Testament present God positively or negatively or both?
8. What images of God from the Old Testament do you like?
9. Of all the Hebrew words discussed which one do you like best?

# Works Consulted

Anderson, Bernhard. *Understanding the Old Testament*. Upper Saddle River, N.J.: Prentice-Hall, 1997.

Armstrong, Karen. *A History of God*. New York: Knopf, 1994.

Boadt, Lawrence. *Reading the Old Testament*. Mahwah, N.J.: Paulist Press, 1984.

Eliade, Mircea. *Images and Symbols*. New York: Sheed and Ward, 1969.

Fantino, Jacques. "Whence the Teaching Creation *ex nihilo?*" *Theology Digest* 46 (1999): 133–40.

Fortman, Edmund. *The Triune God*. Philadelphia: Westminster, 1972.

Gleason, Philip. *The Search for God*. New York: Sheed and Ward, 1964.

Grant, Robert M. *Gods and the One God*. Philadelphia: Westminster, 1986.

Küng, Hans. *Does God Exist?* New York: Random House, 1981.

O'Grady, John F. *Models of Jesus Revisited*. Mahwah, N.J.: Paulist Press, 1994.

Robinson, John A. T. *Honest to God*. Philadelphia: Westminster, 1963.

# CHAPTER 3:
# JESUS—
# THE REVELATION OF GOD

The classical definition of theology, faith seeking understanding, in itself augurs for many traditions of understanding Jesus. Historically, two distinct schools of Christology have characterized Christian theology. The school of Antioch started its theological reflection from below, from the humanity of Jesus, and then developed its understanding of how Jesus was also divine. The school of Alexandria began its Christology from above, starting with the divinity of Jesus. It then developed its understanding of how Jesus was also human. In either approach, depending on the starting point, one dimension of Jesus suffers in relationship to the other. Starting with the humanity of Jesus can eclipse his divinity. Starting with his divinity can eclipse the humanity. Moreover, two other distinctions closely allied to the above two have also characterized Christian Christology: the ontological and the functional. The former concentrates on who Jesus is while the latter focuses on what Jesus did.

For over two thousand years Christian theology has developed many traditions offering explanations of Jesus coming from these two fundamental approaches: the ontological (represented by the school of Alexandria) and the functional (taught by the school of Antioch). But the fundamental Catholic approach to Jesus has been, without a doubt, from above and ontological. Jesus is certainly divine, for Jesus is the Second Person of the Blessed Trinity. Contemporary Christologies offer other possibilities, but no one can ever understand Catholic beliefs and traditions unless they also understand this most fundamental way in which Catholic theology has preached Jesus Christ.

## The Council of Chalcedon

The Council of Chalcedon in 451 stands out in history as the high-water mark for the development of Catholic Christology. At this council the Church reached such a level of clarity that many thought that all subsequent errors in development could be detected by a careful comparison of new ideas with the declaration of the fathers of Chalcedon. Moreover, all subsequent generations could rest secure in the formulation approved by the members of the council. The Catholic Church proclaims that what sufficed for fifteen centuries will suffice for the twenty-first century. Chalcedon's declaration remains the fundamental approach of the Catholic Church for understanding Jesus Christ.

The New Testament presents Jesus as being both human and divine, but never offers any explanation of this phenomenon. The origin of the Council of Chalcedon has roots in the theological controversy in the Eastern Church on the precise nature of the unity in Jesus and the relationship between his divinity and humanity. Were there two natures in Jesus or only one? Did the humanity of Jesus exist first, to be subsequently assumed into a hypostatic union, or was the union concomitant with the existence of Jesus? Is *person* the same as *nature* or not? Can one translate Greek terminology into Latin and vice versa and still maintain clarity on both sides?

Since the matter originally centered mainly in the East, Pope Leo the Great (440–61) did not wish, at first, to be involved. Finally, upon the Emperor Theodosius's convoking a council for August 449 in Ephesus, the pope sent legates and presented his famous *Tomus Ad Fluvium*. Leo insisted on the true and integral human nature of Jesus and the distinction of natures after the hypostatic union, which existed in one divine person. He also described the properties of the human and divine natures, always insisting that it is one and the same divine person who possesses both. Those opposed to Leo's formulation entered this council by force, rejected the position of Leo and approved their own. In the history of theology this was called the *Concilium Latronum,* the "council of thieves." Since the matter was not settled at Ephesus, the Council of Chalcedon was called in 451, with representatives from East and West determined to settle the matter.

## The Definition of Chalcedon

Following then the Holy Fathers, we all with one voice teach that it should be confessed that Our Lord Jesus Christ is one and the same Son, the same perfect in Godhead, the same perfect in manhood, truly God and truly man, the same [consisting] of a rational soul and body, *homoousios* [of the same substance] with the Father as to his Godhead, and the same *homoousios* with us as to his manhood; in all things like unto us, sin only excepted, begotten of the Father before all ages as to his Godhead, and in the last days, the same, for us and for our salvation, of Mary the virgin *theotokos* [bearer of God] as to his manhood. One and the same Christ, Son, Lord, only begotten, made known in two natures [which exist] without confusion, without change, without division, without separation; the difference in the natures having been in no wise taken away by reason of the union but rather the properties of each being preserved and both concurring in one the person *[prosopon]* and one substance *[hypostasis]* not parted or divided into two persons *[prospora]* but one and the same Son, an only begotten, the divine logos, the Lord Jesus Christ; even as the prophets from of old [have spoken] concerning him, as the Lord Jesus himself has taught us and as the symbol of the faith. (Karl Rahner, ed., *The Teaching of the Catholic Church* [New York Alba House, 1967], 153–54)

## After Chalcedon

The Council of Chalcedon had stated that there existed two natures, human and divine, in one divine person, with no confusion of natures. But then how could theology express the unity of Jesus? The answer to this question involved further development of trinitarian theology, with the christological aspect clarified in the sixth century, especially in the works of Leontius, Boethius, Rusticus the Deacon, and Maximus the Confessor. Finally, the matter reached its highest level of development in the scholasticism of the Middle Ages. The contemporary Catholic understanding of Jesus represents a heritage that includes the theologians listed above as well as those who formulated medieval scholastic theology.

Before the development of scholastic theology, however, clarification of the subject reached another plateau in the Third Council of Constantinople in 680–81. The teachings of Chalcedon were reaffirmed in this council with the additional formulation of the belief that two kinds of will operated in Jesus, the human and the divine. With this formulation the Church officially rested its case on the expression of the relationship between the human and the divine in Jesus. Further development would come from the efforts of theologians to interpret and explain this definition. For many Catholic theologians, Chalcedon declared the summit of christological thought beyond which theologians need not speculate.

After more than six hundred years of theological speculation and controversy, the Church expounded a formula of relationship between the humanity and divinity of Jesus. The terminology was not completely clear, since the various factions had different nuances for the same words, but at least a general agreement prevailed on the clearer issues. Now theologians could develop their theology of Jesus based on the profession of faith as developed officially by the Church. The Catholic Church has taught this formulation since that time.

## Medieval Christology

The declaration of Chalcedon never completely responded to the question of the precise relationship between the two natures and one person in Jesus. In an effort to respond to this question in their own time, Catholic medieval theologians, using a method that has continued down to this century, first studied the Trinity and then situated Christology within their understanding of the former doctrine. They would study the

Logos (the Word), the Son, in his relationship to Father and Spirit and then consider the incarnation in light of that relationship. Certain theologians even held the opinion that any one of the divine persons could have become human. The sequence: Trinity-creation-fall-incarnation-death-crucifixion-Church became dominant in Catholic theology and lasted.

The great theologians of the Middle Ages also tended to isolate abstract or ontological Christology from concrete or functional Christology. As already noted, the former deals with the Word of God in relationship to the other persons of the Trinity, particularly the origin of the persons—Father, Son and Spirit, and the precise relationship between the two natures and one person in Jesus. The latter concerns the birth, life and ministry, death and resurrection of the Lord and the presence of Jesus as the savior in the Church. Such a division concurs perfectly with the medieval understanding of the fundamental object of theology: God. The study of God precedes the study of the effects of God's action, the incarnation and redemption, on people. This theology derives from an appreciation of the relationship between the Trinity *ad intra* (within itself) and the Trinity *ad extra* (without, in particular, creation and incarnation). All things originate from God, go forth and then return to the trinitarian fullness. In Christology, in the Word, all things proceed from God. Christology that resulted from the definition of Chalcedon and the scholastic synthesis becomes clearer: all things emanate from and return to the eternal Word of God who had become incarnate in Jesus. Understanding Christology demands first situating Jesus in the presence of the Blessed Trinity. Then the theologian can come to specific conclusions with regard to the actual redemptive qualities of the life and death of Jesus. The redemption remains the means by which the eternal Word brings about the restoration of all things, in the Trinity from whom all things originated.

## Why Did God Become Man?

Along with this fundamental approach of Chalcedon, the Catholic Church also asked the question: "Why did God become man?" God must have had a purpose; some motivation for the coming of the Word into human history. Was the incarnation prompted by the fall of the human race and the need for its regeneration, or demanded by the sheer desire of God to share the human condition? Would the Word of God have become human even if humankind had not sinned?

A study of Thomas Aquinas shows an evolution of his thought culminating in the *Summa Theologica*. In this monumental work Aquinas follows Scripture: "Since in Scripture everywhere the reason for the incarnation is assigned to the sin of the first man, it can be said more fittingly that the work of the incarnation was ordered by God as a remedy for sins so that if sin had not existed, there would not have been an incarnation."[5] This also has become fundamental to Catholic theology, but even in the Middle Ages this was not the only tradition.

Duns Scotus argues that the incarnation should be considered apart from the need for redemption. The incarnation of the Word was, first and foremost, the greatest work of God and should be seen antecedently to and independently of the prevision of sin. Redemption was predestined so that Christ could be the adorer and glorifier of the Holy Trinity, the reason for all things, the final and exemplary cause of all in the natural and supernatural world order. Finally, the Word became flesh so that Jesus might be the universal mediator and mystical head of angels and people.

Both opinions relate the incarnation to the Second Person of the Blessed Trinity. While Aquinas derives his opinion in part from Scripture and sees a redemptive incarnation in the New Testament, at a more fundamental level he situates the incarnation in the Trinity of persons in God. In the all-knowing awareness of everything, God had foreseen from all eternity the fall of humankind and then from eternity destined the incarnation as a remedy for the fall. The three persons in God anticipated the fall and provided the incarnation as the remedy.

Duns Scotus taught that God destined Christ primarily to be the adorer and glorifier of the Trinity. The work *ad extra* was an expression of the work *ad intra*. Since the Word was the reason for all things, the final and exemplary cause of all in the natural and supernatural world order, the essential motivation of the incarnation was the necessary fulfillment of a reality in God, not the historical fact of the fall. In subsequent Catholic theology, however, the opinion of Thomas Aquinas prevailed.

## Adoration Due to the Humanity of Jesus

With these considerations in mind, the Catholic Church also developed an understanding that elevated the humanity of Jesus to an extent that often seemed to contradict prior Church teaching. The human Jesus became the same as the divine Jesus. If Jesus is the incarnation of the Second Person of the Blessed Trinity, then believers must adore the humanity of Jesus. Worship expresses the appropriate relationship between creator and creature. Thus, medieval theologians discussed whether the worship due to God should be afforded as well to the humanity of Jesus. The conclusion, of course, was affirmative. Jesus has the Logos (Word) as his center of attribution. The Logos forms the foundation for the worship due to the humanity of Jesus. Because of the hypostatic union of Christ's humanity with the Logos, the humanity is to be reverenced with the adoration due to God, in itself although not for its own sake.

## Could Jesus Be Tempted or Sin?

This theology of Jesus from above, with its emphasis on ontology rather than function, determines the response to all questions concerning ethical perfection. All questions of sin and temptation must be considered in light of the impossibility of sin on the part of the Second Person of the Blessed Trinity as well as the impossibility of tempting the Logos. When Scripture speaks of the cleansing of the Temple, the cursing of the fig tree, the harsh words to his mother, Jesus' anger with the scribes and Pharisees or his condescending attitude toward the Canaanite woman, all must be explained away. Any sign of weakness or even imperfect moral dispositions cannot be ascribed to the person of Jesus. As the Second Person of the Blessed Trinity, Jesus is not only invulnerable to sin and temptation but may not do anything that could be construed as less than acceptable in polite society. Some other explanation had to be found, and medieval theologians offered their personal solutions. Jesus had to have the fullness of virtue, which was the positive side of his sinlessness. Anything less would be beneath the dignity of the Second Person of the Blessed Trinity.

## The Entrance of Jesus into History

The Catholic traditions also emphasize the supernatural origin of Jesus. The entrance of Jesus into human history raises many questions regarding the virginal conception, the relationship of Jesus to Joseph and Joseph to Mary, as well as the roles of the Holy Spirit and God the Father. In Catholic theology Jesus enters into human history through the full paternity of God the Father, without any human paternity. Theologians talk about the *transitus* of the Son of God, passing from the divine sphere into the human sphere. In the divine sphere he remains the Logos and Son, but by his entrance into the human dimension he becomes man, assuming a historicity, living humanly within human history. The primary source of the activity was God who is Father, but not without the involvement of the other persons of the Trinity. All that was created, and especially humankind, was created through the Word in the Spirit, so that in the Spirit all things participate in the Word. The history of God's dealings with people evolved in historical stages. In these steps the most important moment was the entrance of the Son into history.

Humankind had experienced sin. In spite of human failure God planned to bring humankind into a holy society with divinity. Thus, the Father sent the Son as the Word of God incarnate. While it is primarily the work of the Father, it is also the *kenosis* (emptying) of the Son. Jesus as the Word incarnate entered sinful flesh that he might bear the sins of the world and bring forgiveness and salvation.

Since the source of Jesus was God the Father, Mary, the Mother of Jesus, was a virgin. Catholic theology begins with the thought of the paternity of the Father in the Trinity as the source of the Son, and then naturally Jesus had to be born of a virgin. No need for further paternity existed, since paternity already formed the basis of the Logos's relationship to God the Father.

## Virginal Conception

Christian tradition from its earliest years taught the doctrine of the virginal conception. Both Mathew and Luke teach a conception by the power of the Holy Spirit. Even before the year 200, the affirmation of belief in Christ Jesus was expanded in the old Roman Creed by a reference to his birth from the Virgin Mary. This creedal formula counteracted the heresies of Docetism and Gnosticism that questioned the reality of the humanity of Jesus. The Nicene Creed also affirmed a virginal conception. During this same period the whole question of the relationship of the humanity and divinity of Jesus was being hotly debated. The Church tried to preserve both the divinity and the humanity of Christ in the face of heresies. In such a situation the symbol of the Virgin Mary was ideal. It allowed one to emphasize "virgin" to preserve the divinity while stressing that Mary was a woman to preserve the true humanity. The Catholic teaching on the virginal conception and that on the divinity and the humanity of Jesus are thus a support to one another.

## The Activities and Works of Jesus (Divine Acts)

In traditional Catholic Christology, all the activities and works of Jesus were considered divine acts since they come from the divine person. Many theologians would divide the activities of Jesus into strictly divine acts (miracles and prophecies, which only God could perform) and the daily activities of his life, which are called divine acts only in the widest use of that term.

The medieval theologians used Aristotelian principles in their Christology. Actions belong to the person and derive from the essence. As a result of these principles, all of the activities are predicated of the person of Jesus, which is the divine person of the Word. The Word of God, the eternal Son, raised Lazarus from the tomb, and the Word of God wept because Lazarus was dead; the Word of God prophesied that Peter would deny him three times, and the Word of God washed the feet of Peter.

The activities of Jesus such as eating and drinking, sleeping and walking are truly human, but since Jesus the man is the divine person of the Word, these actions would also be called divine by reason of being acts of a divine person. The theology of Jesus as the Second Person of the Blessed Trinity views all of the actions of Jesus as divine, since all are directed to the person of the Word who gives them their foundation. Theologians concluded from these premises that any action of Jesus could be redemptive, since any action was of infinite value.

Catholic apologetics developed to the point of asserting an obligation to believe in the divinity of Jesus. If Jesus performed miracles and uttered prophecies, then these actions manifested to all that they face more than just an ordinary human being. In Jesus people encounter a divine person. A theologian could read the gospels, which speak of the amazement of the listeners: "We never saw anything like this" (Mark 2:12) and conclude that expressions like these, of which there are many, show that those who knew Christ beheld the deeds he performed in his human nature and realized that he was not just human. They realized that his human nature lay mysteriously but firmly rooted in a person who was far above anything human. Jesus was divine. Once an individual realized the presence of such divine activities and nothing the person encountered contradicted human reason, an obligation to believe in Jesus as divine naturally resulted. This theology and apologetics found its roots in the acceptance of Jesus as the person of the Word, which formed the basis for any understanding of the activities of Jesus in his ministry.

Further speculation on the value of any activity of Jesus concluded that any of his acts would be sufficient to redeem humankind, because all activity reverted back to the person of the Word. The shedding of blood at the circumcision was an activity, which, since it was rooted in the person of the Word, could be sufficient for the redemption of all. To die a human death was a decision on the part of the Word of God, but this activity was in no way necessary for the salvific power of redemption.

Traditional Catholic theology understood all of this through the philosophical understanding of instrumental causality as presented by Thomas Aquinas. An instrument that an artist uses produces an artistic result only if it is closely controlled and united to the artist. The control of the instrument by the artist does not deprive the instrument of its own specific activity nor of its contribution to the final effect produced. Rather, the effect comes simultaneously from the principal cause, the artist, and from the instrumental cause (secondary cause), the material used.

Applying these notions to Jesus, Thomas argued that such humanity becomes a conjoined instrument. The humanity of Jesus preserves its own proper power in its activities and has distinctive characteristics. The principal cause remains always the person of the Word. This explains the theological understanding of all of the activities of Jesus, including the most ordinary, as divine. Even if some of these actions are divine only in a wide sense, all are referred to the principal cause, the person of the Word.

## The Knowledge of Jesus

The question of the knowledge and consciousness of Jesus figures more prominently than all of the other factors mentioned in any discussion of Jesus as Second Person of the Blessed Trinity. The Council of Constantinople defined as a truth of faith the existence of two activities in Jesus, divine and human. As a result, theologians, especially during the Middle Ages, developed the theories of two kinds of knowledge: human and divine. As God, Jesus possessed the divine knowledge of God proper to each person of the Blessed Trinity; as man, he also possessed human knowledge and the human way of knowing common to all people. By his divine knowledge, Jesus knew God in himself and all other things in God. This divine knowledge, the uncreated knowledge of the Word, existed as equal to that of the Father and of the Holy Spirit.

The human knowledge of Jesus differed essentially from the divine knowledge and can be further distinguished. Firstly, from the very moment of his conception, Jesus' humanity enjoyed the beatific vision. This knowledge belonged to his humanity by reason of the hypostatic union. Thus, Jesus had a human knowledge of his divine being and personality. He always had this knowledge, which the saints enjoy in heaven, in the highest possible intensity.

Secondly, Jesus' mind was also endowed with infused knowledge. He knew, as created spirits know, all that was equal to him and inferior to him as human, and he had, moreover, knowledge of God more perfect than any that a human being would have by nature. Fittingly Jesus knew more theology than all of the medieval theologians put together. Following this principle, some later theologians believed that Jesus knew more than all of the greatest minds in the world.

Finally, as a human, Jesus had ordinary acquired and empirical knowledge, which he gained from his contact with others and his earthly experience. Jesus learned like anyone else. But then what need did Jesus have for this knowledge if he already knew everything through his divinity and through infused knowledge? Medieval theologians do not explain precisely the relationship between infused knowledge and experiential knowledge.

Some might think so complete a set of distinctions would reflect a real division in Jesus himself. But since one person remains the source of these types of knowledge, such an analytical approach retains the unity without division. As God, Jesus knew all things and as man Jesus knew all things in God.

Historically, when some theologians objected that such a vision appears incompatible with the suffering described in the gospels, other theologians turned to a physical example to help to understand how suffering could coexist with a beatifying vision: "A storm can lash the sides of a mountain and let loose on it rain and hail and lightning. But nothing disturbs the peace of the mountain heights." The same was true of Jesus.

Today most theologians suggest that since Jesus was fully human, the human knowledge with which he operated could only know of the relationship to the divine Sonship in an undifferentiated and nonconceptual horizon of being. Jesus did not walk around knowing everything about everything. As individuals develop in their self-understanding, so Jesus grew in his self-awareness. This position does not oppose any official teaching of the Church but rather returns to the earlier traditions, which sought to unite the schools of Alexandria and Antioch and the functional and ontological understandings.

## Resurrection

The resurrection of Jesus is at the foundation and at the culmination of all Christology. Yet the resurrection did not always figure so prominently in Catholic Christology. The Church often presented the resurrection as the greatest of the miracles of Jesus. If the person of the Word is responsible for all of the activities of the earthly life of Jesus, then, as the Word of God, Jesus raised himself from the grave. This miracle, the greatest of all, proved to all who would listen that in truth he was the divine Son of God. In the history of Christology theologians related the resurrection to his other miracles, and they understood this culmination of his ministry as the natural outcome of his divine nature. The eternal Word become man, was aware of his divinity even as he lived his human life, performed actions that belonged properly to the Second Person of the Blessed Trinity, understood completely his mission and, finally, after he had finished his task on earth and had been crucified, rose from the dead to prove to all the truth of his mission and person. Some earlier theologians believed that only in this way can believers understand the meaning of Jesus of Nazareth. Today, following the New Testament, theologians see the resurrection as the act of God the Father: "But God raised him up having loosed the pangs of death, because it was not possible for him to be held by it (Acts 2:24)."

In spite of the strong emphasis on Jesus as the Second Person of the Blessed Trinity in the official teaching of the Church, other traditions were never completely forgotten. New approaches continue to affect the meaning of Jesus as the Second Person of the Blessed Trinity. The strong humanizing of Jesus in the past thirty years has affected traditional Catholic theology. Emphasizing the Christology from below represented by the school of Antioch, some current theologies in the Catholic tradition also see Jesus as reflecting God. They refer to Jesus as the human face of God.

## The Human Face of God

Much, but not all, of present Catholic theology focuses on the humanity of Jesus. In the opinion of many theologians today, the uniqueness and universality of the Lord does not arise from his divinity but his humanity. Movement back and forth, from an emphasis on the humanity to an emphasis on the divinity, has always characterized the history of theology. The ancient school of Antioch, emphasizing the humanity, and that of Alexandria, emphasizing the divinity, have had their counterparts throughout history. Both schools exist within Catholic theology today.

Some Catholic theologians today present Jesus in the context of anthropology: Jesus is the point toward which the human race has always been directed; or the humanity of Jesus is a new way of being human; or the deity does not exclude but actually includes humanity; or the human in Jesus is the realization of the divine; or Jesus manifests God as the compassion of God. These new approaches are found in popular magazines as well as in scholarly journals, so the Christian world knows what is being said, even if at times the debate causes confusion and often provides little understanding.

The principle that underlies this approach locates the unique universality of Jesus precisely in his being human. This Christology is not from above and deductive, but from below and inductive. Theologians do not discuss something that is above or below or beside, but a reality that is within: the human expresses the divine. God chose as revelation the human form, the man Jesus. The mystery of Jesus lies in his humanity. The human becomes the localization of the divine. With this perspective theologians must ask, "What does it mean to be human and what does it mean to be divine?"

## The Human and the Divine

At first sight it seems easy to respond to the question, "What does it mean to be human?" On closer scrutiny, the answer is not so evident. What characterizes humanity? Is there a difference between being human as a man and as a woman? Does age affect the meaning of humanity? Do circumstances such as culture or education? Are there limits to what a human being can be? Can what is human be defined as "what humans do"? If so, killing and destroying are as human as love and compassion.

What does it mean to be divine? Everyone has some idea of divinity: power, knowledge, eternity, authority, control, love, mercy—all have been associated with divinity. But what, truly, does divinity mean? If God has created humankind in his image, has the human race done little more than repay the compliment? When people accept a divine revelation based upon faith, how much of the content is the result of human projection, offering God-for-humanity but not God in self? Does the unveiling of God imply a further veiling?

Christianity believes that Jesus revealed God. But how is it possible for the human to be the vehicle of the divine? Can anyone really separate what is human and divine in Jesus? If everything is perceived as both human and divine, does such a prospect lose sight of the divinity, or of the humanity? At the very outset the question poses a problem in trying to discover how the human can be the expression of the divine. If people are not sufficiently clear on the meaning of humanity, then surely no one can completely delineate the meaning of divinity.

## Contemporary Thought

The behavioral sciences in recent years have shown that words like *humanity, human nature* and *human behavior* are empty formulae that can be filled with disparate elements. Humans kill and betray; they lie and cause suffering as well as love and forgive. The most noble qualities can be predicated of being human, as can the most debased. Also, some theologians say that the concept of the divine needs rethinking; that God can be in process. This means that the qualities traditionally associated with God can be forgotten. God can "become" in human history. Change is possible even with God. But does this new way of thinking, termed process theology, also fall into the same trap of creating God in a human image?

The ability to respond to all of the above questions eludes every theologian. Yet, Christians have a faith statement that God is present in Jesus and believers come to know God through Jesus; he is the human face of God. "Philip, he who sees me sees the Father" (John 14:9). Since theology is faith seeking understanding, the faith statement remains. Then the pursuit of the contents of that faith statement is possible, even if the conclusions remain forever limited.

## The Foundation

The examination of Jesus as the human face of God involves questions of anthropology as well as of history. Was Jesus, in a historical moment, the fullness of what it means to be human, the definitive and eschatological man, the new man, the primordial image for all of humanity? Do people learn what it means to be human by observing the life and death of this historical person? These questions presuppose another faith statement: humankind is created in the image of God. "So God created man in his own image, in the image of God he created him, male and female he created them" (Gen 1:27).

Within the Judeo-Christian heritage all people are created in the image of God. They can manifest God; every person can be the vice-regent of God, manifesting some of the qualities of the divine. The image is not limited to the spiritual nature of persons but involves their totality. An inherent dignity results which is humanity's heritage and destiny.

Christians recognize Jesus to be the image of God in an exemplary way:

> He is the image of the invisible God; the firstborn of all creation. (Col 1:15)

> He reflects the glory of God, and bears the very stamp of his
> nature. (Heb 1:3)

But Jesus is not separated from others who are also created in
the image of God. He will always be the firstborn of many
brethren and like us in all things but sin (Heb 4:15). Understanding Jesus as the human face of God depends first upon believing
that every person is created in the image of God and can thus
reflect the same.

To fill out the words *humanity* and *human nature* with content
and then apply them to Jesus, however, is not sufficient. There
will be differences between Jesus and the rest of the human race
as well as similarities. Jesus lived, for example, without the influence of evil and sin. In faith, followers of Jesus learn that the
usual understanding of being human is not adequate. Jesus of
Nazareth infused a meaning to being human that enhances every
human being. Humanity or someone's idea of what it means to
be human is not the measure of evaluating Jesus, but rather his
humanity is the criterion by which people not only judge themselves but even come to realize their potential.

Jesus as the human face of God reveals in a personal way the
meaning of God. The two elements, the human and the divine,
are not disparate or separated, but are united in one historical
person. This implies further consequences. This revelation of
God took place in a personal way, circumscribed within the finite
limits of the human Jesus, the historical person. In Jesus people
may experience the presence of a being at one *with* and the same
time *for* humanity and *for* God.

## Why Jesus Was the Human Face of God

If all people are created in the image of God, if all have the
potential to manifest the divine, then why is Jesus singled out to
be the human face of God in an exemplary way? What is it in
Jesus that differentiates him from millions of others who bear
the face of the human and contain the stamp of the divine?

The human exhibits inherent limitations in attempting to
express the divine. Believers need not try to measure Jesus

against some abstract concept of humanity; no a priori principles need to be established from which deductions will flow about why Jesus is the exemplary image of God. Rather, the procedure begins with the human Jesus and relates his experience to all human experiences. Study his life to discover how, in his living, others experienced the divine. This process will discover what humanity means, or at least what humanity meant to the historical Jesus as recorded by those who believed he was the presence of God.

Such an attempt involves investigating the self-awareness of Jesus. That immediately causes hesitation. How can anyone enter into the personality of Jesus, seeking to unravel the fundamental way in which Jesus is present to himself as an individual? The task of exploring oneself is difficult enough; how much more difficult it must be to attempt to deal with the self-awareness of another. Yet, the words, actions and attitudes of Jesus as recorded in the gospels can teach much about his self-understanding. The study must always be incomplete, but with careful examination of the impact Jesus had upon others some entrance into his personal life can be gained. This helps to situate Jesus in relationship to his personal life and at the same time reveals his distinctive personality.

## Jesus' Concept of God

Most major religions present an image of God as a loving parent, a Father. Judaism recognized the paternity of God, and it was in this atmosphere that Jesus grew up. But Jesus was not content to affirm God as Father in the same way every other pious Jew would address God. For Jesus, God was Abba. God was like the loving parent who responds to a small child. There was an intimate relationship between God and Jesus different from that of other people. Jesus alluded to this difference. He spoke of my God and your God, my Father and your Father, and never our Father (the Gospel of Matthew has the Lord's Prayer beginning with "*Our* Father." Luke does not. Matthew recorded the actual form of this prayer as recited in his community rather than the words of Jesus). The universal meaning of Jesus contained in this unique dependence on God was at the very heart of his message and ministry.

The study of the gospels also discloses a keen sense of dependency upon God. Everything Jesus has he has received from his Father. The Father has taught him all and has given him direction; he has been sent to accomplish the mission of the Father; the Father is greater than Jesus, and it is the Father's will that Jesus will accomplish. In all of religious experience the sense of dependence and creatureliness is significant. The trace of God present in human life is experienced by some, even though denied by others. The awareness of limitations, of a lack of fulfillment in life, the sense of mortality, can contribute to an awakening of the question of God. Do people live in isolation or in need of others? Can personal relations fulfill the need for persons to move out of themselves, or is there another force, a power and an ultimate person who can give the true foundation for dependence and creatureliness? Evidently for Jesus the sense of dependence and creatureliness relates to his self-awareness of God in his life as Abba. Jesus relates to God not with a sense of identity, since he will always maintain the difference between himself and his Father, but in the spirit of revelation. He can reveal God as Father, as Abba, because Jesus is God's Son. The union of willing and even of being makes Jesus present where God the Father is present and vice versa.

## Personal Awareness of Goodness

Everyone experiences moments in life of personal worth and goodness. Jesus had a unique sense of his goodness. He did not live a fragmented life; he possessed a harmony that resulted in a consistency in all of his words and actions. He maintained a tranquility, even in the midst of the greatest conflicts, that evoked admiration. Jesus was aware of his own principles and would not compromise them; he lived what he believed in an integral way.

Many of these qualities are similar to those that all good persons possess, but there is a difference between Jesus and ourselves. The power of evil and sin waxes strong in the world and in the hearts of people. Instead of contributing to a better environment, people, through sinful choices, strengthen the evil in the environment, which in turn supports an increase in personal sin. Lives that are fragmented, out of harmony, lacking in consistency, filled with compromise in the midst of personal turmoil—such lives have characterized the history of the human race. Jesus lived differently.

He did not repay evil with evil; he did not treat people in kind. Jesus decided how he would live his life and would not brook any interference. Jesus did not retaliate against the people who maltreated him. He lived in an environment that contained evil, but instead of contributing to the strength of the evil, he lessened its power by his manifestation of goodness, which absorbed the evil and transformed it. He lived as the compassionate, kind and forgiving friend, even when he experienced rejection, cynicism and resentment. He knew his God, knew his mission and lived accordingly. His life was remarkable because of his ability to express the power of goodness.

## Sin

The goodness that people express has to be viewed in relationship to the evil that also exists in the human heart. A lack of consistency characterizes both the inner human spirit and external actions. Paul recognized this tension when he wrote:

> For I do not do the good that I want, but the evil that I do not want, is what I do. (Rom 7:19)

When faced with goodness, people often react against it. They respond with resentment, or attempt to belittle or deny the reality of that goodness. When faced with evil, people often accept it, even though they know that evil should be resisted. The war of the members against the spirit is fought on the plains of the human heart, and the individual experiences frequent personal casualties.

Jesus seems not to have experienced this internal warfare. What he did was surely learned from his environment, but he appropriated the goodness and rejected the evil. His actions, his words, even his basic attitudes toward human life seemed to have their roots within. Jesus lived by transferring the epicenter of his life to God, to Abba, and thus the externals always expressed the internal principle. This does not mean that he found his center of existence outside of himself; rather he centered his life in relationship to God and thus he could live a harmonious life in which the outward expression flowed from an inner conviction. The closer a person is to God, the more freedom that person experiences. Jesus, the graced man, lived in freedom and in harmony.

## Value and Purpose

Finally, Jesus lived with a definite sense of purpose for his life and with an energy that defies imitation. He was too sure, too definite, too aware of his value and his mission to ever be compared with others. His presence in human history can have a definite effect on every person, especially when it comes to questions about the ultimate meaning of personal life or the meaning of God. In Jesus the fusion of principle and practice met. Jesus saw his purpose and meaning in light of his proclamation of the kingdom of God. He knew that no final response can be given to the quest for meaning unless it includes the presence of God and unless people accept the communion that should exist between God and the human race.

For Christians who struggle to discover personal meaning and the overall purpose of their lives, the unique universality of Jesus will always involve the two poles of his own meaning: his relationship to God and the way he expressed this relationship in his life. To relate to God as Abba, the human person would have to be elevated and somehow participate in the realm of the divine, otherwise the divinity would not become part of personal experience. No one could relate to God as Jesus did unless God invited such a relationship and created its possibility. All people are created in the image of God, and this abstract belief becomes concretized in the actual inclusion of the religious element in the human search for meaning. Anyone who seeks to discover some purpose in life must include the divine, precisely because God created all in the image and likeness of God. Jesus fulfilled this human destiny. He lived for God and all who met him knew it.

## Jesus and Others

Comparisons can certainly be made to other human beings who lived with a sense of dependence, found purpose in the divine or spiritual dimension and expressed some goodness in life. But the life of Jesus involves more than just the sum total of the best of human qualities that have been expressed in history. He founded his life on his self-awareness and his sense of God. He appears to be the man without sin, able to live in the human and sinful environment without feeling its sting and without affirming its presence by personal ratification. His sense of purpose, his mission, exists within and not just without. Nor did he seem to struggle to achieve tranquility and harmony. The level of humanity he reached, all people seek; he remains, even in his unique universality, the firstborn of many brethren.

If the terms *humanity* or *human nature* connote empty formulae that need to be filled with content, the life of Jesus reflects the elements that comprise the human essence in its highest form. If the divine can be expressed to human beings only in a human way, then only the highest example of the human spirit can be the vehicle that God uses for that revelation. To speak of a combination of the human and the divine, or of Jesus as the human face of God still involves a faith statement, but one that has been somewhat unfolded. The New Testament presents some ideas on why Jesus was the human face of God in an eminent way. It also shows how people can still relate him to the universal human potential of being the image of God. Jesus could be the expression of God in this preeminent way, but the question still remains: "How was Jesus the human face of God?"

## How Jesus Revealed God the Father

The gospels make clear how contingent, ambivalent, limited and precarious was the human life of Jesus. He lived as a man, not as a woman and not as androgynous. He lived in Palestine under Roman occupation, with all of the contingencies and limitations that such a narrow mode of existence imposed. He did not benefit from world culture or world knowledge; he did not act and react with people of vastly divergent backgrounds and experiences. He lived an ordinary life in his own historical setting.

The evangelists do not present a biography of Jesus in any sense. But in their writings they offer insights into some aspects of his personality and life that often become overlooked but are important if we are to understand him as the human face of God. He slept, ate and drank, went to parties, enjoyed the company of friends, was part of a family and lived in a small community. He wept over the failure of people to listen to him, felt frustrated with his disciples, grew angry and disappointed. These aspects of his life manifest his humanity and surely do not demonstrate any great originality. He lived as part of Roman-dominated Palestine in an eclectic environment that was home to many philosophical systems and religious strains. In this world of contrasts Jesus stood out, however, as a remarkable person. He caused his listeners to wonder, to be shocked and to be scandalized. At one point even his own family thought he was out of his mind (Mark 3:21). The evangelists are aware of his uniqueness but do not deliberately contrast him with his contemporaries. He seems quite ordinary most of the time. He lived a hidden life for many years, became an itinerant preacher for a brief period and finally was crucified. Yet, when these same writers treat of his power and his influence over people, they show him displaying a quality that far exceeds ordinary human expression. Jesus possessed a transcendence, but one that made itself felt in and through the ordinary.

The gospels narrate both the ordinary and extraordinary in Jesus. The ordinary aspects of life: his relationships with people, his attitude toward Judaism, his sense of forgiveness, his sensitivity toward others, his openness to people's problems, his delight in human friendships, his pain at the lack of understanding of his disciples, his frustration with the hardness of people's hearts, all bear the expression of the divine. As the human face of God, every detail in his life shared in this transcendence. A study of the New Testament should not be concerned with isolating moments of the life of the Lord, but with the manifestations of the divine that have shone through the ordinary elements of his human life.

## Attitudes

The attitudes of Jesus figure significantly in understanding how Jesus reflected God the Father. The heart of his gospel message proclaims that God as Father cares for humankind with a concern for all. Jesus expressed an indestructible certainty that God offers salvation. This reflected his personal attitude, a conviction that salvation, the making whole of humanity and the perfection of the individual are possible and that ultimately the meaning of life involves the fullest expression of personal freedom and liberation. Giving oneself to God paradoxically brings personal freedom. Jesus expressed these attitudes in how he lived and also in how he died. In his attitude toward life he maintained a fruitful tension between the contradictory poles of suffering, evil and sin, and salvation linked with final and irrevocable good. In Jesus the goodness outweighed the evil that surrounded him; thus he could give others an example of how to resist the evil and accept and manifest the good. The basis for this attitude was the belief that God, Abba, is greater than all suffering and grief and greater even than any ability to accept goodness. Creation itself reflects the goodness of God. Such a positive attitude revealed Jesus' personal conviction of how God regarded humankind.

The attitudes displayed by Jesus in his personal concern for the poor, the compassion he offered to those who were the outcasts of society, the kindness he manifested to sinners, to widows, to children, to his disciples and friends—these express the human dimensions of his personality, but they also express God's concerns. Jesus possessed a universality that included the possibility of the conquest of all personal and social forms of alienation. The sense of separateness, the experience of living marginally, the isolation that causes so much pain can be resolved into a harmonious and fruitful life. Peace does not exist only on the interior plane, nor should it be seen as simply a social phenomenon. Rather, it is a combination of the two. Jesus did not retreat from the marketplace of human life, and thus his meaning, his revelation of the healing of the torn fabric of humanity, had to be accomplished in the domains of both the personal and the social. His personal attitude underlines the interrelationship of the two elements. People will know personal hurt in a way that no social or political cure will be able to remedy, and vice versa. The death of a mother or father inflicts pain personally, just as subhuman housing, lack of education, restrictions on travel and the inability to participate in the destiny of one's country cause suffering socially and politically. Jesus, in his attitude toward human problems and human needs, offered a message of universal significance that would respond to the various phases and facets of human alienation. He preached and lived universal reconciliation.

## Freedom and Liberation

Jesus revealed the meaning of God in his attitude toward liberation, freedom and salvation. A feeling of apartness or alienation often causes or contributes to struggle in life, and so Jesus offered an attitude of creative love for all. Based upon the freedom given by God and the salvation promised, Jesus believed that reconciliation was possible, and he actually lived according to this principle. No one was excluded; no one need feel left out. He welcomed into his company prostitutes, widows, tax collectors and sinners as well as the wealthy, educated and powerful. The communion that Jesus preached was experienced in his person and offered to those who would respond to him in faith. Jesus did not offer an absolute principle, but reminded people of a possibility that could be realized. Jesus gave to human history not the final answer to the question of the search for meaning and liberation, but rather the expectation that humanity can be liberated completely, not by seeking something outside of human history, but by seeking something within the human situation.

Freedom and liberation and meaning and God will be discovered not abstractly or only within the narrow confines of the human spirit, but outwardly, bodily, involved with others in the same quest, within social structures as well as in the quiet of one's heart and in the depth of the spirit. Jesus had friends, talked with his disciples about his hopes, encouraged them to make their own decisions with regard to law, ignored social customs when they restricted relationships and also retreated to the mountains to pray alone. The exterior freedom conditioned his interior freedom. Social freedom always includes the encounter with other free people and with God. Jesus answered the God question by helping people to find God within themselves, within others and within their world. Without denying God as Creator and Judge of all, Jesus revealed a God who was like a kind and loving parent ever present to the children. God (Abba for Jesus) encourages those same children to grow and develop, giving them all that was possible in the presence of Jesus and continuing to love those children even when they failed to respond. God was not an absent power or force but was present in human history in the birth of a child, in the presence of family and friends and in a ministry for others.

## How Jesus Died

Jesus had a unique personal experience of God. The core of his message depends on the presence of the saving God in his personal history. God knows intimately the human race. Understanding Jesus, then, involves an appreciation of God's care for all people in human history. The disturbing point, however, in the life of Jesus, as well as in all human lives, is the presence of signs that appear to contradict the loving care of God. How can anyone deal with the suffering and death of Jesus? Why the crucifixion? Why the rejection and misunderstanding and the seeming abandonment of Jesus by God: "My God my God why have you abandoned me?" (Mark 15:34; Matt 27:46)?

The attitudes of Jesus, his words and actions, how he faced suffering and the experience of his death make people rethink the meaning of suffering. The pain of Jesus, his crucifixion and death and all the misunderstanding and rejection he endured did not alter his awareness of the saving presence of God and the nearness of the kingdom. This impels all to examine failure and pain. In the midst of terrible human suffering, Jesus trusted in the salvation and power and goodness of his Father. The death of Jesus, however it might appear, was not a failure. Jesus died as he lived: He trusted in God and believed that eventually liberation, salvation and freedom would be accomplished. God remained present to Jesus as Jesus remained faithful to who he was, to others and to God his Father.

An alternative to the Christian response to suffering and death, seen in some philosophies of the past and present, considers life itself an illusion and concludes that people die as they live, in absurdity. The early Christians, however, believed that in Jesus the benevolent God had the final word. God raised Jesus from the dead. In his dying the Lord committed himself in trust to God. "Father into your hands I commend my spirit" (Luke 23:46). He did not renege on his teaching. Death was the summation of his life, the culmination of his conscious choice for the sake of others. He died as he lived. The value judgments made in his ministry were all completed in that final decision to trust his life to the hands of his loving Father. The outcome was not yet known, but was accepted in faith. The Father responded by raising Jesus from the dead. His suffering and death did not lose their significance by this action, but were seen as the prelude to the establishment of Jesus in power: "This Jesus, God raised up....God has made him both Lord and Christ, this Jesus whom you crucified" (Acts 2:32, 36b).

Suffering in life always causes problems. When people accept Jesus, including his pain and death, they know that God has experienced human suffering and cares about humans who suffer. Israel, in its sacred books, records the divine pathos in its history. Now, in Jesus, God is present in human suffering through the experience of the Son. The sorrow borne brings redemption, since through the faithful acceptance of this suffering the believers can experience aspects of life that are possible only through pain. Love is purified in pain; truth becomes imperative; mortality, limitation and dependence increase in magnitude, loom over the sickbed and stand beside mourners. God knows all pain and sorrow and suffering, for God has experienced the same in Jesus, the Son.

## Life, Death and Resurrection

Happily, the crucifixion culminates in the resurrection. But this final dimension of the meaning of Jesus cannot be separated from the totality of his life. Belief in the risen Lord sees the continuity between this proclamation of God's presence in word and action and the universal significance of Jesus for all people. As risen Lord, God does not only vindicate Jesus; as risen Lord his relationship to God is brought to completion. In his dying in love and obedience to the Father, Jesus revealed the mystery of his relationship to God; and in the resurrection the Father manifested the relationship between God the Father and Jesus. Jesus had committed himself to the Father in his life and then in his death. When the Father raised him, the Father manifested an eternal commitment in return.

The resurrection also manifests liberation from earlier limitations, but the content of this liberation depends upon an appreciation of the earthly life of Jesus. The two cannot be separated. A risen Lord separated from his earthly life is mythical; an earthly Jesus separated from the risen Lord is another human failure. Only through the reciprocal relationship between the two realities does it become clear that the resurrection founds all faith in the earthly Jesus as the human face of God.

## Creative Remembering

The followers of Jesus experienced the risen Lord. As a result of these experiences they gathered together to become the foundation of the Christian community that became the Church. Properly speaking, the resurrection created faith in Jesus as the human face of God because only in terms of the risen Lord could people speak of the exaltation of the earthly Jesus and appreciate the divine transcendence that was present all through his life. The gospels contain formulae or expressions of faith that show some appreciation of the divinity of Jesus, but these must be seen as attempts on the part of the early believers to remember in a creative way what Jesus said and did and then understand the meaning involved. After the resurrection the disciples could see the significance of many of the events of the life of the Lord that they had personally witnessed. Now they could see him as the human manifestation of the divine. His mission revealed the Father, but this was understood only in the light of the resurrection. Since God raised Jesus from the dead, his earthly life took on an importance greater than that which his followers could have understood during their actual experience of his public ministry.

The early believers had to identify faith in the risen Lord with faith in the man Jesus: The raised and exalted Christ of faith had to be seen in continuity with the Jesus of history. The disciples with their Easter faith creatively recalled the major events in the life of Jesus and recognized them as manifestations of the divine. His teachings, the way he treated others, were now invested with the presence of the divine. The apostles saw the ordinary events in the life of Jesus through an additional dimension: the human reflecting the divine. They looked upon Jesus and recognized the presence of God.

## Easter Faith

Easter faith was not newly created by the experience of the risen Lord without a support in the historical experience of Jesus. The foundation in the earthly experience of Jesus by his followers was perfected and understood only through the resurrection. The faith of the disciples can be compared with ordinary human faith, which grows from the fundamental intuition to the point of full acceptance. You meet someone; you like that person, feel comfortable; you talk; you begin to confide; finally you believe in that person and trust that person with your life. Such a thing occurred with Jesus and his disciples in his ministry, but the resurrection led them to the fullness of faith in him. The Easter event was the principal basis for his followers' faith in Jesus.

As with faith in Christ, so the understanding of faith in Christ must be based upon the resurrection. The theological appreciation of Jesus as the human face of God will depend upon the acceptance of the resurrection. Christology rests on the Easter event, which involves not just what happened to Jesus but what happened to the followers of Jesus. The Easter experience lies in the assembling of the disciples in the name of Jesus and in the power of the risen Lord in their midst. The resurrection and the assembling are two facets of one event: Jesus is present to his disciples in a new way— the one who has been accepted by the Father and thus has been changed in the relationship he has to his followers.

In the light of this experience, the disciples interpreted certain sayings of Jesus, along with some passages of the Old Testament, theologically. Members of the early church community coming from a Jewish heritage reflected on many Old Testament passages, in particular the servant songs of Isaiah (Isa 42:1-4; 49:1-6; 50:4-9; 52:13-53) and many of the Psalms such as 110 and 118. Relating these Old Testament traditions to the actual life and death of Jesus enabled the early Church to see the plan of God begun in the Old Testament fulfilled in the life, death and resurrection of Jesus. The meaning of the death of Jesus was understood in the light of the resurrection, which in turn brought a new appreciation of the Old Testament notion of the messiah. Even the cosmic theology of Ephesians and Colossians is founded on the resurrection. Only after his resurrection, when he is Lord in power, does he reign over all (Col 1:15 ff.). The resurrection manifests the conviction of the Christian church that in Jesus as risen Lord the divine presence has taken a human form in history. This human form, the earthly Jesus, has now been accepted by God the Father as the final and eschatological manifestation of the Father's concern for humankind.

## Human and Divine

The precise relationship between the human and divine, however, still plagues any study of Christology. Theology cannot allow the loss of any of Jesus' humanness, nor can there be a loss of the divine. With difficulty theologians and the Church will speak of two components, or two realities. Rather, all should be conscious of two aspects of the one reality. To speak of Jesus as the human face of God does not imply that the human person of

Jesus was just taken up into the Logos. Such statements would convey the idea that Jesus was constituted as a human being and was then taken over by the person of the Logos. The problem lies in the inability to find language that can speak about two total aspects of one reality. How can Jesus, as human, also be called the Son of God? Even the use of "also" gives pause, since it, too, implies a separation rather than a unity in the reality.

In his humanity Jesus intimately lives with the Father, and by virtue of this intimacy he is the Son. The center of his being as a man reposes not in himself, but in God the Father. The center, the support, even the heart of his personality consists in his relationship to God. Jesus was constitutively related and oriented to God as Father and at the same time related to people as brother, as the bringer of salvation and the saving presence of God. Jesus possessed this unique combination, and that distinguishes him and gives him his identity. His autonomy as Jesus of Nazareth and Son constitutes the total relation to the one whom he calls Father: the God whose special love concerns the human race.

Appreciating from whence this experience arose involves understanding the milieu of Judaism under Roman domination. Every human experience, even if thought original, stands in a tradition of social experience. No individual ever draws upon potential inner strengths alone. The consciousness of Jesus was like that of any other human being who lived within the Judaic tradition in Palestine. His experience of God was nurtured by his Jewish traditions as well as by his human awareness of creatureliness and dependence. Unlike his contemporaries, however, he was more concerned with proclaiming the saving nearness of God than announcing God's apocalyptic judgment. It was this saving presence that he identified with himself. Unless he suffered illusions, the only explanation was that God had manifested in Jesus the divine saving presence in a final and definitive way. His followers in fact reacted in this way. In Jesus the divine disclosed itself in a creaturely and human way so that all might call this an instance of human transcendence, or transcending humanity, or even eschatological humanity. But even here no manifestation equals the reality. Jesus discloses the divine transcendence and also veils God, since the created can never adequately reveal or unveil the infinite.

## Philosophical Foundations

This discussion can continue only by involving the various efforts to give a firmer philosophical groundwork to the relationship and the presence of these two total aspects of the one reality of Jesus. The works of the Catholic theologians Karl Rahner, Piet Schoonenberg, Edward Schillebeeckx, Hans Küng and others attempt to deal with this question on a philosophical ground. The agreement that they seem to have reached accepts as fundamental the model of Jesus as the human face of God (John O'Grady), or the sacrament of God (Edward Schillebeeckx), or the human manifestation of the divine (Karl Rahner), or God in Man (Piet Schoonenberg), or the Symbol of God (Roger Haight). In each instance the theologian tries to maintain the foundations of Chalcedon and Jesus as the Second Person of the Blessed Trinity and break out to include other traditions based upon Scripture and human experience as well as contemporary philosophy.

All of these theologians deal with Jesus as the human face of God. In him, in his own person, is revealed both the eschatological (the final, the ultimate, the irrevocable) face of all humanity and the trinitarian fullness of God's being. Jesus, being a man, is God translated for humanity in a human fashion. Existence for others sacramentalizes the proexistence of God or the self-giving of God to creatures. God is God for people and with people. The unique universality of God lies in Jesus' eschatological humanity, as the sacrament of God's love for all. In forgetfulness of self, Jesus identified himself with God's cause, which at the same time was the cause of all people. Thus, Jesus lives as the firstborn of many brethren, since he is the one leaven for humanity who now participates in a different way in the life of the divine.

Jesus did not bring a new system, a new way of being human and a new way of living divorced from the ordinary experience of all people. Every individual has a wealth of possibilities, since every person has the potential for manifesting the presence of the divine. Jesus reminded people of this reality. Nothing that is human is foreign to God. Because of this human richness, the salvation offered by Jesus can never be translated completely into an all-inclusive system. The human face of God revealed in Jesus allows the possibility of many other expressions in other human faces. Everyone has the spark of the divine that the coming of Jesus recalled. Everyone, without exception, is created in the image and likeness of God. Jesus revealed the presence of God in himself, but also reminded all people of their potential to reveal the divine. In him people can see God and also can see their own possibilities.

Catholic theology contains both schools, Antioch and Alexandria. Surely Alexandria has predominated historically but never exclusively. Today Catholic theologies of Jesus also include a liberating Christology as well as Jesus as savior in an evangelical dimension. Understanding CATHOLIC Christology demands a plurality of traditions even if Catholic theology will never ignore the Council of Chalcedon.

> ...for Christ plays in ten thousand places,
> Lovely in limbs, and lovely in eyes not his
> to the father through the features of men's faces.
> (Gerard Manley Hopkins)[6]

## TOPICS FOR DISCUSSION AND STUDY

1. Theology is faith seeking understanding. Why is this important in understanding the many traditions in Catholic Christology?
2. What is the difference between Jesus as the Son of God and people being sons and daughters of God?
3. Can you explain in your own words the theology of two natures, human and divine, in one divine person?
4. What interested you in the study of medieval Christology?
5. Does it make any difference that Jesus could not sin?
6. What are your thoughts on the entrance of Jesus into history?
7. The knowledge of Jesus continues to arouse interest. What makes more sense to you?
8. Jesus is a man. Jesus is divine. Christian anthropology is the reversal of the coin that is Christology. Is this true?

9. The universality of Jesus lies in his being human and divine rather than being divine and human. Does such a statement make sense?
10. What does it mean to be human? What does divinity mean?
11. What is your concept of God? Is it the same as Jesus'?

# Works Consulted

Borg, Marcus. *Jesus in Contemporary Scholarship*. Valley Forge, Pa.: Trinity Press, 1994.

Brown, Raymond. *An Introduction to New Testament Christology*. Mahwah, N.J.: Paulist Press, 1994.

Cook, Michael L. *Responses to 101 Questions about Jesus*. Mahwah, N.J.: Paulist Press, 1993.

Cooke, Bernard J. *God's Beloved*. Philadelphia: Trinity Press, 1992.

Haight, Roger. *Jesus, Symbol of God*. Maryknoll, N.Y.: Orbis, 1999.

McDermott, Brian O. *Word Become Flesh*. Collegeville, Minn.: Liturgical Press, 1993.

Meier, John. *A Marginal Jew*. Vols. 1, 2. New York: Doubleday, 1991, 1994.

O'Collins, Gerald. *Jesus Risen*. Mahwah, N.J.: Paulist Press, 1987.

O'Grady, John F. *Models of Jesus Revisited*. Mahwah, N.J.: Paulist Press, 1994.

Rahner, Karl. *Foundations of Christian Faith*. New York: Crossroad, 1978.

Schillebeeckx, Edward. *Jesus: An Experiment in Christology*. New York: Seabury, 1979.

Schoonenberg, Piet. *The Christ*. New York: Herder and Herder, 1971.

Tavard, George. *Images of the Christ*. Washington, D.C.: University of America Press, 1982.

# CHAPTER 4:
# THE BIBLE–RECORD
# OF GOD'S REVELATION

The Bible records people's religious experience. Beginning with Abraham through Moses and the prophets and finally to Jesus of Nazareth, these many books over many centuries documented how some individuals experienced God. Each person had his or her personal relationship with God and then preached to others not only about how they understood God but also about how God had changed their lives. Like all Christians, Catholics turn to the Bible to help in their own personal journey with God and to God. Most of the images that today's Catholics have of God, including those of Jesus and his early followers, first appeared in the recorded religious experience of Jews.

Old cliches never seem to die. Although Bibles were often chained in medieval times, Catholics were never forbidden to read it. The "locking up" was not to discourage people from reading the Bible but to protect its few copies from theft. Before the printing press Bibles were hand copied and were therefore both rare and of great value.

Other historical circumstances, however, did discourage Catholics from reading the Bible. During and after the Reformation, when Protestants had translated the Bible into the vernacular and made their own interpretations of its meaning, the Catholic Church became fearful that loyal Catholics would misinterpret the Bible and fall into what was considered the heresy of Protestantism. As recently as the last century, Pius IX in his encyclical *Quanta Cura* condemned the Bible societies in the world that wanted to have vernacular Bibles in every home. Pope Leo XIII took up the same cause in 1878 in his apostolic constitution against noxious books. Second after the writings of heretics and schismatics came the vernacular Bible. All Bibles published in the vernacular by non-Catholics were "strictly forbidden." Although difficult to understand today, such restrictions made some sense in their historical period. The Catholic Church feared encouraging its members to read the Bible without guidance of proper ecclesiastical authorities. Especially since the Lutheran principle of Sola Scriptura (only Scripture) invited private interpretation, the Catholic Church thought it best to keep vernacular Bibles away from its members.

In the United States the Catholic Church began as an immigrant Church. Many people came to this country with little or no education. The clergy were the only educated Catholics. They would read the Bible and then give a careful and accurate interpretation for their flocks. The people had their rituals, their prayers and especially the sacraments, which sufficed to enhance their faith. The Church encouraged devotions to Mary and the saints and the use of sacramentals such as holy water and holy pictures. With such helps, along with a full sacramental system, church leaders saw no need to emphasize the Bible. In fact, most Catholic clergy ignored the Bible as much as their flock. For the Protestant tradition, which did not retain such a developed sacramental system, the Bible became the heart and soul of worship. No wonder Catholics would always say that their Protestant friends knew the Bible and they did not. Given the renewal movements within many of the Christian churches since the 1960s, Protestants are becoming more sacramental, using many of the symbols and rituals of the Catholic tradition, and Catholics are becoming more interested and conversant with the Bible. For both Catholic and Protestant, the Bible remains always the Word of God.

# Words

Some words divide: *black* and *white, rich* and *poor.* Some words unite: *sister, brother, friend.* Some words are sad: *death, illness;* and some words are happy: *party, celebration.* Some words cut and some words heal. Some words are great and some words are small. The poet speaks the great words: *fire, love, kiss, sky, earth,* and *water.* The great words enter into the very depth of reality and pull up something that can lead to an appreciation and love of life.

> The world is charged with the grandeur of God
> It will flame out like shining from shook foil
> It gathers to a greatness like the ooze of oil crushed
> Why then do men not reck his rod?
> Generations have trod and trod...
> (Gerard Manley Hopkins)[7]

> How sharply our children will be ashamed
> taking at last their vengeance for these horrors
> remembering in how so strange a time
> common integrity could look like courage.
> (Yevtuschenko)[8]

*World, charged, grandeur, God, shine out, ooze of oil, children, ashamed, integrity, courage*–each word is a great word used powerfully by the pen of the poet. Great words uplift, enliven, celebrate and soothe. In the hands of the poets they transform.

# The Word of God

In the Christian tradition Jesus is and speaks the great Word: God is present in human history and God loves the human race. Of course, this Word of God existed before Jesus. In ancient times, however, it remained a question as to whether God loved the human race. People were ambivalent. They wondered and came to differing conclusions. To assure them that the gods and goddesses loved them, they developed intricate rituals, hoping to placate what were often thought to be angry deities. Some early tribes or nations believed that their gods and goddesses loved them but not other peoples.

With the advent of Judaism the one God of Abraham, Isaac and Jacob, Sarah, Rebecca, Rachel and Lea established a covenant: This God of the fathers and mothers would be their God and they would be God's people: A chosen race, a royal priesthood, a people set apart (Exod 19:6). The people of Israel also believed that God was always present in creation. With Judaism an ordered world came into being by the very Word of God (Gen 1:1ff.). Throughout the history of Israel different individuals heard this one Word of God, made it their own and preached this Word to others. Moses, when he had his religious experience, asked God: "What is your name?" (Exod 3:13). God replied by not replying: *ehyeh asher ehyeh.* As already noted, Hebrew has no system of tenses, unlike English. The principal tenses are action completed and action not completed. Recall that in the past these Hebrew words were translated as: "I am who I am." But they can also be translated as: "I will be who I will be." The latter makes more sense. God would not reveal the sacred name, for knowing a person's name gives too much information. The people of Israel will discover who God is in their own history. Their religious experience helped them to know something of God but not everything.

During the period of the prophets the Word of God frequently came to individuals with the imperative to both live the Word and preach the Word. For many the Word was both salvation and judgment, but in fact the Word brought only salvation. People brought judgment upon themselves when they failed to listen to the Word of God and live it. God spoke a Word of creation and of judgment based on how people responded.

In the Exodus experience God entered into a covenant *(berith)* with the Israelites. In the past people interpreted this covenant as a reciprocal contract. The word *berith* has been translated as "covenant" but in fact it might better be translated as responsibility, not on the part of the people but on the part of God. God called the people to abide by the commandments, but throughout the history of Israel God remained faithful even when they failed to do so. God never changed. God remained the God of the people of Israel. God manifested the virtues of compassion, kindness, mercy and fidelity in the presence of the opposite vices on the part of the holy people of Israel. Again and again God offered a covenant, an unconditional covenant of love and pardon expecting love and fidelity from the people of Israel. Again and again people refused to listen, but God never changed. The people of Israel then and now remain God's holy people, for God has so promised.

## Jesus the Word of God

Jesus not only spoke the great Word of God; Jesus was the Word of God. In his ministry, his teaching and his activities Jesus demonstrated the love of God for all people, both Jews and gentiles. The resurrection of Jesus was the great experience for the followers of Jesus. Through this marvelous event they saw with new eyes the ministry of Jesus, including his crucifixion and death. The life, preaching, actions, death and above all the resurrection of Jesus became the material from which the chosen group of early believers preached the new way to listen, to understand and accept the one Word of God.

Jesus offered a new covenant with God based on the same covenant of old. Jesus himself showed the kindness, the compassion, the mercy and fidelity of God. No longer would people be unsure of their relationship to God. "If God has given us his son, is there anything God will deny us?" (Rom 8:32). The faithful God of the Old Testament became human in the historical existence of Jesus of Nazareth. Through the experience of Jews, Jesus and Christians, the one Word of God became part of human history. The Bible records that experience of God's Word.

## The Bible

People usually think of the Bible as one unified book. In fact the Bible consists of many books from different collections, various sources and many separate literary units. The word itself comes from the Greek word *biblia,* which means "books." Jews and Christians disagree on precisely how many books are in the Old Testament just as many Christian churches either disagree on how many books are in the New Testament or assign different values to some of the books.

Jews accept books written only in Hebrew. Many other of their sacred books written in Greek or Aramaic do not form part of the Jewish Scriptures. Many Protestants accept this decision by the Jews. Catholics accept all of the sacred books of the Jews, which formed part of the Greek version of the Jewish sacred books called the Septuagint, whether or not they were originally written in Greek, Hebrew or Aramaic. In the New Testament Catholics accept twenty-seven books. In the past some Protestant churches accepted only twenty books as canonical and seven others as deuterocanonical, which means that the New Testament had two levels of sacred books. Today most Christian Churches accept all twenty-seven books of the New Testament.

In all probability the first written works of the Old Testament were composed seven or eight hundred years before Christ and reached some finalization in the sixth century before Christ. The legends, traditions, sagas stretch back further in history to the time of the Exodus around 1250 B.C. The New Testament was written over a period of some 60 to 75 years. As with the Old Testament, there was first an oral tradition. Stories and traditions about Jesus circulated by word of mouth for 20 to 25 years before they reached their final written form.

## Authorship

For many years the Catholic Church accepted the authorship of the first five books of the Bible by Moses and the authorship of the four gospels by apostles or disciples of apostles. Today the Catholic Church accepts Moses as the inspiration for these books rather than the actual author. The books attributed to Moses were not written until some 600 or 700 years after his death. Anonymous authors also wrote the gospels, although there exists the possibility that the Gospel of John was written by an eyewitness disciple of Jesus (not one of the twelve apostles). Paul wrote most of the letters attributed to him. But some of the letters bearing his name in the New Testament probably come from unknown authors. In fact the vast majority of the books of the Bible come from anonymous authors. Some scholars even attribute certain books of the Bible to women authors. Because of the low social status of women in the community at the time, the female authors would not have been able to lay claim to authorship.

## The Bible and Church Teaching

In 1943 Pope Pius XII published his encyclical *Divino Afflante Spiritu,* giving Catholic scholars complete freedom to interpret the Bible as they saw fit, within the confines of contemporary scholarship. "The Instruction by the Pontifical Biblical Commission on the Historical Truth of the Gospels," in 1964, gave further latitude dealing with the historical Jesus and the development of the understanding of Jesus within the early Church. The decree of the Vatican Council on divine revelation, *Dei Verbum,* supported these earlier decisions by the Catholic Church to give scholars free range in interpreting the Bible according to the guidelines of contemporary scholarship.

At the turn of the century the Biblical Commission specified that certain parts of the Genesis story should be taken literally, including the appearance of the devil in the form of a serpent and the historical existence of Adam and Eve. In 1955 the secretary of the Roman Pontifical Biblical Commission announced that Catholics had complete freedom with regard to these earlier decrees except where they touched on faith and morals. More recently the present Pope John Paul II noted the solidity of the theory of evolution. Commenting on the encyclical of Pius XI in 1950, *Humani Generis,* the present pope commented: "Today, nearly half a century after the publication of the encyclical, new knowledge leads to the recognition of the theory of evolution as more than an hypothesis." The Book of Genesis and the works of Darwin are not in opposition, but are discussing different things in different ways. The Bible should never be interpreted as a scientific document nor should it be interpreted literally.

## Catholic Interpretations

Biblical scholarship in the Catholic Church includes the many and varied interpretations given to the Bible over the past two thousand years. Some interpretations have come and gone. Some of the early fathers of the Church used an allegorical interpretation of the Bible. Many took a literal approach, which lasted into this century. Some today support an advocacy interpretation; for example, some women scholars want to read the Bible from their perspective, giving new insights into texts that have been, for centuries, interpreted only by male commentators.

Scholars may choose to evaluate the Bible as literature, studying the various techniques the authors used to accomplish their purpose. How does a book written in the sixth century before Christ relate to books written before or after? How do the books of the Old Testament relate to the New Testament? Paul speaks of faith over works (Rom 3:28). James praised the value of good works and decries a faith that is simply intellectual (Jas 2:24, 26). How do these ideas relate to each other? How can knowledge about an author's background, sources, personality and the problems and situations he faced (including his immediate listeners or readers) affect the actual written work? What did the author really want to say and to whom was he writing or speaking? All these questions form part of the concern for contemporary Catholic scholars. And all affect our understanding of the Bible.

Two extremes exist in biblical interpretation: on the one hand, fundamentalism, or a literal interpretation of every aspect of the Bible; and on the other, a view that the Bible consists of what might be called freely composed fairy tales, with no historical value. The Catholic Church maintains a centrist position. Scholars will use many systems of interpretation, including literary, historical, reader-response, sociological and feminist. Each offers some appreciation of what the Bible may mean to the contemporary believer.

# The Bible: Experience and Traditions

The Bible records the experience of chosen men and women: what they suffered, and what they celebrated and what they passed on to their children. The Exodus from Egypt created Judaism. The people experienced the departure from Egypt, the revelation of God at Mount Sinai, the wanderings in the desert and finally the land-taking. They recorded their religious experience in hymns, poems, legends, sagas and historical narratives.

Christians experienced the resurrection of Jesus. Through this marvelous event Christianity became a movement within Judaism and eventually a separate religious tradition. If Jesus has not been raised from the dead, Christianity would not exist. With the experience of the risen Lord, the early followers became emboldened preachers, eventually reaching to the city of Rome, where Paul "preached the kingdom of God and teaching about the lord Jesus quite openly and unhindered" (Acts 28:31).

The ministry of Jesus in Palestine became not just his own religious experience but a support to his followers as they preached to others. Parables, miracle stories, sayings, episodes of healing and forgiveness, the driving out of demons, all formed part of the traditions about Jesus. All formed the basis for the New Testament gospels.

The preaching of Paul, his relationship with the churches he founded and his response to various problems contributed to his own religious experience on the road to Damascus. His reflection on these circumstances eventually found inclusion in the New Testament. Other early Christian writers made their contribution through letters and sermons.

Such external experiences helped to create the Bible. But similarly, prophetic and mystical experiences of God, visions, dreams and the experience of the Holy Spirit contributed to religious experience. Those experiences were also recorded in the Bible. The combination of prayer and worship, the internal and external experiences of God, created the Psalms and many sections of the New Testament. The Bible also contains a record of social customs and reflects influences from other traditions and cultures. The Wisdom literature of the Old Testament comes largely from other Near Eastern cultures as viewed through the eyes of the faith of Judaism. In the New Testament, the traditions of the early Church such as the anointing of the sick, baptizing in the name of the Father, Son and Holy Spirit, the confession of sins and the breaking of the bread were all part of the experience of the first Christians. All of these influences join with the recollections of the ministry of Jesus as recorded in the gospels to form the New Testament.

## The Human Authors of the Bible

Different people wrote the various books of the Bible. Someone actually wrote the Book of Revelation and the Epistle to the Romans. Individuals were also responsible for many of the prophetic books, and the Psalms, too, had a literary author even if the actual writing took place after a period of fixed oral tradition. Some books had editors. Other books are compilations, such as the Book of Proverbs. The evangelists used sources. Some works are ascribed to authors who had no influence on the actual work. Paul did not write Hebrews and probably not the Pastoral Epistles but his name became attached to these letters. As already noted, perhaps women wrote some books, but they did not circulate with feminine names because of the subordinate role of women in ancient society. All the books of the Bible come from people of faith, who inspired, edited or wrote them.

Within the various books of the Bible a literary process also took place. The traditions contain legends, laws, oracles, parables and confessions of faith that were first preached and then written down. In the Old Testament people handed on the stories of their origins, the main events of their history, gathered their laws into collections and then recorded them for future generations.

In the New Testament, the early church writers first recorded the passion of Jesus. The various collections of sayings of Jesus were written down as well as collections of parables, miracles and stories from his ministry. Eventually someone or some ones put these various books together, resulting in the New Testament.

The book of Isaiah is composed of writings from different periods. Later someone combined these different sections into one book, which became applied to the Southern Kingdom of Judah. New Testament writers applied some sayings of Jesus to the actual condition of the early Church. The parable of the sower originally ended with the thought that the harvest will be great, no matter what happens. The early Church added the interpretation given in the gospels to explain how some people did not accept or remain faithful to the Word of God.

Some editors also elaborated earlier texts. The Book of Chronicles reworks the material of Kings. Wisdom, chapters 10 through 19, reworks the story of the Exodus. The stories of the origins of Jesus in Matthew and Luke come from an application of certain verses and traditions from the Old Testament woven together with a nucleus of historical facts. This literary process further explains the complexity of the Bible and its origins and the need to use various methods of interpretation.

## Inspired by God

Catholic tradition teaches that God inspired the Bible. This distinguishes the Bible from all other sacred books and gives to it an authority and power as the norm for all Christian communities. But what does inspiration mean and how does this belief agree with all that has been said about the origin of the Bible? Did God actually inspire each written word? Who was inspired— preacher, writer, editor or everyone involved?

Inspiration involves a process, under the guidance of the Spirit of God, that eventually created the Bible. Inspiration, human and not miraculous, does not prescind from the ordinary development of traditions and human procedures. The Bible has both a human and divine dimension. As a human document the Bible was composed from the contributions of many people over a long period of time. They used their histories, talents, backgrounds and experience as best they could. As divine, the Bible expresses the relationship of God to all people. The Bible is God's Word in human words.

The Bible makes sense only to a faith community. God blessed some individuals with a gift to interpret the meaning of events, and God blessed some to communicate this meaning to others. Nourished by the faith of the community, which they shared, these authors expressed that faith in a literary form. The Bible contains not just the record of an event but the development and interpretation of what happened to a group of people. The individual author used his or her own genius to create the literary work from the facts commonly known. A special consciousness of inspiration was not necessary beyond the awareness of faith he or she wished to express in the actual writing. Poets or musicians are inspired to create an artistic work. They are inspired even if what they have created in reality comes from something already known. There is a community aspect in the process of inspiration as well as a full literary process with the genius of an inspired individual. Through the great words of many poets, the one Word of God became known and recorded.

The actual process of inspiration was probably casual and contingent. Other gospels exist that have never been accepted officially by the Church. Paul probably wrote some letters that were lost. Jews accept some books as sacred but the Catholic Church accepts more than those contained in the Jewish Scriptures. The power of the Spirit guided the faith expressed by the community and raised up individuals who expressed and recorded this faith for future generations. The Holy Spirit used these individuals not as mere instruments but as human beings, each with his or her own particular talents for communication and expression. Together, over a long period of time, they contributed a wealth of individual and communal faith expressions that achieve a unity within the completed Bible. The whole process need not have been understood at the time and surely involved many people. Nothing essential perished, since the whole Bible expressed the faith of committed people. The Holy Spirit inspired the book and continues to guide its interpretation.

All of the above does not deny that God was involved in the origin of the Bible. Rather, God, who despises nothing human, uses human beings for the actual enrichment of humanity and the creation of the Bible. God established the context within which human words can be the extension of the divine even as they remain very human. This process enriches the human race and manifests the goodness and power of God. Without poets, without people who could use the great words, who could reach down into the very depth of reality, the Bible would never have existed.

## Inerrancy

No survey of Catholic teaching on the Bible can avoid the question: Is the Bible free from errors? If God is the principal author and God does not lie, surely the Bible can never contain any errors or mistakes. But the human authors are not God. The words of the Bible are true only in the sense in which the human authors conveyed them, and surely the authors themselves were not without error. Since the Bible came from a particular time and place, no one today should presume that its authors possessed our own scientific knowledge. Nor did they necessarily think as Western people do today. The Catholic Church firmly teaches that "The books of scripture must be acknowledged as teaching faithfully, and without error that truth which God wanted put into the Sacred Writings for the sake of our salvation" (*Dei Verbum*, no. 11). Beyond that, the Bible, like any human endeavor, contains the imperfections and limitations of all things human.

Religious experience gave the world the Bible. Certain individuals had an experience of God. They lived their lives open to the possibility of accepting in faith the presence of God. Once they realized the great benefits proceeding from faith in a loving God, they wished to assist others in reaching a similar plateau in human life. From many gods and goddesses to one God in history, the Bible records the human odyssey, reaching its completion in the belief that God had entered into human history in the life and person of Jesus of Nazareth. The one Word of God expressed in many words throughout history became incarnate in Jesus. Eventually this one Word in the history of Israel and Christianity became recorded in the Bible.

In many and various ways, God spoke of old to our fathers by the prophets, but in these last days he has spoken to us by a Son whom he appointed the heir of all things through whom he also created the world.

(Heb 1:1–2)

## TOPICS FOR DISCUSSION AND STUDY

1. The Bible is the Word of God. What does that mean to you?
2. Has the manner in which the Bible been presented in this chapter affected your understanding of it?
3. The Bible is not revelation but the record of revelation, or the record of people's relationship to God. What are your thoughts on this proposition?
4. The Bible is inspired, but God did not inspire every word. In what sense can this be true?
5. The Catholic Church does not advocate fundamentalism in the interpretation the Bible. How does the Catholic approach to the Bible differ from fundamentalism?
6. The Bible teaches God's Word in human words. What are its most important teachings?
7. Catholic biblical scholars and Protestant biblical scholars share the same basic methodologies. Are there any differences?
8. Appreciating poetry helps people to appreciate the Bible. Why might this be the case?

# Works Consulted

Barton, John. *People of the Book: The Authority of the Bible in Christianity.* Philadelphia: Westminster, 1989.

Brown, Raymond. *Biblical Exegesis and Church Doctrine.* Mahwah, N.J.: Paulist Press, 1985.

———. *Biblical Reflections on Crises Facing the Church.* Mahwah, N.J.: Paulist Press, 1975.

———. *The Critical Meaning of the Bible.* Mahwah, N.J.: Paulist Press, 1981.

———. *An Introduction to the New Testament.* New York: Doubleday, 1996.

———. *Responses to 101 Questions on the Bible.* Mahwah, N.J.: Paulist Press, 1990.

Collins, John J., and John Dominic Crossan. *The Biblical Heritage in Modern Catholic Scholarship.* Wilmington, Del.: Michael Glazier, 1986.

Gnuse, Robert. *The Authority of the Bible.* Mahwah, N.J.: Paulist Press, 1985.

Montague, George T. *Understanding the Bible.* Mahwah, N.J.: Paulist Press, 1997.

O'Collins, Gerald, and Daniel Kendall. *The Bible for Theology.* Mahwah, N.J.: Paulist Press, 1997.

O'Grady, John F. *The Four Gospels and the Jesus Tradition.* Mahwah, N.J.: Paulist Press, 1989.

# SECTION II: THE ROMAN CATHOLIC CHURCH

# CHAPTER 5:
# IMAGES OF THE EARLY CHURCH AND THE NEW TESTAMENT

*Custodial* is a word that connotes guarding, protecting, regulating, controlling. It also involves management and organization through rules and regulations. The word *charismatic* connotes creativity, spontaneity and spirit-filled freedom. A charismatic personality avoids rules and regulations and often sees little need for management and organization. People tend to be one or the other of these two personality styles. In a family situation the balance of having one parent who is more custodial and the other more charismatic often helps create a healthy environment for all. But if both parents are very custodial, this invites rebellion. A household in which both parents are charismatic, on the other hand, encourages chaos.

Institutions often tend to be custodial. Organizations like rules and regulations and clearly defined structures. Yet if an institution does not also allow for the presence of a freer and more creative approach to life, the institution will stagnate, shrivel up, wither and die. Like the family, however, no institution can survive without some aspect of the custodial. Organization and regulation insures survival. Free spirit-filled movement insures vitality.

Over the past two thousand years Christianity has had many periods of regulation and custodial activity and other moments of spirit-filled charismatic activity. Christianity began as an enthusiastic movement of people filled with the Spirit of God calling all who would listen to a life of freedom as God's children. Soon however, this same Christian community inevitably moved into an organized body with clear lines of leadership and carefully crafted rules and regulations. Christianity survived precisely because of the custodial nature of some early Christian communities.

The Catholic Church is custodial. Such a statement does not imply that the Catholic Church does not also include some charismatic elements. But by and large the Catholic Church concentrates on authority, hierarchy, rules and regulations. Its code of church law rivals and often surpasses the legal system of any other large international organization. Such may not look like the community described in the New Testament but on careful analysis the New Testament also testifies to the inevitable movement toward organization and control.

## Early Christian Communities

Jesus began his public ministry by preaching and healing, casting out demons, forgiving sins and proclaiming the presence of the reign of God. After his resurrection his ministry of preaching, healing, casting out demons and forgiving sins continued through the efforts of those who believed in Jesus. They had experienced the risen Lord and became bold in their proclamation of Jesus as Lord and Christ (Acts 2:36). Like Jesus, these first missionaries led the life of traveling preachers waiting in expectation the speedy return of Jesus in glory. Although their original mission was to the Jews, these Christian preachers quickly extended their preaching of the gospel to Gentiles. With the passing of time, as the teachings of Jesus spread, institutional forms and structures became tighter. What began as a gathering of enthusiastic Jews who believed in Jesus evolved into local churches of both Jews and Gentiles. Before the end of the first century this movement had become a Church dominated by Gentiles.

In recent years many scholars have attempted to describe this development. Unfortunately they all face the lack of "hard facts." They have only been able to provide possible interpretations and hypotheses. One fact seems clear: The Church we now experience developed slowly. Christianity arose as an enthusiastic movement, which presupposed a fundamental solidarity and equality among believers and turned away from master-servant relationships. Such a theory need not exclude authority and leadership and the actual exercise of that authority, but the basis remains forever solid. The baptismal declaration of Paul: "...there is neither Jew nor Greek, freeman or slave, for you are all one in Christ Jesus (Gal 3:28)" remains forever the foundation of the Christian community.

A clear picture of the development of the Church from the death and resurrection of Jesus to the organization of Christian communities such as those led by Ignatius of Antioch and Clement of Rome still eludes us. Complete historical records do not exist, nor does a clear sociological analysis. The twentieth-century believers have only the writings of the New Testament, other early Christian writings and some knowledge of Greco-Roman organizations and Jewish institutions. Through these documents, scholars attempt to analyze the practices in the early Christian community in comparison with the social and cultural context out of which they arose.

## Church—*Ecclesia*

In the common Greek of this period *ecclesia* (church) denoted the assembly of the free male citizens of a city. In Hebrew *kahal* signified the assembly of the Lord. When the Old Testament was translated into Greek, *kahal* was sometimes translated as *ecclesia* and other times as *synagogos*. The Christians began to refer to themselves as *ecclesiae* of the Lord. The term had many uses. It meant the free association of Christians assembled at the house of someone, as well as the various house communities of a city (the Church in Corinth), and could mean the Christian communities in several cities and, finally, all Christians in the world.

The word *ecclesia* can then refer to the actual assembly of Christians or to the Christian group itself, whether local or dispersed in the form of many house communities all over the world. For Christians of the twenty-first century the word *Church* usually refers to the worldwide organization. Envisioning the Church in this way would be anachronistic when considering the use of this word in the New Testament.

The early Christians made the *oikos* (house) the pastoral basis for the early enthusiastic Christian movement: The Scriptures refer to the *ecclesia* of the house of Aquila and Priscilla (1 Cor 16:19), of Prisca and Aquila in Rome (Rom 16:5) and the house of Nympha (Col 4:15). The earliest structure in Christianity followed the general unit of civic life—the household. Such a household contained members of the family as well as servants and slaves. Early Christian groups built their proper structure on already existing relationships, both internally (members of the household) and externally (friends and acquaintances). Different households existed within the city, giving rise to various approaches to the Jesus tradition.

The house in these early Christian communities provided the forum for preaching and instruction. It was the place where Christians gathered and ate and drank and celebrated the Eucharist (Acts 2:40–47). The heads of these households were wealthy citizens who placed their houses at the disposal of the communities. The communities themselves, however, consisted of various levels of society. Such a structure continued down to the third century. In the early fourth century Christians would have separate church buildings but until then, the basic unit of society formed the structure into which the early Christian community fit.

## Hierarchy and Patriarchy

In Roman and Hellenistic society the father of the house exercised the authority for all. The structure in ancient times was clearly hierarchical with a patriarchal order. Initially, the Christian community broke up these hierarchical and patriarchal structures since the community consisted of brothers and sisters united in one faith, one Lord and one baptism. Lydia seems to have been the head of a household and probably head of the local church (Acts 16:14–15). This would have made eminent sense in an enthusiastic movement. Eventually, the hierarchical and patriarchal model predominated as the Church developed specific structures even as early as the end of the first century.

Eventually these house communities faced the questions of structure and authority that confront any society. Who is in charge? How are conflicts resolved? Who establishes relationships with other house churches? Who sets the rules and how must they be followed? If anyone thinks that the early Christian community existed without conflict, they have only to read carefully the Acts of the Apostles, the letters of Paul and, finally, the other writings of the New Testament. Conflict may not have predominated, but it flourished even among the leaders of the Christian community.

## Paul and Antioch

The first fundamental conflict arose in Antioch at the beginning of the missionary work of Barnabas and Paul. Christianity struggled with the split between those who saw the teachings of Jesus as a system of doctrine and a code of ethics dependent upon Jewish law and those who saw the teachings of Jesus as a proclamation of the redemptive act of God in Jesus by which God opened the way through faith to justification and reconciliation. The former position predominated in Jerusalem under the leadership of James. Paul taught the latter. The earliest conflict involves Jewish/Christian relationships as well as Jewish/Christian and Gentile/Christian relationships. During the initial period of the Gentile mission, no effort was made to coordinate that mission with the type of Christianity associated with Jerusalem. The Jerusalem community saw the Jesus tradition as an outgrowth of Judaism, and it continued to observe the Jewish law. Soon, however, the law-free gospel of Paul and the Gentile Church came into conflict with the legal framework of Jewish

Nyack College Library

Christianity. The dispute came to a head at Antioch with the conflict portrayed in Galatians 2:11–13.

## The Council of Jerusalem

The Council of Jerusalem convened (Acts 15:1–29), and the members determined that Gentile Christians were free from circumcision but were obligated to observe those laws required by Leviticus of non-Hebrews living in the midst of Hebrews. Harmony was restored and Paul was free to continue his missionary activity in good conscience, free from any harassment by those who wanted all Christians to first become Jews. All of this is recorded in Acts 15. Paul continued his successful activity as a missionary. But for his arrest in Jerusalem, he would have continued his preaching. Although the time sequence that Acts describes may not be accurate, it does record the successful resolution of the conflict between Paul and the leaders of the Jerusalem Church.

The resolution of this conflict shows the beginning of some established line of authority that can resolve conflicts: Church leaders assembled together have some authority over households of Christians existing in different and distant cities. The Church at Jerusalem has authority since James, apostle but not one of the twelve and the brother of the Lord, is accepted as continuing the accurate interpretation of the Jesus tradition.

## An Alternative Explanation

The above description provides the traditional understanding of the resolution of this conflict. Yet another interpretation is also possible. The Apostolic Decree of Acts 15 can be understood not as the result of the conflict in Antioch as recorded in Galatians 2:11–14 but as the cause. Following the hint given in Luke that the dispute between Paul and Barnabas which resulted in their separation (Acts 15:36–40) was subsequent to the Jerusalem conference, then possibly the dispute at Antioch was the result of this conference. Thus, no future conference restored the unity that was fractured in Antioch. The scenario may have been the following:

1. Paul goes to Jerusalem to see James, Peter and John (Gal 2:6b–10), resulting in freedom for the Gentile Christians. The leaders of the Jerusalem Church remind Paul to remember the poor. No other obligations are involved.
2. The Apostolic Decree is formulated (Acts 15); Paul was not present.
3. Paul learns of the Apostolic Decree and confronts Peter, Barnabas and the men sent by James in Antioch. Paul loses. Peter and Barnabas and others withdrew from table fellowship with those Christians who do not observe the Jewish law.

Up to this point Paul felt secure that he was preaching a gospel with the support of the Jerusalem Church as well as the Antioch community. After the dispute, Paul lost his power base in Antioch and (as Acts confirms) he had to travel farther west hoping to find acceptance for his missionary preaching. He wrote to the Romans, modifying his views but still maintaining his fundamental gospel of freedom. The tension between Jewish and Gentile Christianity, present from the beginning of the Christian mission, as reported in Acts, was never resolved. Thus Paul never preached to the Gentiles without harassment from those who disputed his understanding of the Jesus tradition. He may have ended his career as an isolated figure whose theological insights and emphases were destined for decline in subsequent centuries.

## Paul and His Teaching

Obviously the defeat of Paul at Antioch did not mean that Paul was eliminated from the memory of the Church. Acts portrays him as a hero, and his letters have come down as a chief part of the New Testament. He was remembered as an apostle, a missionary and a martyr for the faith. But the latter remains more common in the tradition than his teachings. The dispute at Antioch meant that an interpretation of the faith other than that of Paul became normative for Christian ministry. Luke in particular portrays this in the Acts of the Apostles. Luke, in Acts, replaces the Paul of Galatians and also (in a limited fashion) of Romans with the Paul who will compromise his view for the sake of the unity of the Church and its authorities. Luke presents Paul as the theologian who gives full support to the Apostolic Decree and dutifully returns to Jerusalem to submit himself to Church leadership (Acts 21:20–26). This will fit in well with the images of the Church in the Pastoral Epistles. Christianity was quickly becoming an organized Church with a system of doctrine and code of ethics rather than an enthusiastic movement acknowledging God's redemptive acts in Jesus present in a gathering of disciples.

The recollection of this unresolved dispute did not disappear with the composition of the canonical New Testament. Marcion, for example, seems to have justified his preference for Paul by referring to Paul's condemnation of Peter. For Marcion, Paul rather than Peter espoused the true Christianity. The Valentinians, an early Christian heretical group, also shared this view accepting Paul as the superior apostle. Ultimately those who favored Peter were seen to be right, or "orthodox." Further evidence might be found in Matthew 16:17–18 wherein Peter is exalted as the "rock of the church." Perhaps this combated the self-exaltation of Paul and his authority in Galatians 2:11–13. The Church followed the Apostolic Decree, with its emphasis on doctrine and ethics, and ceased to adhere to Paul's theory of salvation by grace through faith.

Paul lost in his effort to influence the theological understanding of Christian ministry in the early Church. The community preserved his letters but often interpreted them in a way different from his intention. The later Church even attributed to his pen the Pastoral Epistles, which clearly differ in style and viewpoint from the early letters of Paul. Although he may have lost the battle, Paul's teachings in Galatians and Romans continue to challenge the Church to recall the fundamental aspect of the Jesus tradition, which emphasizes justification through faith alone. This Pauline teaching formed the foundation for the challenge posed to the Catholic Church by Martin Luther when he nailed his ninety-five theses to the doors of the Church at Wittenberg in 1517. On October 31, 1999, Vatican and Lutheran

World Federation officials signed a joint declaration on Justification, demonstrating that a consensus in basic truths of the doctrine exists between Lutherans and Catholics.

For the first thirty years after the death of Jesus the early communities struggled with authority. The move toward increased organization often proved useful in resolving conflicts. These early communities also faced the thorny question of their relationship to Judaism. They found themselves embroiled in a future complicated by the long delay of the expected Second Coming as well as by the influx of Gentiles into their ranks. In many ways these conflicts remain unresolved. Even the development of the "Church" in the final third of the first century and the first quarter of the second century could not answer all of these profound questions. Certain decisions were made from which developed what is now known and experienced as the Catholic Church. The system of doctrine with orthodox teachers and the code of ethics with careful observation became the hallmarks of Catholic Christianity along with an authority structure to help resolve conflicts, both doctrinal and disciplinary.

## The Church of Matthew

Although Mark was the first written, the first gospel with a clearly developed ecclesiology is Matthew. Matthew alone among the gospels uses the word *ecclesia* (church). Often scholars call it the ecclesial gospel and through the centuries the Church used this gospel for liturgy and for catechetical purposes. The Roman Catholic Church in particular has favored this gospel. Not until the reforms of the liturgy of the Second Vatican Council have Roman Catholics listened to the other gospels in their liturgy on a regular basis. All Christians have heard of the Sermon on the Mount. Few realize that the Gospel of Luke contains a similar sermon given by Jesus on his way to Jerusalem. Everyone knows of Christianity's eight beatitudes (Matthew); they fail to realize that Luke lists four. No doubt Matthew has influenced centuries of Christian history.

The community of Matthew probably flourished in the seventies in Antioch. It was a mixed community of Jewish and Gentile

Christians. The author, probably a scribe, may have recognized himself in Jesus' saying that "every scribe who has become a disciple of the reign of God is like a householder who brings out of his treasure what is new and what is old" (Matt 13:52). This follower of the Lord realized that the future of Christianity belonged to the Gentiles. He also accepted the delay of the Second Coming and prepared for future generations by offering guidelines for an established, organized and even hierarchical Church. Once Paul lost out in Antioch he retreated to Asia Minor, where he could preach his gospel more freely. The Gospel of Matthew represents a compromise conciliating the more stringent position of James and the more liberating opinion of Paul. The law continues to bind but must be radically interpreted by the Jesus tradition. This compromise by Matthew continues throughout the centuries. The Church flourishes when efforts at compromise and conciliation permeate its structure.

Matthew expects Jewish and Gentile Christians to live in peace. He begins his gospel proclaiming that Jesus is both son of David and son of Abraham. He is both Jewish and open to all nations. Magi come from the East to worship the newborn king of the Jews (Matt 2:1–5). He ends his gospel with the command: "to make disciples of all nations" (Matt 28:19). Throughout the gospel the author makes reference to Jewish traditions while being open to Gentile development. This wise Jewish Christian seems to have seen both sides of an issue and patiently sought resolution by compromise and conciliation.

## The Pastoral Gospel

The ecclesial gospel also becomes the pastoral gospel. Luke comes down hard on the rich. Such is not the style of Matthew. The rich may find it harder to enter the kingdom of God (Matt 19:23) but they can always be poor "in spirit"(Matt 5:3). If not physically hungry, they can hunger after justice (Matt 5:6). Even the weeds that grow in the Church should not be torn out but tolerated with patience and mercy. (Matt 13:24–30). The story of the coin in the mouth of the fish (Matt 17:24–27) also exemplifies this tendency to compromise. Although the followers of Jesus are not obliged to pay such taxes, this exercise of Christian freedom should be avoided if it causes offense. This also seems to have been the principle at issue in the dispute between Peter and Paul at Antioch. Paul proclaimed that Christians need not observe the dietary laws of the Jews. Peter evidently went along but backed away when this caused problems. Peter preferred to compromise rather than destroy unity. Even with respect to Church authority Matthew seeks a middle position. He recognized the need for authority and leadership but chose Peter, who was acceptable to both Jewish and Gentile Christians, as his model. Matthew, in chapter 16, asserts the power to bind and loose on Peter. In chapter 18, which is directed in particular to Church leaders, he also refers this power to the Church (Matt 18:18).

## The Ecclesial Chapter

The community of Matthew exhibits great respect for law and authority, as his gospel attests. He also seeks conciliation and compromise wherever possible. In the past many readers of Matthew looked upon this gospel as rigid. If the emphasis remained only on law and authority, the gospel *would* be rigid. The presence of the conciliating spirit changes an authoritarian gospel to one recognizing the need for nuances and compromise. Without the aspect of compromise, the Matthean community would have been tempted to legalism and authoritarianism. Matthew allows no such conclusion. His ideas in chapter 18 demonstrate this concern. Many scholars call this chapter the ecclesial chapter of Matthew. It begins with the question of who is greatest in the reign of God or greatest in the Church (Matt 18:1–4). Jesus responds by offering the example of a child. The one who is dependent upon God and on others is greatest. The church leader, the church member who recognizes the need for relying upon God and upon the members of the community is the greatest in the Church.

The next section (Matt 18:5–9) deals with scandal in the Church. All, especially leaders, should take care about harming those who are most vulnerable in the community. Scandals given by church leaders can hurt the most. Sometimes those who are weakest can be hurt the most and be lost to the community forever.

The chapter continues with an injunction to seek out the lost sheep (Matt 18:1–14). Both church leaders and members must always seek out the one who has strayed and welcome that person back. The Church that cares little for the one member who has wandered off no longer continues the tradition of Jesus.

In dealing with discipline in the Church Matthew offers guidelines (Matt 18:15–20). When problems arise, go first to the party involved. Seek reconciliation personally. If that fails, then call in a few others. If these methods prove fruitless, then finally the leadership of the Church will settle the question. If no resolution occurs, the person is to be treated "like a Gentile and tax collector" (Matt 18:17). Some have interpreted this as an expulsion with the shunning of the former church member. The officially repudiated Christian should be totally shunned. Or is he to be the subject of outreach and concern in imitation of Jesus, who was so interested in searching out tax collectors that he was accused of being their friend (Matt 11:19)?

The final section involves forgiveness (Matt 18:21–35). Christians, both leaders and members of the Church, are to forgive without limit. The power to forgive must characterize Christianity more than does the power to excommunicate. People will not turn from Christianity if it is too forgiving. People have turned from Christianity in droves because they found it unforgiving. The unforgivable sin is to be unforgiving.

The Church of Matthew needed organization to survive in a sinful world. Someone had to be in charge. Rules had to be made and observed. Structures had to be established. The presence of all such elements in Christianity must never, however, take away from the call of Jesus to respond to the lost with an infinite abundance of forgiveness. The Church of Matthew never settled for black or white. Gray often permeates in life, and when things go askew, Jesus calls us to forgive seventy times seven. And, finally, in the last judgment the only criteria will be: "Whatever you did to the least of my brethren you did to me" (Matt 25:45).

## The Community of Luke

Chronologically the next Christian community exemplified in the New Testament gospel tradition comes from the Gospel of Luke and the Acts of the Apostles. From the opening prologue, the author centers on continuity. The believing community in the 80s must feel comfortable that what they accept as the meaning of the Jesus tradition, in fact, can be traced back through ministers of the Word to eyewitnesses to Jesus (Luke 1:1–4). The same continuity persists in the development of Acts. The gospel ends in Jerusalem. Acts begins in Jerusalem and concludes when Paul preaches the gospel of Jesus in Rome, "openly and unhindered" (Acts 28:31).

## The Spirit

The sense of tradition roots this continuity, and the Spirit makes it all possible. Throughout the gospel and Acts, the Spirit figures prominently. The gospel begins with the Spirit coming upon Mary (Luke 1:35). The same Spirit inaugurates the Church at Pentecost (Acts 2:1–5). Luke uses the word *pneuma* (Spirit) seventy times in Acts. It is here that Peter and Paul are remembered not primarily for their personal exploits but as vehicles of the Spirit. The disciples must not look longingly for Jesus in the heavens (Act 1:11) but recognize the power of the Spirit on earth. This Spirit will accomplish the spread of the Jesus tradition to the center of the known world. With the experience of Pentecost, the apostles become bold in their proclamation. Subsequently, all those who become followers of the Lord will be endowed with the Spirit from on high (Acts 2:38; 8:15–17; etc.). This same Spirit directs Peter to the house of Cornelius, gives the impetus for the missionary activity of Barnabas and Paul and is proclaimed as the inspiration for the Apostolic Decree in Acts 15. Paul goes to Rome through the guidance of the Spirit (Acts 19:21) and when he leaves Asia for Europe, the Spirit provides presbyters for the flock (Acts 20:28). Every step in the development of Christianity from a small group in Israel to the worldwide Church results from the activity of the Spirit.

It is evident from reading Acts that the community of Luke takes pride in its origin and its accomplishments. The community moves from triumph to triumph until the gospel reaches Rome. All is made possible through the power of the Spirit, which continues to live in the Christian community. Christians may walk tall, secure in their foundations and confident in the future. Setbacks are temporary, for no one can thwart the positive and forward movement of the Spirit.

Such a viewpoint of the Christian Church, however, has its drawbacks. Triumphalism recurs frequently in the annals of the Church. Such an attitude differs significantly from the awareness of the power in weakness, which lies at the root of the Jesus tradition. Christianity does not go from triumph to triumph in spite of all efforts to whitewash failures. A community of the Spirit makes eminent sense, provided that community does not lay claim to controlling or limiting the Spirit. If only Church leaders have the Spirit, if only Church leaders can interpret the Spirit, then failures are inevitable. The Spirit surprises and even allows one generation of Christians to pay for the foolishness of an earlier generation. A Church of the Spirit in which all have the Spirit also offers problems. If all share in the same Spirit, then the Church needs neither authority nor leadership. This approach to the Church has led to anarchy. Luke reveals his vision for the future Church. A sense of pride and accomplishment is good. An awareness of the powerful presence of the Spirit invigorates. One approach, however, is not enough, for the Jesus tradition shines more brilliantly than any one facet of it can reflect. Luke makes his contribution to ecclesiology and allows others to make theirs.

## The Community of John

The Johannine tradition of Jesus differs from the other gospel traditions. The same is true for the Johannine sense of Church. The Beloved Disciple and his community offer specific understandings for the Church as it continues the mission to remain faithful to Jesus and his tradition. The unique approach that this community takes toward Church should remain, just as the testimony of the Beloved Disciple will remain (John 21:23). Historically, the witness of the Fourth Gospel has frequently proven troublesome to the organized Church. For many decades into the end of the second century this gospel was considered suspect. Eventually it became part of the canon as an authentic interpretation of the Jesus tradition.

The community of the Beloved Disciple emphasized the individual relationship to Jesus and the love of the brethren. These two elements manifest the essentials of the Jesus tradition. With them, all else is possible. Without them, nothing is possible. The gospel also deemphasized the ritual of baptism and the Eucharist in favor of the faith foundation for these sacraments. Baptism by water makes sense only if the Spirit has baptized the individuals in faith. The Eucharist can be celebrated only if the community first believes in the Lord and has committed itself to Jesus. Authority exists primarily in the Spirit. In the epilogue, (chapter 21) the community accepted the apostolic authority of Peter but on the conditions that he love Jesus and die for the sheep.

The Church of the community of the Beloved Disciple emphasizes individual faith, the love of the brethren and an egalitarian spirit that gives full reign to freedom, spontaneity and creativity. The weakness of such an approach is evident. This community did not ultimately survive in a sinful world. Structure and organization protects, even if it can also stifle. And yet this community provides an alternative approach to the organization of Matthew and the triumphalism of Luke. Its members believed that faith in Jesus, the love of the brethren and the presence of the Spirit sufficed to ground their Christian identity. This belief gave them an extraordinary sense of freedom. Even though this Johannine community did not survive more than a century, its example of freedom continues to remind the organized Church of one of the essentials of Christianity.

## Colossians and Ephesians

Whether Paul actually wrote Colossians and Ephesians remains disputed. If Paul did not write Colossians, in all probability it may have been written within a decade after the death of Paul. The style may not be Pauline but the content is so similar that some hold that it is Paul's thought transcribed with stylistic adaptations by a secretary. Whether Paul wrote Ephesians is also disputed. But if Paul is not the author, the actual author clearly knew the other letters of Paul.

In both letters the author gives authoritative guidance to the communities to whom he is writing. An awareness of the enthusiastic aspect of early Christianity figures in Ephesians 4:11, and no emphasis on apostolic succession can be detected. Instead of relying on leaders to deal with problems, both epistles seem to present the Church as a growing entity, a spiritual presence that transcends. The Church functions best as a loving community, modeled on the love of Jesus for his followers and an awareness of holiness. This holiness of Christ lives in the Church, which is his body being built up in love (Eph 5:31–32).

The Church as the body of Christ allows for fluidity and an acceptance of many charisms. This suits the earlier Paul in Corinthians. The Church becomes more personal than institutional. In it, people can experience and manifest a love similar to that which Jesus offered in his ministry. The love of a spouse for the bride exemplifies the love that persists in the Christian community. Even pain and suffering fit in, for through them the individual fills up what is lacking for the body of Christ (Col 1:24). As Christ gave himself up for the Church, so Church members do likewise (Eph 5:25). The personalized Church encourages people to give of themselves. This self-offering can then pass from generation to generation.

The author of Ephesians knew the other letters of Paul and surely was aware of the sinfulness in the early Christian communities. Paul frequently had to deal with the failures of believers. Yet this same author could see the Church as a spotless bride, holy and without blemish (Eph 5:27). The mystical Church as the body of Christ must be holy, for Jesus is holy.

These characteristics of the Church communities portrayed in Ephesians and Colossians present a lofty ideal: love and holiness. The structure of the Church is not as important as the mystical identity with Jesus. Whether Paul wrote these epistles or not, the basic Pauline theology continues. A more enthusiastic and charismatic Church community belonged in early Christianity. It also must remain as an ideal of what the Church might yet become.

But enthusiasm and mysticism bring their weaknesses as well as strengths. Survival in an often cruel and sinful world needs more than just enthusiasm. Surely, the New Testament gives evidence for both the charismatic and enthusiastic communities as well as custodial, organized structured communities. Eventually the latter become the norm without ever losing sight of the important witness of the former. The Pastoral Epistles not only follow the development of Luke/Acts and Matthew but also further the movement to organization and authority.

## The Pastoral Epistles to Timothy and Titus

The Church of the nineties produced other approaches to the community, which would continue the Jesus tradition. The Church had moved from an enthusiastic climate in Corinth. One word will characterize these letters more than any other—*structure*. The expectation of an imminent Second Coming has passed. Christianity may well have a long life to lead, and as a religious movement it needed to preserve its traditions and its teachings. Apostolic succession offers the means for such preservation. Christianity needed structure and the author of these epistles had a clear plan. Written with the mantle of the authority of Paul, these letters offer a remedy to avoid disintegration. Presbyter-bishops must be appointed in each town. These individuals will guard against false teachers (1 Tim 4:1–2; 2 Tim 3:6; 4:3; Tit 1:10). They provided stability, preserved the authentic teaching of Jesus and ruled their communities with power. They taught sound doctrine (Tit 2:1) and maintained continuity (2 Tim 3:14). These epistles arose in a moment of crisis as Christianity dealt with encounters with the larger world and settled in for a long wait for the coming of the Lord. The call for control and structure became the norm for most Christian Churches. The presbyters-bishops alone teach, alone carry on the tradition, alone provide the vision for the future.

The laying on of hands mediates the charism of presbyter-bishop. Such ritual has its roots in the Old Testament with the ordination of Joshua by Moses (Num 27:18,123; Deut 34:9).

> Do not neglect the charism which you have, which was given to you by prophetic utterance through the presbyteral laying on of hands.
>
> (1 Tim 4:14)

> I remind you to rekindle the charism that is within you through the laying on of my hands.
>
> (2 Tim 1:6)

Nothing in the Pastorals focuses more clearly on the change from the authentic letters of Paul than the use of the word *charism.* In Paul's lifetime the word meant the gift of the Spirit granted freely with diversity to all Christians. Now the word became united with an ordination ritual, the laying on of hands. *Charism* had become indicative of an office, an official designation and an appointment authenticated by ritual.

The apostolic delegate preserves the deposit of faith, teaches and governs. These charisms mentioned in 1 Corinthians 12:28 and Romans 12:6–8 become the responsibilities of the apostolic delegate. Such a designation does not mean that only such delegates can teach but because of apostolic succession the teaching and leadership roles in the Church enjoyed by the apostle are passed on to succeeding generations.

The Pastorals also establish a college of presbyters (1 Tim 3:1–7 Tit 1:5) who become associated with the author in his ministry. Later in the letters of Ignatius of Antioch the presbyters become subordinate to the bishops, a further stage of development. What had been charisms of the Spirit in Corinthians has become part of the apostolic succession in the Pastorals.

The tradition passed on by the apostle to his followers changes from a living *paradosis,* a process of adaptive interpretative tradition in which the apostle functions as one link in a chain, to *parathaekae,* a precious object entrusted for safekeeping, to be forever unchanged. The delegate fulfills his function by handing on what he has received. He guards and renders faithfully the message coming from the apostle.

Strong leadership with a central control has worked well in the history of Christianity, especially in the Roman Catholic tradition. This facet of the Jesus tradition has shone more brilliantly than others. In fact, for some Catholics this is the only facet of being Church. Yet, while the Pastorals offer much that merits acceptance and adoption, they do not offer everything. Christianity began with a loosely united group of followers of Jesus and within a hundred years had evolved into a well-organized hierarchical Church. Because this is the way the Church had developed by the conclusion of the first century does not necessarily mean that this is the only model of value to the Christian Church. Each understanding of how the Church might function has had its merits. We can learn from them all, even today.

## Models of the Church

Some twenty-five years ago Avery Dulles, S.J., wrote his classic work, *Models of the Church.* In this book he proposed five models: The Church as Institution, Mystical Communion, Sacrament, Herald and Servant. He later added a sixth: A Community of Disciples. Certainly the Christian Church and the Catholic Church possess all of these dimensions. In this same work Father Dulles wrote of the difference between models and paradigms. Although taken from science, when used in theology a model can deepen understanding, synthesize what is already known, account for many of the strands in the Bible and in tradition and fit with what people have experienced. When one particular model does this better than other models, then the model becomes a paradigm. For Catholics the paradigm has been the institutional model.

# The Catholic Institutional Church

In the sixteenth century in the midst of the reformation controversy Robert Bellarmine offered his classical definition of the Catholic Church:

> The one and true Church is the community of men brought together by the profession of the same Christian faith and conjoined in the communion of the same sacraments under the government of legitimate pastors and especially the one Vicar of Christ on earth, the Roman Pontiff.[9]

One faith, one sacramental system, under legitimate authority resting on the pope as the vicar of Christ—this definition has characterized the Catholic Church ever since. During this same period theologians thought of the Church as a perfect society, subordinate to no other society and lacking nothing for its own institutional completeness. Both descriptions emphasize the structure of the Catholic Church, in particular the rights and power of its leaders (chiefly the bishops and the pope). The Catholic Church perdures in history as hierarchical. Such a model has aided the Church greatly in its missionary activity and has ensured a sense of stability and continuity with the past.

The Church as institution functions by teaching, sanctifying and ruling. The Church clearly divides hierarchy and laity. Since the bishop has been given the primary teaching office in a diocese, the faithful are conscience-bound to follow what the bishop teaches. Since the pope is the primary teacher for all the Church, all are obliged to accept what he teaches. The pope and bishops assisted by priests and deacons also fulfill the role of sanctification. Governance remains rather simple: from pope to bishops to pastors to laity. When the hierarchy teaches, rules and sanctifies, they perform service functions.

In this model the Catholic Church responds to the many troubling questions in life, offering a stable and certain environment in a confusing and contradictory world. Security comes from listening to what the Church teaches. Even when faced with contradictory views or explanations, Catholics could dismiss these opinions as the result of ignorance, sin or a lack of true faith. The Church as institution gives its members a strong sense of identity and security.

Such a custodial model, although often based on the Gospel of Matthew and the Pastoral Epistles, does not fit completely with the general tone of Jesus and the entire New Testament. The New Testament supports a custodial approach to the Jesus tradition and also emphasizes a community of disciples united by the same faith under the guidance of the Holy Spirit. But in the recent past the Catholic Church has been more custodial than necessary. The Scriptures call to the Church to model the image of a loving and caring mother who recognizes the Spirit in all. The Church should teach without hesitation the need for faith and love as the foundation for any Christian community, even one that still remains hierarchical. Catholic traditions offer several approaches to understanding the Church. Certainly survival demands authority and organization. Christianity, however, involves more than these. Faith and love and the presence of the Spirit bring a charismatic element to the Church. Somehow all of these traditions belong. The communities of Matthew, Luke, the Beloved Disciple, Colossians and Ephesians and the Pastorals all belong to the Catholic heritage and offer a multitude of traditions.

## TOPICS FOR DISCUSSION AND STUDY

1. What are the advantages and disadvantages to a custodial approach to life? A charismatic approach?
2. Enthusiasm explains the origin of Christianity.
3. Matthew preserved the old and was open to the new. Do you like being a centrist in life?
4. Can Christianity do without clear lines of authority?
5. The community of the Beloved Disciple emphasized faith and love. Too simplistic or not?
6. Luke stresses the Spirit. How does the Spirit continue in the Church?

7. Does anyone read the epistles to the Colossians and Ephesians? Have you ever heard anyone preach on these letters? What can they offer to the contemporary Church?

8. What model do you accept and live under? One or many? Which model predominates? for you?

# Works Consulted

Achtemeier, Paul. *The Quest for Unity in the New Testament Church.* Philadelphia: Fortress, 1987.

Brown, Raymond, and John Meier. *Antioch and Rome.* Mahwah, N.J.: Paulist Press, 1983.

Brown, Raymond. *The Churches the Apostles Left Behind.* Mahwah, N.J.: Paulist Press, 1984.

———. *The Community of the Beloved Disciple.* Mahwah, N.J.: Paulist Press, 1979.

Dulles, Avery. *Models of the Church.* New York: Doubleday, 1974.

———. *The Resilient Church.* New York: Doubleday, 1977.

Küng, Hans. *The Church.* New York: Doubleday, 1967.

O'Grady, John F. *Disciples and Leaders.* Mahwah, N.J.: Paulist Press, 1991.

———. *Pillars of Paul's Gospel: Galatians and Romans.* Mahwah, N.J.: Paulist Press, 1992.

Schillebeeckx, Edward. *The Church with the Human Face.* New York: Crossroad, 1987.

# CHAPTER 6:
# POPE, BISHOPS
# AND HIERARCHY

The Catholic Church traces its foundation to Jesus and the apostles. An unbroken and defining link binds the present Church to the Church of the apostles:

> You form a building, which rises on the foundation of the apostles and prophets, with Christ Jesus himself as the capstone. (Eph 2:20)

> And they devoted themselves to the apostles teaching and fellowship, to the breaking of bread and the prayers. (Acts 2:42)

This unbroken continuity not only gives assurance of the relationship between the present Church and the early Christian community, but also promises a link to the future. The once and future Church are one and the same since all go back to the original followers of Jesus. The Second Vatican Council declares that "the bishops by divine institution have taken the place of the apostles as pastors of the church" (*Lumen Gentium,* no. 24). The Church rests upon the apostles. The unity of the Church includes some relationship to the earliest followers of the Lord, especially the apostles, and through them present believers can rest assured of the relationship to the actual ministry of Jesus.

The author of the Gospel of Matthew knew the need for authority and organization. He recognized that the future of the

Church depended on the Gentile rather than the Jewish Christians and evidently had also concluded that the Church will be present in human history for many years to come. In the conclusion of his gospel he professes a line of authority through the apostles to Jesus.

> And Jesus came and said to them, "All authority in heaven and on earth has been given to me, Go therefore and make disciples of all nations, baptizing them in the name of the Father and of the Son and of the Holy Spirit, teaching them to observe all that I have commanded you and lo, I am with you always to the close of the age."
>
> (Matt 28:18–20)

No one can say for certain the origin of this passage from Matthew. The presence of the liturgical formula, with baptism in the name of the Father, Son and Holy Spirit, points in itself to a later origin for this saying than the ministry of Jesus. The need for an organized Church also supports the view that the passage more likely comes from the time of Matthew than Jesus. The idea behind the passage, however, the need for succession, probably arose quickly in the early Christian communities. The actual historical remembrance of Peter as a spokesperson and chief among the twelve gives sufficient foundation to the role of Peter as dating back to the time of Jesus.

Although always apostolic, the Church is not necessarily rooted in the twelve alone. In the New Testament the word *apostle* can never be used interchangeably with the *twelve*. Paul was clearly an apostle but not one of the twelve. The same can be said for other early followers (2 Cor 8:23; Phil 2:25; 1 Cor 12:28; Eph 4:11). The study of the New Testament demonstrates that the apostles, in fact, had no successors, nor did the twelve. Apostolic ministry, however, must continue (*Louvain Studies* [Summer 1996] is devoted to apostolic continuity of the Church and apostolic succession). In fact the ministry of the Church involves more than just an unbroken chain of authority. The ministry of the Church today involves the spiritual ideal of the disciples and apostles, the dedicated and enthusiastic commitment to preaching embodied in Paul, the virtues of presbyter/bishops and the sacramental ministry, especially the breaking of bread. The Church maintains apostolic ministry in a most complex way.

Too often in the past the understanding of apostolic succession as the link between bishop and apostles through the imposition of hands was too narrow. The more recent *Lima Document,* from the World Council of Churches in 1982, presents apostolic succession in a broader context:

> Apostolic tradition in the Church means continuity in the permanent characteristics of the Church of the apostles: witness to the apostolic faith, proclamation and fresh interpretation of the gospel, celebration of Baptism and the Eucharist, the transmission of ministerial responsibilities, communion in prayer, love, joy and suffering, service to the sick and needy, unity among the local churches and sharing the gifts which the Lord has given to each. (Geneva, 1982, no. 28)

The above statement can seem too broad, especially when compared to the usual understanding of Apostolicity in Roman Catholicism. In an ecumenical document, however, such might be expected. especially when the underlying element is the validity of ordination and true succession among the many Christian Churches. The Church needs continuity. No one can doubt that. But precisely how this continuity can be maintained, especially in the light of two thousand years of history, needs further examination.

Irenaeus's understanding of apostolicity offers us guidance today:

> True doctrine ought to be found in the tradition received from the apostles, by the bishops or the presbyters instituted by them and who have transmitted it to their successors up to the present time. (*Adv. Haer.,* III, 3,1)

Apostolicity involves true teaching. Apostolicity involves the very "roots" of Christianity. If no one can feel comfortable that what is taught and happening in the Church today has some connection to Jesus through apostolic succession, then Christianity becomes completely relativized. Roots in the past assure confidence in the present and in the future.

## Apostolic Succession

The apostolicity of the Church can never be reduced to apostolic succession, however close they may be related. The apostolic college certainly continues in the college of bishops. The early fathers of the Church, Clement, Ireaneus, Tertullian, Cyprian, Hippolytus and others all relate bishops to the apostles. Today bishops are the principal teachers of the Church and thus carry on an apostolic ministry. As principal teachers they offer guidance and direction especially when they gather as a college, such as at the Second Vatican Council. Something similar can be said for the gathering of national conferences of bishops. The question of the relationship between apostles and bishops in the New Testament can be divided according to two viewpoints, those of Luke and Paul.

## Luke

Debate continues on the precise relationship between the twelve disciples and apostles. Some believe that the title *apostle* refers exclusively to the twelve in Luke. Others see the term *apostle* is used of the twelve more as a primary title than as an exclusive one. Further discussion centers on the role of the twelve in the early Church. Certainly Luke does not view them as missionaries but perhaps for him they had a certain power to approve missionary activity. For Luke, Paul is the great missionary.

In Luke the twelve are not depicted as bishops. Luke offers no evidence in Acts that any one of the twelve ever presided over a local Church. It is also generally agreed that James the leader, not called a bishop, of the Jerusalem community was a brother of the Lord, and so not the same as James son of Alphaeus (one of the twelve). Peter is sometimes called the bishop of Antioch, but no evidence of this exists in Acts. Most Roman Catholics suppose that Peter was surely the first bishop of Rome. However, no evidence from history or archeology attests definitively to such a position. Luke does not present the twelve as bishops nor local leaders. The apostolate of the twelve and the presbyterate-episcopate existed at the same time with different functions.

Some believe that the connection of the twelve to bishops lies in the sacramental powers to baptize, to celebrate the Eucharist and to forgive sins. The New Testament offers no evidence that the apostles handed on such powers to anyone. The conclusion from the New Testament seems clear: There were no successors to the twelve. The symbolism of the twelve responsible for the founding of the renewal of Israel was unique. They served a definite purpose in the life of the Church and then passed into history.

Yet Luke does have them fulfill distinct roles in the Acts of the Apostles. The problem of the Hellenists in Acts 6:1–6 was far more serious than the distribution of goods. The Hellenists were not great supporters of the Temple and other Jewish Christians were. Although this is not a definitive belief, many think the Hellenists were Jewish converts to Christianity who lived in the Diaspora among the Gentiles. The decision to give the Hellenists their own leaders paved the way for the future Gentile Church. The implications became evident when persecution broke out: The Hellenists were scattered but those loyal to the Temple, (the Apostles, the twelve?) were not. In fact the Hellenists probably became the first missionaries among the Gentiles.

The second great decision within the early Church involved the observance of the Jewish law. Gentiles did not need to become Jews first and then Christians. The law was no longer binding. The twelve figured prominently in these decisions. In Acts 6:2 the twelve call together the multitude and propose a solution to the problem of the Hellenists. In Acts 15:4 the twelve welcome Paul and Barnabas to discuss the relationship between Christianity and Jewish law. Luke presents the twelve as a kind of council presiding over matters of consequence for the future of Christianity.

Some say that Luke invented the whole scenario. Luke cannot always be trusted as a historian in spite of his protestations that such was what he desired. With the recent discoveries from Qumran, however, it seems plausible that the early Church took over for its own structure the organization of the sectarians at Qumran. Thus Luke presents the twelve, those closest to Jesus, as a kind of council, which convoked sessions to deal with major problems. The Lucan apostle, since he was the companion of Jesus, could have been the guarantor of the Jesus tradition for future generations. In particular, as apostles, they could establish future direction for the developing Church. Today's successors of the twelve live on in the college of bishops, particularly when it assembles to deal with matters affecting the whole Church.

## Paul and the Apostles

Paul held a different viewpoint of apostles. Paul had experienced the risen Lord; he had been given a mandate to be a missionary to the Gentiles and he imitated the death and resurrection of Jesus in his personal life. In his own understanding, this made Paul an apostle. Paul clearly admitted that Peter was an apostle and even would accept the role of the other apostles but never without his personal claim to be an apostle as well. (Gal 1:18-20; 2:1-21). Since Paul was not an eyewitness he could never give testimony to the words or actions of Jesus personally. Yet his conviction that he had been given a mandate from the risen Lord assured him that he could also make decisions with regard to the future development of Christianity. Paul brought to the fore the problem of what obligations were expected of Gentile Christians and whether they were different from those expected of Jewish Christians. Rather than following any words or practices of the earthly Jesus, Paul drew his conclusions from his own understanding of the risen Lord. Paul, as the innovator, sought the approval of the apostles in Jerusalem. They, as guarantors of the tradition, agreed with Paul, at least to some extent. When, to the mind of Paul, they reneged, he confronted Peter and followed his own interpretation (Gal 2:11ff.). Later he would modify this position. Since the approach he articulated in the letter to the Galatians seems to have failed, Paul eventually wrote Romans, which represented a compromise in the relationship of Jewish law to Christianity.

Like the other apostles Paul does not seem to function as a local bishop. He founded churches and probably left other people in charge, yet always displayed a special solicitude for the churches he founded. While the other apostles expressed a concern for the whole Church, Paul had a special concern for those communities he had established. Paul expresses this concern in the many letters he wrote to churches he founded.

The reading of the New Testament does not demonstrate that the presbyter-bishops described in the Acts and letters were direct successors of the twelve apostles. Eventually, however, they would succeed to the pastoral care of the local community in the fashion of Paul and the general care of the whole Church in the manner of the twelve apostles. These presbyters-bishops may or may not have been appointed as such by the missionary apostles. Historians find it difficult to trace the presbyter-bishops to the twelve but perhaps some of them can be traced to apostles like Paul. Some relationship exists among the twelve apostles, other apostles and eventually presbyter-bishops, but the development took place slowly with some churches having such a structure early in history and eventually all the churches adopting a similar structure in imitation of one another. The structures evolved slowly, but yet a monarchical episcopacy existed at the end of the first century. The Church developed primarily under the guidance of the Holy Spirit and the development also included some anthropological and cultural forces. Just as God uses human beings to preach the one Word and produce the sacred Scriptures, so God used ordinary human events and social structures to contribute to the development of the Church.

Timothy and Titus as disciples of Paul the apostle could be viewed as second-level apostles. They might intervene or interfere in church affairs just as Paul did, but eventually the presbyter-bishops rose to the level of authority in a local community, and with the death of the apostles and second-level apostles, the leadership structure became that of presbyter-bishop. Perhaps this structure began as a collective authority and eventually evolved into a monarchical episcopacy in certain cities. Antioch may have had this kind of structure before other cities, such as Rome.

It has become more complicated for today's ecclesiastical leaders to exercise a concern for the whole Church as did the twelve in the early Church. Bishops throughout the world can gather in ecumenical councils such as Vatican II, which bear a concern for the whole Church. Church synods and national conferences are other ways the bishops can gather to focus on common concerns.

But each causes problems: Ecumenical councils cannot be called regularly; synods are infrequent and regional conferences only deal with a particular region. Roman Catholicism has settled the question with the bishop of Rome assuming the position of Peter for the care for the whole Church. For the community of Luke, the twelve made the decisions that affect the whole Church. The bishop of Rome (more commonly known as the pope or the Holy Father) principally fulfills this function today.

## The Successor of Peter: The Ministry of the Bishop of Rome

Many Roman Catholics assume that after the death of Peter every bishop of Rome was aware of the special authority he inherited as the successor of the chief of the apostles. To explain the lack of any evidence of the exercise of such a universal power, apologists replied that the circumstances did not merit any intervention. But these apologists nevertheless believed that the authority did reside in the office of the bishop of Rome, just waiting to come into great prominence.

Contemporary theologians are more aware of the lack of conclusive evidence documenting any understanding in the early Church of a universal role for the bishop of Rome. The earliest fathers of the Church cited to support these views, Clement of Rome, Ignatius and Irenaeus, do not offer undisputed evidence and therefore their arguments cannot be used without some reservation. An understanding of the eventual exercise of papal authority need not presume that the postapostolic Church was in such full possession of itself, and in particular of its structure, that it immediately asserted and exercised a primacy in authority given to the bishop of Rome.

Just as the early Church gradually developed an understanding of Jesus as recorded in four gospels and the various other writings of the New Testament, so with time the Church began to understand its own structure and its form of authority. The need for a central authority became more evident when divisions in the Church and among the bishops made it apparent that a single sign and cause of unity for the universal Church could best fulfill the continuation of the mission of the Lord.

Gradually the bishop of Rome began to fulfill a ministry similar to that which Peter fulfilled in apostolic times. Such an experience caused a rereading of the Scriptures in the light of this historical necessity. The Church began to see in the bishop of Rome a manifestation of the Petrine function of "strengthening the brethren" (Luke 22:32). Today most Roman Catholic theologians and historians recognize the interplay among historical factors or anthropological needs as well as the divine commission to preach the gospel to the whole world to explain the origin of papal ministry. The role of the Holy Spirit also figures in the development of the role of the bishop of Rome. Other factors such as the place of Rome as an imperial city contributed to the development of papal authority. Christ did not institute the structure of the Church in a direct fashion. The Church structures that gradually emerged were guided by the power of the Spirit. They included some elements that stemmed from Christ and others conditioned by the time and space of their origin. This does not imply that the papacy itself is the result of merely historical processes but that these processes were part of the divine plan for the Church. Once part of the faith community, believers can recognize in historical and anthropological elements the will of God. For most Roman Catholic theologians the papacy with its full exercise of office shares in the mystery of the Church and thus forms an object of faith. The study of the origins of Christian ministry in the New Testament offers a possibility that the office of the pope may itself continue to change. The understanding of the role of authority in ministry in the present world, especially when the historical factors of the history of Christianity have already altered the understanding of the authority of the papacy, offers possibilities for further changes.

## The Leonine Tradition

The reign of the emperor Constantine (285–337) marked the transition of the Christian Church from a persecuted people into a legal, corporate personality within the framework of established Roman law. When the Christian Church became the official state religion, its leaders assumed a role not unlike that which the emperor played in civil affairs. Thereafter, the Church took on more of a structure based on the form of the Roman Empire. The line between Church and state was often transgressed. Christian emperors sometimes treated the Church as a department of civil government and Church leaders reacted to the state as an institution inferior to that of the Church. The relationship between the authority of the Church and the authority of the state continued to present problems throughout the Middle Ages and do so even down to the present day. As the temporal power of the empire declined, many governmental functions of administration and protection devolved upon the office of bishop and, in particular, the bishop of Rome.

Bishops became prince-bishops and had both a civil and ecclesiastical authority. Leo the Great, the bishop of Rome, went out from Rome to meet Attila the Hun and protected the city and its population. Theologians agree that this same pope formulated the doctrine of papal primacy and authority that had been present in seminal forms for the previous two centuries. Leo clearly formulated his belief on the precise relationship between Jesus and Peter, and then Peter and the bishop of Rome. These views founded the Western understanding of the role and office of the bishop of Rome as an office of primacy in authority. Of particular interest are the arguments that Leo used in describing the authority of the bishop of Rome. He was trained in Roman law and explained succession through the use of the legal concept of heredity. In Roman law the heir had the same rights, authority and obligations as the one he replaced. Thus the pope could exercise the same authority and power that Christ had entrusted to Peter. Leo's interpretation of Matthew 16:18–19 demonstrated that he believed the authority of Peter over the apostles was a sharing in the absolute authority of Jesus himself. To the idea of juridical continuity taken from Roman law Leo added his understanding of a mystical or sacramental continuity: "Peter in heaven continues to govern the Church through his heir and vicar, and in this sense the pope is Peter himself mystically continuing to exercise his authority in human history."[10]

This same period saw the rise of monasticism. In this new form of Christian life a spiritual and charismatic type of ministry could continue to function. Monks enjoyed an independent type of authority often in opposition to what had come to be seen as the hierarchical and juridical authority. This freer approach to creative ministry was more prevalent in the East and indeed continues to exist in the Eastern Church. In the eighth century, especially after the monothelite and iconoclastic controversies in the East, the monks assumed more of the role of authority figures as "men of God" and exercised their power outside the normal channels of church life. In the West a similar development occurred as abbots and monks created their own sphere of influence. Such a development did not create a total opposition between the authority as exercised by bishops and pope and that exercised by holy men and women, since the bishops themselves were often chosen from the ranks of the monastic clergy. And sometimes popes were also chosen from this group.

Although Leo's teaching on the papacy continued to dominate Roman Catholic theology up to the present time, not every member of the Church adopted the teaching nor was it accepted everywhere in Christianity. Several centuries passed before Leo's theory became practice. Even the title "Papa," a word used earlier for all bishops, did not become reserved for the bishop of Rome until the sixth century, and then only in the West. Gregory VII still had to assert in 1075 that only one pope existed in the world. Even the title Vicar of Christ, used by contemporary popes, was a late development. For the first millennium the title used was Vicar of Peter.

The study of early history, both in the New Testament and in other early Christian writings, offers no definitive proof that Peter was ever considered the first bishop of Rome. Yet Peter has long been associated with the Church at Rome. Clement of Alexandria refers to the Church at Rome founded by Peter and Paul, and Papias in the second century suggests that Mark recorded the teaching of Peter in his gospel. The recent excavations under St. Peter's demonstrates the veneration rendered to Peter on that site as early as the second century. Even if history can not definitively establish Peter functioning as bishop of Rome, his New Testament ministry did continue. The Gospel of Matthew (Matt 16:16–19) saw a need for clear lines of authority, and the Gospel of John (John 21:15–19) recognized that Peter, and then presumably his successors, had some role to play in the developing Church. Certainly this function need not have been attached to an episcopal city but in fact, that happened. The city where Peter died eventually developed its own monarchical episcopacy and began to function as the center of the Petrine ministry for the twelve. Matthew (16:17–18) had entrusted the keys of authority to Peter. Luke (22:32) acknowledged the task of strengthening the brethren. John (21:15–17) admitted pastoral care. All this became the ministry of the bishop of Rome.

Originally Peter functioned along with the other apostles, including Paul the missionary apostle, in dealing with matters affecting the whole Church. The successor of Peter still speaks both in the name of the whole Church and in the name of Jesus. To truly continue this Petrine function, however, the pope speaks not only in the name of Jesus and the Church but includes the other bishops in the concerns of the worldwide Church.

## Divine Institution

The Catholic Church teaches that the papacy is of divine institution. The study of the New Testament, the references already mentioned in Matthew, Luke and John point to some divine foundation for the Petrine function. The modern papacy, however, has developed over two thousand years and is still evolving. Some influences come from the role and trappings of medieval monarchs and a reaction to Protestantism by the papacy. The Petrine function has been attached to the city of Rome and to the person of its bishop. Some think that nothing prevents this function from being fulfilled in another place and by several people or a council. They believe that the function should be institutionalized but that it can also change as the Church changes in history.

# Jurisdiction

According to the First Vatican Council, the pope as successor of Peter exercises a jurisdiction that is universal, ordinary, immediate, truly episcopal, supreme and full. *Jurisdiction* is a legal term derived from a judicial tradition. With the development of papal authority the pope took on many features of a political power. This jurisdiction of Rome differed considerably in the history of Christianity. In the early centuries Rome functioned with strict authority over the bishops of Italy but in the rest of the West intervened only in special cases. The Eastern Churches had their own authority figures who eventually became the patriarchs. The churches outside of the Roman Empire had little relationship to the bishop of Rome. In the Middle Ages the Church of Rome took on a more universal jurisdiction. Thomas Aquinas in the thirteenth century and Francesco Suarez in the sixteenth century regarded the Church as a strict monarchy in which all of the bishops depended upon the pope for their own jurisdiction.

The term *jurisdiction* is not the most felicitous since it seems to juridicize the authority of Peter. The New Testament does not give to Peter alone the authority to make laws and without this authority the meaning of jurisdiction has little significance. The fathers of the First Vatican Council debated the concept of jurisdiction, intending to avoid a strictly legal interpretation. Federico Zinelli, a leading theologian and official church reporter for *Pastor Aeternus,* contended that the term *episcopal* should make it clear that the pope exercises authority as a pastor whose mission it is to feed the flock entrusted to his care. Just as individual bishops are missioned to feed the particular flocks committed to them, so Zinelli argued, the pope is commissioned to pasture the whole flock of Christ. The pope should not be seen as a universal and absolute ruler but as the bearer of an authority modeled on that of the earliest followers of Jesus, who in turn modeled their own authority on the service of Jesus himself. The authority given to Peter as attested in the New Testament should not be seen as primarily jurisdictional nor can it be seen as merely honorary. A better designation would be sacramental. Today some Catholics continue to question the appropriateness of the term *jurisdiction* as applied to the kind of authority that the pope should have over other bishops. Vatican I posed the question in terms of an opposition between two types of primacy—honor and jurisdiction—so that the term *jurisdiction* was used to exclude a mere primacy of honor. The authority of Jesus, which according to Matthew 16:17–19 was transmitted to Peter, cannot be suitably called either honorary or jurisdictional. There is a third kind of primacy, properly theological in nature, which might be called ontological or, in a wide sense, sacramental. In the writings of Leo the Great, sacramental themes of primacy predominate over the juridical themes that later became so prominent. In a sacramental view of primacy, the notion of papal power moves away from jurisdiction in the legal sense toward a style of leadership based on charism and moral authority. The pope, like a patriarch, functions as a bishop among bishops. He exercises a primacy not *over* bishops but rather *among* bishops and is, in that sense, a first among equals. This special service given to the pope has been explained in the Second Vatican Council as the authority "to preside over the assembly of charity," (*Lumen Gentium,* no. 13) and to foster collegial relationships among the regional bishops and the particular churches.

Frequently in the history of Christianity the Eastern Churches, and the Protestant Churches as well, have bristled at the position by the Roman Church on jurisdiction. The ideas as presented above would help considerably to assuage some of these historical fears. The concept of papal primacy could be interpreted more in accord with the testimony of the New Testament, less legalistically and more in accord with the collegial and conciliar view of the Church. The present pope has actually called for a rethinking of how the authority of the bishop of Rome can be exercised in the Church today.

> When the Catholic Church affirms that the office of the bishop of Rome corresponds to the will of Christ, she does not separate this office from the mission entrusted to the whole body of bishops, who are also vicars and ambassadors of Christ. The bishop of Rome is a member of the "college" and the bishops are his brothers in the ministry.

> I am convinced that I have a particular responsibility in this regard, above all in acknowledging the ecumenical aspi-rations of the majority of the Christian communities and in heeding the request made of me to find a way of exercising this primacy which, while in no way renouncing what is essential to its mission, is nonetheless open to new situations.
>
> (*Ut Unum Sint,* May 30, 1995, no. 95)

# Infallibility

Paul VI seemed to imply that dogmas are historically condi-tioned. He frequently mentioned the need of the Church to adjust to the times:

> To what extent should the Church adapt itself to the histori-cal and local circumstances in which it has to exercise its mission? How is it to guard against the danger of relativism which would make it untrue to its own dogmas and moral principles? And yet, how can it fit itself to approach all men and bring salvation to all becoming on the example of the Apostle Paul "all things to all men" that all may be saved?
>
> (*Ecclesiam Suam,* no. 87)

Does language always remain the same? Is a vernacular transla-tion of Hebrew, Greek or Latin the same? Can content remain the same with a change in form? All such questions remained unanswered in any definitive way. All cause problems for infalli-bility. Whatever the negative notions associated with the term, it implies something positive. Because Jesus is present in the Church and because the Holy Spirit guides the Church, no possi-bility exists for the Church to ever fall away from the truth of Jesus Christ. Much may change but that can never change. But how can this truth be maintained? How can the pope teach apart from the rest of the Church? What has happened to the continu-ing function of the twelve other than Peter? Does infallibility involve what is believed by the faithful in the Church or what is believed by a segment?

Ordinary infallibility belongs to the Church when bishops, even though as individuals they are not infallible, do proclaim infallibly the doctrine of Christ. "Even though dispersed throughout the world but preserving the bond of unity among themselves and with Peter's successor, in their authoritative teaching concerning matters of faith and morals, they are in agreement that a particular teaching is to be held definitively and absolutely" (*Lumen Gentium,* no. 25). The pope also can exercise his ordinary magisterium and teach infallibly even without the formal declarations as stated above.

During the First Vatican Council in 1870, the assembled fathers declared in its dogmatic constitution, *Pastor Aeternus,* that the Pope possesses "the infallibility with which the divine redeemer willed his Church to be endowed in defining the doctrine concerning faith and morals." Previously this unfinished council had also spoken of the papacy as a divine institution, with a primacy of jurisdiction over all churches, pastors and believers.

No doubt this council was affected by the historical currents of the times. Europe had experienced both the French Revolution and the rise of Napoleon. Italy experienced an antipapal and anticlerical attitude. The enlightenment had affected all scientific study. German romanticism had called into question many of the older tenets of both theology and philosophy. Where the Church would fit into this New World needed to be delineated, and a strong papal authority in all matters would help. While the discussions were never completed, four conditions were affirmed to be necessary before a pope pronounced infallibly: (1) the pope acts as supreme pastor and teacher of all Christians; (2) he uses his authority as successor of Peter; (3) the subject matter concerns faith and morals, that is, doctrine expressing divine revelation; (4) he expressly indicates that the doctrine must be held definitely by all. Moreover, the declaration also states that these definitions are "irreformable of themselves and not because of any consent of the Church."

The Second Vatican Council adds to the teaching on infallibility by stating that "the whole body of the faithful who have an anointing that comes from the holy one (cf. 1 John 2:20, 27) cannot err in matters of belief. This characteristic is shown in the supernatural appreciation of the faith of the whole people, when, from the bishops to the last of the faithful, they manifest a universal consent in matters of faith and morals" (*Lumen Gentium,* no. 12).

## Vatican II and Catholic Traditions on the Papacy

Prior to the Second Vatican Council the authority of the bishop of Rome was interpreted in the same manner as throughout the early and later Middle Ages: Christ promised and conferred an absolute authority upon Peter; this primacy in authority continued in the Church and can be found in the exercise of the authority of the bishop of Rome. This recent council did not alter the notion of supreme authority of pope and bishops over the Church but did claim that this authority is to be exercised as service and in a collegial way (*Lumen Gentium,* no. 18). Pope and bishops will use their authority and power but only to build up the flock (*Lumen Gentium,* no. 27). The Church has developed in its understanding of authority but ultimately has returned to the notion of authority as service, as witnessed in the New Testament.

The authority of the papacy for most Roman Catholics symbolizes the authority of the Church. Even for Protestants, the popes of recent times have exercised authority not only within the Roman tradition but also beyond the confines of the Catholic Church. The pope has become an authority figure for Christianity even if some aspects of Christianity have problems with certain elements of the papal authority structure. Certainly the life of the Christian, Roman Catholic or not, should center primarily upon Jesus. But the presence of the pope within the Roman Catholic community and his influence outside this community both in religious and world affairs necessitates a study of his role in the past and the present. Then all Christians can look forward to what a renewed papacy would mean for the Christian Church.

A renewal of the Church based upon the return to the biblical traditions as sanctioned by the Second Vatican Council includes a rethinking and restructuring of the office of the bishop of Rome. The First Vatican Council defined that the papacy is of divine institution and that the pope enjoys a primacy of jurisdiction over all particular churches, pastors and believers, and when he speaks "ex cathedra" as successor of Peter he is blessed with infallibility. This council appears authoritarian, especially when its pronouncements are compared with the documents from the Second Vatican Council. This more recent gathering of the bishops of the Roman Church manifested an openness, a return to a biblical tradition, a concern for pluralism and adaptability and a suggestion that the Holy Spirit operates throughout the Church. This same council often seemed to substitute an attitude of service, self-criticism, adaptability and friendliness for the strong defensive and authoritarian attitude of the First Vatican Council. As a result of this change in attitude, many Catholics see a need for a revision of papal authority and an examination of its use of power. As already noted, the present pope, John Paul II, specifically calls for a rethinking of papal primacy in his encyclical *Ut Unum Sint.*

## Recent Developments

The study of the New Testament roots of episcopal authority and the gradual emergence of this office in the Church implies that the divine institution of the papacy must be seen in the context of the historical needs of the Christian Church. Rather than speak of divine institution, many prefer to speak of the Petrine office, ministry or function within the Church. In theory most Christians will accept the need for this ministry to continue to exist within the Church, but how it is exercised could be further adapted based upon the historical needs of the Church. A single individual will probably continue to hold this office, but it is not impossible that a group of individuals could divide its judicial, legislative and administrative powers. Since both Vatican councils left unanswered the proper interrelationship of the pope, the universal episcopacy and ecumenical councils, further discussion within the Roman tradition seems necessary, and this discussion need not be locked into the authority structures of the past, provided the function of Peter continues in the Church. The change in geopolitical realities in recent years also calls for an examination of the operations of the papacy. In theory, the pope has supreme control over all of the agencies, secretariats and congregations. But as is true with all bureaucracy, they tend to have a life of their own apart from the pope (who yet bears ultimate authority and responsibility). With the pope spending more time outside of the Vatican, a division of authority seems inevitable if the Church does not wish the bureaucracy to move into a vacuum created by other circumstances.

The decision at Vatican I to avoid a declaration stating that the primacy of Peter is irrevocably attached to the see of Rome leaves open to question whether some day the primate of the Roman Catholic Church will be one other than the bishop of Rome, even if today this seems most unlikely. The institutionalization of this Petrine function remains paramount. Only then can the Church have an effective sign and cause of unity. Having an individual to fulfill this function strongly symbolizes this unity, but whether this is the only possibility for the future should not be accepted as a given.

Whatever the future form of apostolicity and the authority of bishops and pope, certain principles should always remain. Based upon the teachings of the New Testament and the earliest traditions of the Church, diversity, collegiality and subsidiarity should underpin the authority of the Catholic Church. While these principles have never been consistently honored, they have become essential aspects of Church authority over the past two thousand years.

## Diversity

The presence of the Holy Spirit promised by Jesus (John 16:13) has given rise to different forms of theology, law, spirituality, liturgy and piety in the Church. Diversity persists in the midst of unity. In fact unity becomes strengthened in diversity and perfected. The recent synods of Asia and Oceania have pleaded for greater diversity in the Church. The Catholic Church should never be understood as Western and European. Already the Catholic Church has over two dozen rites, some even within the Latin Church, for example, the Ambrosian rite of Milan. Theologies differ from East to

West, from an Aristotelian-based theology to the more phenome-
nological and personally based theology of the present pope, John
Paul II. Spirituality also ranges from the charismatic Spirit-filled
approach to the Christian life (including the more mystical dimensions of Teresa of Avila or John of the Cross) to the spirituality of
ordinary daily life. Diversity should continue and include regional
as well as cultural and ethnic differences. Unity in its very being
moves to multiplication and diversity, which forms both the resolution and perfection of the original unity.

## Collegiality

*Collegiality* means, "to bind together different elements." The
sharing of authority, power and responsibilities has characterized the Catholic Church in the past thirty-five years. One ecumenical council, nine ordinary synods, numerous extraordinary
synods, five extraordinary consistories and frequent meetings of
approximately one hundred episcopal conferences—all have
become part of the actual functioning of the Catholic Church.
Lay men and women function on every nonsacramental level of
the Catholic Church, including as heads of offices, chancellors
and even administrators of parishes. Shared authority and power
will continue to develop in the Church.

All collegial bodies, whether councils or synods or consistories or conference meetings, operate differently. Far from being
a threat to the power of the pope, today they are accepted as
helping the pope fulfill his functions. Because these bodies are
often too large and meet too infrequently, they can accomplish
only limited results. Each group, however, brings to the central
offices of the Church different perspectives. This was evident in
the recent synods of Asia and Oceania. The Synod of the Americas brought bishops from both American continents together for
the first time and created a sense of unity in the Americas. Contemporary culture today demands consultation and discussion.
The Catholic Church shares the same need. Although collegiality does not mean democracy, these structures provide both a
safety valve and a reality check within this large international

institution called the Catholic Church. Although organized primarily as a hierarchy consisting of pope and bishops, the Catholic Church has changed its face and not just cosmetically. Who knows what the next thirty years will bring?

## Subsidiarity

What a lower level can accomplish should not be taken over by a higher level. Micromanaging never helps an institution but often stifles creativity and development. The Church does not function like a multinational corporation, with the pope as the CEO and bishops as middle managers. Each bishop functions as the sign and cause of unity in his own diocese by sacramental ordination and not just by papal appointment. The local level knows the problems and in most instances knows better the solutions. Certainly consultation with the larger Church should always characterize diocesan decisions, but ultimately the principle of subsidiarity teaches that what can be handled locally should be handled locally.

Subsidiarity also presumes collaboration. Bishops work together with the pope and Roman offices and vice versa. Bishops work together with clergy and laity. Decisions affecting the whole Church presuppose the collaboration of all members of the Church, just as decisions for a diocese rests upon the mutual working together of the diocesan family. The new Code of Canon Law calls specifically for such collaboration in parish councils, diocesan pastoral councils, presbyteral councils and the regular synods of bishops. Consultation and collaboration may also bring deliberative decisions involving all members of the Church. The future alone will show how.

### TOPICS FOR DISCUSSION AND STUDY

1. Apostolic succession remains essential for the Church. What does this mean for the relationship of the Catholic Church to other Christian Churches?

2. The Petrine function must continue. The bishop of Rome is both sign and cause of unity for the whole Church. How can this function serve all of Christianity?

3. Luke and Paul have different perspectives on apostolicity. What are the values of each approach?

4. What does infallibility of the pope mean to ordinary Catholics?

5. How does the Holy Spirit function in the development of church structures? Can anthropological, historical and sociological needs explain church structure?

6. Diversity characterizes the Catholic Church in membership. How should this be present in structures?

7. *Collegiality* and *subsidiarity* are terms frequently used in management. How can they be applied to the Church?

8. How can the Catholic Church remain authoritative and hierarchical and yet be pastoral?

# Works Consulted

Bermejo, Luis M. *Infallibility on Trial: The Church, Conciliatory and Communion.* Westminster, Md.: Christian Classics, 1992.

Brown, Raymond. *Priest and Bishop.* Mahwah, N.J.: Paulist Press, 1970.

Dionne, J. Robert. *The Papacy and the Church: A Study of Praxis and Reception in Ecumenical Perspective.* New York: Philosophical Library, 1987.

Dulles, Avery. "Toward a Renewed Papacy." *The Resilient Church.* New York: Doubleday, 1977.

Fries, H., and J. Finsterholzl. "Infallibility." *Sacramentum Mundi.* New York: Herder and Herder, 1967–69, vol. 3, 132–38.

Granfield, Patrick. *The Papacy in Transition.* New York: Doubleday, 1980.

Grisez G., and F. Sullivan. "The Ordinary Magisterium's Infallibility." *Theological Studies* 55 (1994): 720–38.

Klausnitzer, Wolfgang. "Roman Catholicism and the Papal Office." *Theology Digest* 45 (1998): 233–37.

Lima Document. *Baptism, Eucharist and Ministry.* Geneva: World Council of Churches, 1982.

Miller, M. *What Are They Saying about Papal Authority?* Mahwah, N.J.: Paulist Press, 1983.

Orsy, Ladislas. "Magisterium: Assent and Dissent." *Theological Studies* 48 (1987): 473–97.

Quinn, John. *The Reform of the Papacy.* New York: Crossroad, 1999.

Rahner, Karl, ed. *The Teaching of the Catholic Church.* Cork: Mercier Press, 1966.

Rebeiro, M. "The Ongoing Debate on Infallibility." *Louvain Studies* 19 (1994): 307–31.

Reese, Thomas. *Inside the Vatican.* Cambridge: Harvard University Press, 1996.

Ricca, Paolo. "New Possibilities for the Papacy." *Theology Digest* 46 (1999): 48–52.

Ullmann, W. "Leo I and the Theme of Papal Primacy." *Journal of Theological Studies* 2 (1960): 32–41.

# CHAPTER 7:
# THE LITURGY AND
# THE SACRAMENTS
# OF THE CHURCH

All religions involve worship. Every religious tradition promises some contact with the divine through the use of symbols and ritual. In the Catholic tradition, since things can express something other than what appears to the eye, the use of certain elements in the context of prayer adds a dimension that promises the individual communion with the divine. The presence of God in an individual's life, grace, becomes a reality through the sacraments in the Catholic tradition. Jesus, the Son of God, the definitive presence of God in human history, becomes present in many ways. As Jesus was the sacrament of God to the human race, so the Church is the sacrament of his presence to all times and places and expresses itself in seven sacraments. Worship involves priest, congregation, prayers, ritual and material things that contain the reality they express, even if never completely. In recent years the Catholic Church has chosen the word *liturgy* to express the many different elements involved in the worship of the one true God through Jesus Christ by the power of the Spirit.

## Jesus as Liturgist and Priest

Jesus is the only true priest in Christianity. He offers the true worship to God. In the continuation of his presence through the Church individuals join in this one offering. Jesus is the first liturgist:

> But now Christ has obtained a ministry [liturgy] which is much more excellent than the old as the covenant he mediates is better since it is enacted on better promises.
>
> (Heb 8:6)

The author expresses the superiority of Jesus especially when he remarks:

> We have such a high priest, one who is seated at the right hand of the throne of the majesty in heaven, a minister [liturgist] in the sanctuary and the true tent, which is set up not by man but by the Lord.
>
> (Heb 8:1-2)

Jesus does not stand before the Lord God but sits at the right hand in majesty. The worship offered by Jesus surpasses that of the Old Testament.

## Spiritual Meaning of Worship

The word *liturgy* involves the work of the people carrying a sense of the spiritual, not to the exclusion of the external, but with an emphasis on the internal. For example, in Acts 13:2 we read: "While they were worshiping the Lord and...fasting...." For some this refers to liturgical action such as prayers or chants or even the Eucharist. Others see the meaning as private prayer and to still others it refers to a true liturgical action, an act of worship. But if the meaning was private and general prayer, the author could have used a different word. He chose not to. The presence of fasting should also be considered in seeking the meaning. The context is Antioch, and Luke wishes to show how this new teaching spread. He begins by referring to prophets and teachers. They would be the chief protagonists of the new mission. The context of the community is a liturgical service, which is joined to fasting. In the midst of this action, Luke narrates the election of Paul and Barnabas. The narrative closes with Paul and Barnabas being sent out to proclaim the Word (Acts 13:4–5). Liturgy involves prayer and action propelling believers to preach the Word.

## Paul and Worship

Paul's letter to the Romans also offers an important understanding of the practice of the early Church:

> Because of the grace given to me by God to be a minister of Christ Jesus to the Gentiles in the priestly service of the gospel of God, so that the offering of the Gentiles may be acceptable, sanctified by the Holy Spirit.
>
> (Rom 15:16)

Paul is a sacred minister and his responsibilities involve sacrifice. The use of the word *priestly* and the reference to offering refer to sacred actions. Paul functions as the priest who sows the seed of the gospel in the hearts of the Gentiles and completes his work in the offering of the Gentiles to God. The Gentiles become an acceptable sacrifice. Liturgy has gone from temple to synagogue to the preaching of the Word of the gospel, to the worship of God through which the Gentiles become spiritual offerings to God through the Spirit.

## Liturgy

The word *Leitourgia* (liturgy) contains in itself nothing that necessarily refers to Christian worship. It came from usage in the Old Testament and from a pagan word meaning public work. The lack of a specific Christian meaning becomes more evident when one realizes that the word came into Latin being translated as office or ministry or celebration or sacred action. Even the original sense of the term, "public work," is insufficient as a term for worship. And the sense of worship of the people also is not expressed by the word since originally it meant service *for* the people and not *by* the people. Some would also say that the word *liturgy* connotes more the external aspect than the internal aspect.

In Church literature from the sixteenth century on, the term *liturgy* referred more to rubrics without any sense of external expression of internal worship. As late as 1958 the meaning referred principally to regulations. Even references to the Roman liturgy or the Maronite liturgy or the Byzantine liturgy usually refer primarily to the rites and how they are carried out, rather than to an internally experienced worship.

## *Latria*

In the New Testament *latria* always means worship due to God (Matt 4:10; Luke 2:37; Acts 26:7; Rom 1:9 Heb 8:5; 9:14) and carries an emphasis on the internal aspect of worship. Also in the New Testament, the writers used *latria* to indicate more the interior disposition of the person rather than external ceremonies. *Latria* gives value to the ancient liturgy. Otherwise it remains purely ceremonial. In the New Testament true worship expresses the spirit, not only the human spirit but also the Holy Spirit, which is given by the Lord.

True Christian worship is always *latria*, which emphasizes the internal but not without the external. The word can indicate both. The difference between Christian worship and worship of the Old Testament or pagan worship often centers on the meaning of sacrifice. The Christian does not need victims since the Christian offers the self to God in an interior and spiritual union with Christ through the Spirit. The chief offering belongs to Christ and the Christian shares in this one offering.

## Definitions of *Liturgy*

Historically the definition of *liturgy* has usually been taken from Pius XII's encyclical *Mediator Dei* (1947). "Liturgy is the whole public worship of the mystical body of Christ, head and members." The pope rejects in this encyclical the concept of liturgy as purely external and ritualistic as well as the notion of liturgy as juridical. Both had been part of the traditional notion of liturgy. The encyclical also rejects the meaning of liturgy as being fundamentally an aesthetic experience. Liturgy is the worship of the Church, not just any worship but that which belongs properly to the Church. It has its origin in Christ and in some ecclesiastic order.

In this century many have struggled with descriptions of liturgy, emphasizing one element over the other. Certainly it involves both the priesthood of Jesus and the official ministers. The result or end of liturgy always involves the worship of God and human sanctification. Although not the most fundamental aspect, aesthetics, expressed in apt ritual, remains important. Such becomes obvious in every church ceremony.

Liturgy also involves how people live. The spiritual sacrifice of a good life belongs to liturgy. The mission of the Church, the mission of Jesus continued in the lives of his followers form the substance of what the Church brings to its worship of God. The one offering of Jesus includes the offering of his followers in the Church.

Liturgy involves mystery. First the worship of the Church involves the mystery of God's plan for all creation through Jesus and then the mystery of how Jesus remains in the Church. The mystery also involves how the Church experiences itself and how it experiences the presence of the crucified and risen Lord. Mystery here does not imply that people know nothing, but rather that people know something but not everything.

True worship, true liturgy, rests first on the perfect worship offered to God by Jesus, the one priest and mediator of the new covenant. This worship fulfilled the worship of the Old Testament. Jesus lived his whole life as worship of God and wished that his relationship to God might continue in the Church inviting others to join in this one communion.

## The Worship of Jesus

The Church shares with Jesus the task of worshiping God. The Lord had given to the Church his own personal worship as a continual gift. The Church worships God through participating in the worship of Jesus, the one priest.

> The liturgy is considered as the exercise of the priestly office of Christ. In the liturgy the sanctification of man is manifested by signs perceptible to the senses and is effected in a way which is proper to each of these signs. In the liturgy full public worship is performed by the Mystical Body of Jesus Christ, that is, by the Head and its members.
>
> (Constitution on the Sacred Liturgy, no. 7)

The liturgy of the Church continues the liturgy of Jesus and joins to this one act the Church's own desire and efforts to render appropriate service to God.

Jesus worshiped God by proclaiming the kingdom, by sanctifying himself so that others may also be sanctified (John 17:19). Jesus manifested the glory of God and brought about the sanctification of people. In fact, the sanctification of people renders worship to God. The service given to God is the holiness of God's people made possible through the proclamation of the gospel.

The sanctification of people does not mean a moral holiness but a participation in the saving mystery of Jesus through living as Jesus did. Jesus makes people holy, and so they live the spiritual sacrifice of a good life. Moral activity flows from what people are, rather than people becoming holy through moral activity. Jesus has sanctified his followers. This comes first.

Liturgy is the act of worship of Jesus joined to the personal worship of the Church, which brings about the sanctification of people expressed in ritual. Worship forms the principle aspect of liturgy not only as social but also as the personal act of Christ and then of the Church joined to Christ. Since the one true liturgy precedes the Church, the Church exists first passively and then actively. The liturgy of the Lord becomes constitutive of the Church itself. The Church becomes most the Church when it worships God through the continuous offering to God of Jesus. The Church offers the only true worship to God since it continues the worship of Jesus. Christ offered the true worship by proclaiming the good news to the poor, caring for them and serving them. He became the sign of salvation for all and continues this role in the Church.

## Vatican II

The Second Vatican Council began its work with a renewal of the Liturgy. The church fathers began by placing liturgy in a theological and biblical perspective. Liturgy makes sense only in the context of the eternal plan of God for the salvation of all people through Jesus. This one plan God has revealed through the prophets and then in Christ, whose humanity becomes the instrument of salvation for all.

The salvation of Christ consists in the reconciliation of people with God and the worship of God completely and perfectly. In the Constitution on the Sacred Liturgy the council fathers introduce the paschal mystery as a theological factor to be integrated into the full understanding of what liturgy means and what the Church does in its liturgy.

> In the restoration and promotion of the sacred liturgy this full and active participation by all the people is the aim to be considered before all else.
>
> (Constitution on the Sacred Liturgy, no. 14)

## The Paschal Mystery

The paschal mystery of Jesus has brought liberation and salvation. Now Christ transmits the liberation and salvation once promised to Israel through his Church and to all people. The liberation and salvation constitutes the heart of the liturgy of the Church and involves the mystery of the Church. The Constitution on the Sacred Liturgy of Vatican II places the liturgy on the same level as the whole mystery of salvation in the incarnation of Jesus. Liturgy involves the mystery of redemption and the glorification of God and actuates God's eternal plan for all. Liturgy creates the last and the eschatological moment of the incarnation under the aspect of the paschal mystery. The ritual associated with liturgy signs and effects its meaning. Through this sign, God expresses the eternal will for salvation, and people participate and receive salvation. The worship of Christ in his paschal mystery now involves the worship of the faithful followers.

In his paschal mystery Christ worshiped God in truth. He did not just offer a ritual. His priesthood differs substantially from all other priesthood. Thus, his activity differs as well. Through the sanctity that Jesus possessed he offered perfect worship to God his Father. He made himself holy and offered himself to God (John 17:19). The worship of the Church contains this true worship in sign and symbol. The true worship of Jesus transcends any ritual enactment, but the heart of the worship of Jesus continues in the Church in its sacred acts of worship. What Jesus offered the Church offers.

Liturgy is the perpetual actuation of the paschal mystery in which the priestly work of Jesus, through efficacious signs, continues in the Church. In this paschal mystery he fulfills the promises of old, enacts the new covenant and creates the new people of God. He has moved from earth to heaven and to God his Father. The redeemer has sent his Spirit as a reminder of what has already happened, what is happening now, and what is yet to come.

## Sacred Action

Liturgy involves a sacred action through which in ritual the priestly work of Christ, the sanctification of people and the glorification of God is exercised and carried on in and through the Church. As sacred action liturgy involves not only the interior *(latria)* but also an external action. The ritual expresses humanly the willingness to receive salvation and redemption. As Christ was willing to worship God through his accomplishment of the salvation and sanctification of people, so the Church does likewise.

Liturgy remains instrumental, a means, not an end, and not any sacred action but one in which Christ functions as the principal agent. This sacred action participates in the actions of Jesus. The Church does what Christ wishes to be done. The Church in liturgy always serves the will of the Lord.

Ritual is important. The rite signifies and effects what it signifies. As Jesus was the symbol of the Word of God, so the liturgy of the Church signifies the Church as continuing the saving presence of Christ. Words and actions and things and movement and place all contribute to the effective sign of God's saving will made possible by Jesus in the Church.

## The Priestly Work of Christ

The priestly work of Christ continues. The total work of Christ was priestly inasmuch as he always mediated God to others and always offered himself to God. His actual sacrifice on Calvary, or his paschal mystery, completed what he had begun in his incarnation. Through this sacrifice Christ summed up his life. The final priestly activity constituted his holy people, his own royal priesthood. The Church continues this same activity in its liturgy.

Jesus glorified God through the sanctification of people. By his ministry and his death and resurrection Jesus gave glory to God. He continues this glorification and sanctification in the liturgy of the Church. His whole life, including his death and resurrection, are now made present in the worship of the Church. As the Body of Christ the Church becomes the place where Jesus as head of the Church functions. Because the Church exists first as the subject of liturgy, the Church receives through its liturgy. The priestly work of Christ moves to his Church and then people are part of this one body. Just as the Eucharist makes the Church, so liturgy makes the Church. Without liturgy, the Church is not.

## Christ Acts through the Church in Worship

Christ acts now through his Church. The priestly work of Christ has become present, now, through the participation of the work of the Church as the Body of Christ. The liturgy pertains to the Church constitutively. Through the Church, Christ becomes present in the world. Through the Church the priestly work of Christ becomes actuated in every time and place. The Church offers worship.

The celebration of the Eucharist best exemplifies the liturgy of the Church since it culminates the union of people with God through Jesus present in the ritual and sacred meal. Liturgy also includes other expressions, in particular the official prayer of the Church and the entire sacramental system. The paschal mystery of Jesus becomes more evident to believers when they live out this mystery through the liturgical year, joining personal prayer to the official prayer of the community.

The service rendered to God in worship creates liturgy. The actual living out the spiritual sacrifice by individual believers becomes the human content, added to the one offering of Jesus. Through many actions and the use of ritual actions and things, people become sanctified and complete the one priesthood of Christ. The community gathers, bringing with it a spiritual sacrifice of its service in the world. The community then responds in faith to the Word of God and worships by offering the liturgy of the Church.

## Sacraments

The proper celebration of liturgy is supposed to bring a marvelous and wonderful renewal of all things Catholic. But in spite of the renewed liturgy, the sacraments in English, innovation and experimentation with music and renewed architecture, the large mass of Catholics do not seem renewed, or at least the harvest of new life promised after the Second Vatican Council for sacramental life has not materialized. While the sacraments may be celebrated more frequently, the sacraments themselves may have become stranger to those who share in them. For the younger generation, despite the fact that they have experienced only the renewed liturgy, sacraments seem to have less meaning. Yet sacraments form an essential part of the structure of the Catholic Church. The Church itself lives as the fundamental sacrament after Jesus. As sacraments are so essential to the Church's structure, the institutional Church must offer ritual actions that express its concern for the individual believer.

## Sacraments as Pledges

The Latin word *sacramentum* has a curious history. Originally the word meant the sum that two contending parties deposited in court when they had entered into a lawsuit. The deposit might be grain, oxen, sheep or other material goods. The successful party received the deposit back while the loser forfeited the deposit. Frequently the forfeited pledge was used in whole or in part for religious purposes. Hence, *sacramentum* came to mean a sacred thing with the basic meaning of a pledge.

Later in Roman history the word came to mean a promise or the particular military oath or pledge that a soldier made when joining the Roman army. The Roman military administered this pledge solemnly. One person offered the pledge and others came forward affirming the pledge personally. In imperial times all loyal citizens took the *sacramentum* to the emperor and renewed it yearly.

Life is full of pledges and promises. Politicians pledge to uphold the constitution. Couples pledge love and fidelity. Soldiers continue to pledge allegiance to their country to the point of dying in its service. Christianity also presupposes a pledge to Jesus. In this sense all Christian churches have sacraments. For the Catholic, sacraments are religious pledges, which involve commitment and thanksgiving and much more.

## *Mysterion*

The etymology of the Greek work *mysterion* (from which we get the English word *mystery*) lies in the shadows of history. It might come from the Greek word *myein* (to hide) or from *myeo* (which means to initiate someone into something hidden or secret or even sacred). The use of the word in Christian theology may come from its use in Hellenistic mystery religions. In this context *mysterion* involved cultic celebrations in which some representation of the deity appeared. In certain sacred rites, performed only in the presence of the initiated, the participants gained some contact with the divinity. Those who wish to participate must first experience the initiation rite. Then the actual participation in the *mysterion* promises salvation through the joining of the human with the divine through symbols and ritual actions, including washing and eating.

In Christianity *mysterion* at first meant the whole mystery of salvation, with its various phases. *Mysterion* gradually came to signify, in a more restricted sense, the Christian understanding of sacraments. In the sacramental system of the Church the great history of salvation finds expression, and through the sacraments, the *mysterion,* the Church offers salvation to its members.

Since before the twelfth century theologians did not agree precisely on the meaning or number of the Christian sacraments, only gradually did sacramental theology develop. The combination of *sacramentum* from Roman culture and *mysterion* from Greek culture coalesced into an understanding of how the Church expresses itself in significant moments in the believer's life bringing the faithful to God and God to the believer through the sacramental life of the Church.

## Sacraments: Expressing a Spiritual Reality

Sacraments are signs, objects and rituals that reveal some truth or reality beyond themselves. Karl Rahner describes a sacrament as an instance of the fullest actualization of the Church's essence as the saving presence of Christ's grace for the individual at moments critical for salvation. *The Catechism of the Catholic Church* describes sacraments as "efficacious signs of grace, instituted by Christ and entrusted to the Church by which divine life is dispensed to us. The visible rites by which the sacraments are celebrated signify and make present the graces proper to each sacrament. They bear fruit in those who receive them with the required dispositions (no. 1131)."

Thomas Aquinas, in the thirteenth century, added his understanding of sacraments by the use of Aristotle's thought on matter and form. The matter became the elements used (e.g., water for baptism or oil for anointing) and the form became the words used in the actual celebration. This added an ontological understanding of sacraments with particular application to the Eucharist. The substance of the bread and wine was changed into the substance of the body and blood of Jesus with only the accidents remaining, that is, the appearances of bread and wine. Aquinas attempted to explain the presence of the spiritual reality through the use of philosophy.

Sacraments express or reveal some truth or reality beyond themselves. Sacraments in themselves involve nothing particularly mysterious or theological since sacraments are part of life. Poets use words to express this reality. Artists use marble or paint.

> The quality of mercy is not strained; It droppeth as the gentle dew from heaven upon the place beneath. It is twice blessed. It blesses him who gives and him who receives.
>
> *(The Merchant of Venice)*[11]

Michelangelo demonstrated compassion in his *Pietà*. A nurse or doctor in a hospital writes no poetry, creates no statue, but offers mercy and compassion to a sick patient. All are signs and symbols of a spiritual reality and in each case the expression never fully realizes the quality of compassion. The spiritual seeks expression on the level of the physical and material, but the expression never equals the task. For all people, if the spiritual quality never finds its expression it dies. Love between two people that is not expressed in word and action does not grow, but withers and dies. Signs, symbols and sacraments pervade the fabric of life.

Sacramental elements permeate life. People experience the sacraments both as a pledge and as an expression of a spiritual reality. The existence of sacraments in life, however, does not necessarily mean that people understand the sacraments in the Catholic Church. Sacraments are also mystery in the New Testament sense of that word—inexhaustible intelligibility. People today seem in need of growing in their understanding of the Catholic sacramental system.

The early Church knew the need for instruction. *The Treatise on the Apostolic Constitution of Hippolytus* (c. 170–c. 236) states, "Let a catechumen be instructed for three years." While undertaking a pilgrimage, Egeria (a Spanish nun in the fourth century) describes the services she experienced in Jerusalem: "The bishop spent forty days going through the Scriptures, explaining them first literally and then unfolding them spiritually. He would also teach them about the resurrection and about all things concerning the faith." Egeria also describes the long instruction prior to baptism and the Lord's Supper. Without instruction and guidance the sacraments degenerate into formalism, superstition or even ritual lies.

## Sacraments and Ordinary Experience

In the ancient world everyone knew sacred meals. The Jews had the Passover; the Greeks had mystery religions, which shared sacred meals in the presence of the gods. Both hoped for some union with God or the gods through the ritual eating and drinking. Sacred meals offered, in the words of Evelyn Underhill, "access to the Ultimates." Today even the family meal is long gone, never mind the sacred meal. Authority is passed on by letters of appointment and not by the laying on of hands. The sacrament of penance, however, has found some counterpart in the world of the psychiatrist and psychologist. If people think they have sinned, they can go to a priest. If they never heard of sin, they can go to a psychiatrist. The sacramental principle belongs to life but often the way sacraments are celebrated in the Catholic system seems to come from a different age. This causes confusion for some contemporary Catholics.

## Sacraments and Faith

Sacraments express a reality already present. Sacraments presuppose faith. People receive according to what they bring. But today seems less an age of faith than an age of questioning. American culture cultivates enquiry and uncertainty rather than conviction and commitment. Many today find themselves unable to bring to the sacraments what the sacraments demand. Surely the sacraments nourish faith but also make no sense without faith. In the final proclamation before the reception of the

Eucharist in the Catholic Mass the priest declares: "Happy are we who have been blessed with the gift of faith." All rests upon faith.

## The Sacraments and the Individual

People live dialogically. One individual lives open to another and seeks communication. An individual becomes a person only through interpersonal exchange. Every person is open-ended, ever led into new situations and drawn to a summons that determines one's existence as an integrated person. Destroy the dialogical structure and the human being no longer exists. Sacraments function as dialogical encounters with Jesus Christ in the Church. Sacraments involve meetings and exchanges. Participation in the sacraments means little if the individual does not experience an encounter with the Lord. The ritual, the elements used, the atmosphere—all contribute to the final meeting between the individual and the Lord within the Church.

## Problems with the Eucharist

In the history of the Catholic Church some members interpreted the words of eucharistic institution literally and in a physical sense. The bread and wine became the physical body and blood of Christ rather than the real and sacramental body and blood of Christ. In the eleventh century Berengarius of Tours maintained belief in the real presence of Jesus in the Eucharist but denied that any material change in the element was needed to explain it. In 1054 Berengarius was forced to profess and sign the following:

> The bread and wine placed on the altar are after consecration not only a sacrament but also the true body and blood of our Lord Jesus Christ and that these are sensibly handed and broken by the hands of the priest and crushed by the teeth of the faithful not only sacramentally but really.
>
> (*Mansi*, XIX, 900)

Berengarius signed in Tours, but before the document was finally accepted by the pope, all references to "sensibly handed...and crushed" had been removed. Today some Catholics still think of the Eucharist as a physical presence of Jesus rather than a real presence. Others following a more Protestant tradition pay more attention to a spiritual presence. The Eucharist in Catholic tradition really expresses the presence of Jesus among his community within the context of a sacred meal.

## Myth, Ritual and Symbols Today

All worship involves myth, ritual and symbol. In ancient religions the myths offered the doctrinal element of religion. They affirmed in story form that the human race actually has contact with God. The ritual enacted the myth with a hope for further contact. The gods and goddesses used symbols to reveal themselves to people and people used symbols to express and receive communion with the gods and goddesses. The creation myths of Babylon, the fertility rites and the water and food and dance of these ancient religions held together myth, ritual and symbol. People today have not changed in the need for symbols to express life's deepest meanings. But they have changed in what they understand to be effective symbols for today's world and they have a different understanding of how union with God finds expression in myth, ritual and symbol.

Today people see themselves either as the symbol or as the participatory reality. Human dignity, freedom, tragedy and joy carry the possibility of some relationship to God. People can be the symbols for divine contact. Such thinking does not fall far from the teaching of Matthew 25:40: "Truly I say to you as you did it to one of the least of my brethren you did it to me." Theater and motion pictures and music offer new myths for contemporary people. The best of these concern the meaning of life, the search for self, the problem of relationships, hope for the future, apologies and angst from the past. Ritual has become the service offered for others after earthquakes or hurricanes or any other major or minor human tragedy. In such a situation, what do the sacraments mean in the Catholic tradition?

# Baptism

Christianity begins for the individual at baptism. Baptism begins a process, which ends in the death of the Christian. Sometimes individual Christians view baptism as a once-for-all ceremony. Parents take their newborn to the Church. The Church community welcomes the infant. The priest pours water and baptizes the baby. Baptism, however, is more than a ceremony of the past. Baptism begins the Christian life and marks the start of a constant effort to live a life fashioned on the life of Jesus.

The Gospels of Matthew, Mark and Luke record the baptism of Jesus. The gospel of John does not actually mention the event but seems to imply it. Jesus accepted a baptism of water for repentance at the hand of John the Baptizer. Jesus, filled with the Holy Spirit, began his ministry. In the past many Christian theologians claimed that Jesus did not need a baptism for repentance, and so he underwent this ceremony for the sake of example. But since the New Testament depicts this event as inaugurating the public ministry of Jesus, the baptism by John the Baptist must have had great significance for Jesus. The way in which the Spirit came, rested and remained upon him reveals Jesus to have been an extraordinary person. This should cause the reflective reader of the gospels to wonder about the meaning of the baptism of Jesus.

After his baptism Jesus preached the kingdom of God: God was present in human life, and God loved all people. With the beginning of his ministry, Jesus began the journey that would lead him to the cross and the outpouring of the Spirit of God on all humanity. The gift of the Spirit continued in the preaching of the apostles. Peter preached after Pentecost, and the people repented, believed and were baptized in the Spirit. As the early followers of Jesus preached about him people accepted in faith that Jesus truly spoke in God's name. They began to live a life modeled upon the life of Jesus and received the Spirit of God within themselves. Baptism meant being blessed with the Spirit of God.

Early Christians also knew that allowing the Spirit of God to influence them was a lifelong event. Overcoming evil and conquering sin entailed a daily struggle. Being filled with the Spirit of God meant allowing the presence of God to fill up all the facets of the human personality, not picking and choosing but being open to all that God desires. Baptism begins life in the Church, where individual believers overcome sin with the help of others, with the guidance of the Word of God and with the assistance of the sacraments. The Christian life contains its level of difficulties but also offers joys as the Spirit of God builds up the Church making it the tangible sign of the presence of God in the world today.

Baptism includes some relationship to sin, not only in the sense of original sin but also in being filled with the love of God, which destroys all sin. Christians do not limit the effects of baptism to original sin and see it only as a ceremony that commemorates a past event. Rather, Christians view baptism as the beginning of the struggle against all evil and sin that is completed only with death.

Every person has his or her pet vices and sins. People willingly open themselves to God in one area but not in another. People have the secret areas of their lives where no one may enter, not even God. People sin because they are afraid to open themselves to God and to others for fear that they will lose what they already have. A Christian takes a chance and trusts God to heal the bitterness and hurt and the unhappy memories that everyone possesses. Yet this sacrament is really about gain rather than loss. To trust in God causes pain, since most people associate giving of themselves with losing themselves and become afraid. But instead of losing, when an individual gives himself or herself to God, God blesses them with more than they had ever hoped to receive.

Baptism begins the process of living in faith. Baptism begins the acceptance of God in a person's life. Baptism points to death, when the individual gives himself or herself completely into the hands of another, God. Baptism points Christians toward the future even as it reminds them of their origins. Recalling their own baptism, they look forward to what will come for all who are baptized in the name of the Father and of the Son and of the Holy Spirit.

## The Rite of Baptism

The renewal of the sacraments after Vatican Council II revolutionized the understanding of baptism in the Catholic tradition. Some see the baptismal understanding as reflected by and incorporated into the Rite of Christian Initiation of Adults as a Copernican revolution in sacramental interpretation. In this Vatican document the Church teaches that adult baptism is the norm for the sacrament. This does not mean that the Church will not baptize infants but that to clearly comprehend the meaning of the sacrament and the rite demands an understanding of adult baptism.

The rite of baptism begins with the signing of the cross on the forehead of the candidate by the priest or deacon, followed by the same gesture by parents, godparents, family and friends. By this signing all those present promise to teach the candidate the love of God and neighbor. The scriptural reading, followed by a brief homily, centers on the meaning of Baptism, especially as the rite of entrance into the church community. After a renunciation of evil and sin and a profession of faith by those present, the priest or deacon baptizes by the pouring of water or by immersion in the baptismal bath.

As Jesus was anointed priest, prophet and king, so the priest or deacon anoints the newly baptized with sacred chrism, oil blessed by the bishop during Holy Week. He covers the child with a white covering and gives a lighted candle to parents and godparents. The rite concludes with a special blessing for parents.

## Confirmation

Historically confirmation concluded baptism. For some, baptism and confirmation are one sacrament, not two. The coming of the Spirit in Acts 2 brings a social dimension to Christian faith. The disciples boldly preach the gospel of Jesus empowered by the Spirit. As already noted, the Spirit founds the apostolate and drives the preaching of the early apostles until the known world has heard the message of Jesus of Nazareth. Some find instances of confirmation in the imposition of hands by Peter and John on the converts of Samaria in Acts 8:14–17 and by Paul on the disciples at Ephesus (Acts 19:107). The New Testament also refers to the laying on of hands in Hebrews 6:2 and makes frequent mention of sealing with the Spirit (2 Cor 1:20; Eph 1:13; 4:30). Once a person has received the Spirit he or she has accepted the obligation to become the means of giving the Spirit to others.

## The Rite of Confirmation

Although closely related to baptism, confirmation becomes a separate rite by the fourth century. The bishop, who in earlier times took a personal interest in every new convert, found that the number of those seeking admission into the Church increased significantly, so that he was unable to personally baptize all. The parish priest then took on the function of baptizing and the bishop, at some other date, anointed the newly baptized with oil. The disappearance of the catechumenate by the sixth century also influenced the separation of these rites of initiation. The Eastern Church continued to confer both sacraments at baptism and even gave the Eucharist to the newly baptized. Infants received all three sacraments in the same ritual.

Theologically some see confirmation as an integral part of baptism. Others regard it as a new outpouring of the Spirit to strengthen the candidate as he or she begins an adult life. This affects the age of confirmation. Since 1971 the National Conference of Bishops in the Catholic Church has decided the age of confirmation, with the general practice in the United States being to celebrate the sacrament in a person's early teens. Usually the bishop administers this sacrament, but in special instances a priest may also confirm.

The symbol is the same oil, sacred chrism, used in baptism. Oil means strength and nobility. The coronation rites of kings and queens included an anointing with oil. The individual requests a sealing with the Holy Spirit, and the bishop traces the sign of the cross on the forehead, adding: "Be sealed with the Holy Spirit, in the name of the Father, the Son and the Holy Spirit." The bishop then wishes the newly confirmed the gift of peace.

The history of this sacrament goes back to the many outpourings of the Spirit in the early Church. The readings recall Pentecost. As the Church began through the giving of the Spirit by Jesus, so the contemporary Church calls its youthful members within the context of the celebration of the presence of Jesus in the Eucharist to accept the challenge to live according to the Spirit and be a means for others coming to the same Spirit.

The ritual brings the young person face to face with the bishop, the leader of the local Church. They pray together, the bishop lays his hands on the candidate and the confirmed rises to face the challenges of the Christian life. Sponsors stand behind the candidate. Individuals who have helped shape the young person's life of faith again pledge to support their candidate in living the gospel of Jesus.

## Reconciliation, Penance, Confession

In the Catholic Church in the United States it is customary to refer to the "sacrament of reconciliation" as well as a "reconciliation room." For most Catholics it remains confession or penance. In the past Catholics went to confession weekly. For many American Catholics today the practice of weekly or frequent confession has passed. People know they need God's forgiveness but find that they experience it in ways other than private confession to a priest. Even with strenuous efforts to encourage private confession, most American Catholics ignore the many calls to return to this sacrament frequently.

The New Testament attests to the power of Jesus to forgive sins: "That you may know that the Son of Man has authority on earth to forgive sins..."(Mark 2:10). The New Testament in Matthew also records this power given to Peter: "Whatever you bind on earth shall be bound in heaven; whatever you loose on earth shall be loosed in heaven" (Matt 16:19). The author gives this same power to the Church: "Truly I say to you whatever you bind on earth shall be bound in heaven and whatever you loose on earth shall be loosed in heaven"(Matt 18:18). The Gospel of John also cites the same power as being given to the disciples gathered in the upper room after the resurrection: "Receive the Holy Spirit. If you forgive the sins of any they are forgiven; if you retain the sins of any they are retained"(John 20:22–23). How the Church has exercised this power, however, has differed considerably over the centuries.

The history of this sacrament offers more shadows than light. By the third century a system of public confession had developed as, in effect, a second baptism. After the sinner, either voluntarily or because it was demanded under threat of excommunication, enrolled in the order of penitents, the Church expected certain activities. The person was forbidden to receive communion and had to undergo a rigorous regime of prayer, fasting and almsgiving. At the end of a period of time, the length of which was determined by the gravity of the sin, the Church reconciled the sinner at the celebration of the Easter Vigil. He or she then rejoined the congregation as a member in full communion. Penance could be experienced only once in a lifetime, and afterward the Church often imposed a lifelong continence. The combination of enrollment in the order of penitents, the rigorous public penance, the once-in-a-lifetime possibility and the penalties broke down the system. The sinner happily postponed penance until the eve of death.

In the seventh century Irish missionary monks developed another system administered through penitential books. These books for confessors contained prayers, questions to be asked and a list of sins with appropriate penances. They were more flexible than the previous system and became the norm for the celebration of the sacrament. Even in this new system the penance remained rigorous, but the confession of sins was private and absolution, originally given when the penance was completed, gradually began to be given before the penance was begun. From this grew the modern practice of confession, absolution and light penance. The Fourth Lateran Council (1215) sanctioned this practice and required every Catholic to receive penance at least once a year if conscious of mortal sin. In 1973 the new Rite for Penance provides for general absolution in some circumstances without previous individual confession of sins.

Penance comes from the Latin word *poena*, which means punishment. The early Church believed that sin hurt not only the sinner also others as well. Atonement was necessary. The Church never lost sense of the atonement accomplished by Jesus on the cross but wished the sinner to join to Jesus' sacrifice personal acts that would atone for the evil brought into the world and into the Church by personal sin. Individuals should also regulate their lives so that sin would be less likely in the future. The penance became medicine for the soul, which healed the wounds inflicted by sin. Often the penances included long prayers, fasting, almsgiving, floggings, pilgrimages and continence. Since these often interrupted the ordinary aspects of daily life, gradually a system of commutation developed. A sinner could commute many days of penance into one day through almsgiving or even saying a prayer repeatedly in a physically uncomfortable position. From this practice also came indulgences, which the Church could apply from its treasury of good works to the case of a particular sinner in need of reconciliation.

## The Rite of Penance

The rite begins with a blessing by the priest:

> May God, who has enlightened every heart,
> help you to know your sins
> and trust in his mercy.[12]

Although the Catholic Church allows for a reading of Scripture and a brief homily, in practice this is not followed in individual confession. The person acknowledges sin and the need for forgiveness. The priest suggests a suitable penance, usually in some way related to the sin committed, and prays the prayer of absolution:

> God, the Father of mercies, through the death and Resurrection of his Son has reconciled the world to himself and sent the Holy Spirit among us for the forgiveness of sins; through the ministry of the Church may God give you pardon and

peace, and I absolve you from your sins in the name of the Father, and of the Son and of the Holy Spirit. Amen.[13]

The priest concludes with the following or another final prayer:

May the passion of our Lord Jesus Christ, the merits
of the Blessed Mother and of all the saints and whatever
good that you may do or sorrow you may endure be
the cause of the remission of all your sins, help you to
grow in holiness and reward you with eternal life.
God bless you. Go in peace.[14]

The rite may also include a laying on of hands as the priest offers the prayer of absolution.

Penance as a sacrament has had many forms over the centuries. The penitential rite beginning most Masses has been considered as a form of the sacrament of penance by many within other Christian churches. Some Catholics use this as a personal expression of sorrow for sins. Remnants of this rite as an expression of the sacrament of penance can be found in the two prayers after the confession of sins found in the ritual in the Latin Mass:

May almighty God have mercy on you, forgive you
your sins and bring you to everlasting life. Amen.
May the merciful Lord grant you pardon, absolution
and remission of all your sins. Amen.[15]

In the revised Order of the Mass of Paul VI, the second of these prayers has been dropped. Some thought that when this prayer was translated into English, it could give people a sense that the penitential rite was sufficient to receive absolution. For this reason it was dropped. In the mediaeval tradition, however, the very celebration of the Eucharist included the forgiveness of sins.

The present Church actually has three forms of the sacrament. First, a rite for the reconciliation of individual penitents, which most Catholics have experienced; a second form consists of the reconciliation of several penitents with individual confession and absolution. This occurs in many parishes several times a year, especially during Advent and Lent. The third form, reconciliation of many penitents with general confession and absolution, became frequent in the United States during the seventies. Again, individual parishes celebrated this rite usually during Advent and Lent. In more recent times this third form has been used less frequently depending on the custom of individual dioceses.

## The Eucharist

Sacred meals have always been part of worship. The Christian sacred meal differs considerably from any other sacred meal since Christians believe that the divine Son of God is truly and really present in the bread and wine. Other sacred meals promise to bring about some union with the divine by means of the food and drink. Offering food and drink to the gods has characterized human worship for millennia. Most instances of these sacred meals included the notion of thanksgiving. The title "Eucharist" for this central act of Christian worship may come from Jesus' act of giving thanks as he instituted this sacred meal (1 Cor 11:24; Matt 26:26–28; Mark 14:22–24; Luke 22:17–20) or because this sacred meal expresses in a most profound manner the thanksgiving of Christians to God for the gift of Jesus. From the Greek, the word *Eucharist* comes from *eu,* meaning "good," and *charis,* meaning "gift" or "grace." The first mention of this sacred meal being called the Eucharist can be found in the late-first-century letters of Ignatius of Antioch and the early second-century document the *Didache.* Over the centuries Christians have also called this ritual meal Holy Communion or the Lord's Supper. Catholics call it the Mass, probably from the Latin word for the dismissal concluding the ritual.

The four accounts of the institution of the Eucharist from the New Testament differ but not substantially. Paul's version (1 Cor 15:3) has more in common with Luke's (Luke 22:17–19). Mark (Mark 14:22–25) and Matthew (Matt 26:2629) seem to come from the same source. The early Christian community at Jerusalem celebrated the Eucharist (Acts 2:42, 46), as did Paul on his visit to Troas (Acts 20:7). The Fourth Gospel alone, although having the longest section on the last supper, does not record the institution of the Eucharist. Eucharistic teaching however exists especially in chapter 6:51–58.

The acceptance of the Eucharist as the presence of the body and blood of Christ characterized early theological belief. Even when theologians referred to the elements as symbols or anti-types, they affirmed the belief in the reality of the presence of Jesus. From the fourth century, language on the *how* of the Eucharist began to become general. Some, however, thought the bread and wine continued to be present, while others held the bread and wine to be no longer present but only the body and blood of Christ. Eventually the doctrine of transubstantiation affirmed no longer the presence of bread and wine but only their appearances with the substance of the bread and wine becoming the substance of the body and blood of Jesus. In the early Middle Ages, when Berengarius of Tour's notion that the true symbol contained the reality it represented gave way to the symbol being seen as not containing what it represents, the references to the Eucharist as the symbolic presence of Jesus dropped out of theological vocabulary or were simply denied. As already noted, the Fourth Lateran Council (1215) taught the actual transformation of the bread and wine into the body and blood of Christ. In the following century Thomas Aquinas made more precise the meaning of transubstantiation by the use of Aristotle's teaching on matter and form. The substance changed but the accidents (the appearances of bread and wine) remained. During this same period eucharistic devotion received considerable attention. Urban IV (1261–64) established the feast of Corpus Christi and faithful Catholics celebrated the real presence more by adoration than by the actual reception of the eucharistic bread and wine.

The Reformation returned to the earlier controversy on what remained after the prayer of consecration. In general the Reformers maintained that the bread and wine continued to be such along with the real presence of Jesus (Luther) or that the Eucharist was only a memorial to Jesus with no change in the bread and wine (Zwingli). The Council of Trent reaffirmed the teaching on transubstantiation but avoided any formal teaching in the Aristotelian and Thomistic sense of substance and accidents. Since Vatican

Council II Catholic theologians have also used the ideas of transfi-
nalization and transignification to explain the "how" of the
Eucharist. These hold that both the purpose and meaning of the
bread and wine have changed in the eucharistic prayer. Pope Paul
VI, in his encyclical *Mysterium Fidei* (1965), reaffirmed and emphasized the teaching on transubstantiation while also adding, "...as a
result of transubstantiation the species of the bread and wine
undoubtedly take on a new significance and a new finality."

Catholics also refer to the Eucharist as a sacrifice, taking their
cue from the New Testament. The words used in the institution
narrative of the eucharistic liturgy, *covenant, memorial* and *poured
out* all contain some sacrificial elements. For many centuries the
precise meaning of the Eucharist as a sacrifice remained unclear.
The Council of Trent, in opposition to the Reformers, who
rejected any notion of sacrifice, affirmed that the sacrifice of the
Mass is propitiatory, availing for both living and dead. It does
not, however, detract from the sufficiency of the sacrifice on Calvary. The heart of sacrifice in Scripture is the offering. The
offering remains once and eternal.

> He has no need like those high priests to offer sacrifices
> daily for his own sins and then for those of the people; he
> did this once for all when he offered up him.
>
> (Heb. 7:27)

Within a Catholic tradition the offering of Jesus exists eternally,
and when the Church celebrates his eucharistic presence, the
eternal offering becomes present, as Jesus is present. To this one
eternal offering the Church joins the offering of the people. The
Vatican Council remarks:

> At the Last Supper...our Savior instituted the Eucharistic
> sacrifice of his body and Blood....he did this to perpetuate
> the sacrifice of the cross throughout the centuries until he
> should come again and so to entrust to his beloved spouse
> the Church a memorial of his death and resurrection.
>
> (Constitution on the Sacred Liturgy, no. 47)

The contemporary retrieval of eucharistic thought and practice has focused on a recovery of the meaning of symbol. The

symbol contains the reality it expresses, even if never completely. This renewed theology of the Eucharist also concentrates on the understanding of the role of language, focusing in particular on the memorial aspect of the Eucharist. The sacred meal recalls the past, the death and resurrection of the Lord, celebrates his presence in the sacred meal and looks forward to his future coming. The language of the sacrament celebrates this mystery and brings people into contact with the past saving mystery, which continues into the present and leads people into the future.

> Christ has died.
> Christ has Risen.
> Christ will come again.
> (*Sacramentary of the Roman Missal*)

Other choices are available, such as this response often sung in American liturgies: "We remember how you loved us to your death. And still we celebrate for you are with us here. And we believe that we shall see you when you come in your glory Lord. We remember, we celebrate, we believe" ("We Remember" by Marty Haugen, GIA Publications).

## The Ritual of the Eucharist

The ritual of the sacred meal begins with pardon and the assurance of forgiveness by the priest. The opening prayer leads the people into an opening of mind and heart to express and strengthen faith. The readings from the Bible follow. The priest or homilist bridges the gap between the liturgy of the Word and the liturgy of the Eucharist. The assembly makes a profession of faith. The first part of the ritual concludes with the preparation of the gifts and with a prayer for transformation not only of the bread and wine but of the participants as well.

The liturgy of the Eucharist begins with a prayer of praise and thanksgiving, leading the people to proclaim the holiness of God and of the Son. The priest then prays the eucharistic prayer, which contains the words of institution from the New Testament. After a profession of faith by the people, the priest prays for the

Church and calls for the communal expression of faith by the people in the recitation or singing of the Great Amen. In preparation for communion the congregation recites the Our Father, offers to one another the sign of peace and then personally affirms faith by the response of "Amen" before the reception of communion. The rite concludes with a final prayer to realize the presence of the Lord Jesus in daily life within the community and a concluding blessing.

The reform of the ritual after the Vatican council has added greater variety through the use of a three-year lectionary cycle for Sundays and a two-year cycle for weekdays. This affords the congregation a greater familiarity with larger sections of both Old and New Testaments. With the addition of many new eucharistic prayers, including two written especially for children, the rite offers a variety while maintaining its repetition of patterned behavior to make people feel comfortable in the ritual celebration.

## Anointing of the Sick

Catholics of an earlier time called this sacrament extreme unction or the last rites. As a sacrament the priest anointed the dying person on the five senses in preparation for death. When the Catholic Church in 1972 changed the name to the anointing of the sick and recommended it for anyone who is sick, whether physical or mental, American Catholics liked the name change. Now most Catholics are used to the idea of having a priest anoint them when sick, whether near death or not, and many parishes provide a communal anointing of the sick.

The New Testament refers to the anointing of the sick in Mark 6:13, but the classical scriptural reference comes from the letter of James:

> Is anyone among you sick? Let him call for the elders of the Church, and let them pray over him anointing him with oil in the name of the Lord; and the prayer of faith will save the sick man and the Lord will raise him up, and if he has committed sins he will be forgiven.
>
> (Jas 5:14–15)

Hippolytus (c. 170–c. 236) writes of a prayer for the blessing of oil for anointing. So does St. Serapion of Thmuis in the fourth century. From the fifth century on, liturgical books and writings of theologians and popes make frequent references to anointing, with both spiritual and physical effects. From the tenth century anointing becomes part of sacramental theology. By the time of Thomas Aquinas a full theology of anointing has become part of the Catholic tradition, and in the Council of Trent anointing becomes officially one of the seven sacraments of the Catholic Church.

Since the Second Vatican Council the Catholic Church has expanded this sacrament to include a sense of pastoral care of the sick. During the Middle Ages the sacrament had become closely associated with repentance and the penitential system so that it was postponed until death approached. The renewed rite of 1972 not only changed the name of the sacrament but also emphasized the healing and underlined the acceptance of sickness as part of ordinary human life. The Church responds to the needs of people when they find themselves reminded of their mortality in the experience of sickness. Even ordinary ailments remind people of death. How often people, when ill, even if only with a minor illness, say: "I just wanted to die." In such circumstances the Church expresses its care and solicitude for the sick person through the ministry of the sacrament of anointing.

## The Rite of Anointing

The rite includes a blessing of the room with holy water, the reading from James and some penitential rite, including absolution. Then the person receives an anointing on the forehead and on the palms of the hands. The rite concludes with a prayer for healing, the Lord's Prayer and a special blessing.

## Matrimony

Marriage as a human institution certainly anteceded Christianity. The Church, however, added two distinctive elements to the marriage not present in Jewish or pagan marriages: the equality of man and woman in the marriage and the indissolubility of the marriage bond. Even today, with the presence of annulments in the Catholic tradition, the presupposition in favor of the marriage always exists. (The annulment process will be discussed under Catholic morality.)

In the Old Testament the woman became in effect the property of the husband in marriage though he could not sell her (Exod 21:7ff.). The woman could neither own nor inherit property and could not divorce her husband, although the man could divorce the woman (Deut 24:1). Polygamy existed, especially in the patriarchal period, sometimes with the consent of the woman as in the case of Abraham and Sarah (Gen 16:20).

Jesus taught a restoration of the lasting marriage bond and monogamy (Mark 10:2–12; Matt 5:31; 19:3–9; Luke 16:18). Mark and Luke allow of no exceptions. Matthew allows for one. Paul reasserts the teaching of Jesus in Romans 7:2 and 1 Corinthians 7:3–14. The author of Ephesians, whether Paul or one of his disciples, compares the union between Christ and the Church to the union between husband and wife (Eph 5:22–33). 1 Peter assigns the governance of the household to the husband and emphasizes the duty of love toward the wife as an equal partner. Like Matthew, Paul admits of one exception (1 Cor 7:3) in the case when the non-Christian will not live in peace with the Christian.

In Catholic theology marriage has two purposes: the continuation of the race through procreation and the mutual love of the spouses. Up to the Second Vatican Council the first was considered primary, with the mutual love in community as secondary. Today the Catholic tradition sees an equal importance to both the ends of marriage. From at least the ninth century, theologians considered marriage a sacrament, and in the thirteenth century Thomas Aquinas taught that marriage as a sacrament conferred a special sacramental grace upon the couple as they assumed their new relationship and responsibility for each other. In a sacramental marriage each spouse accepts responsibility for the other in his or her relationship to God. Together they live out their calling to support each other in their spiritual development.

# The Rite of Marriage

Unlike the other sacraments, the ministers of this sacrament are the couple themselves. Whether the marriage takes place within Mass or not, a liturgy of the Word begins the ceremony. After the readings and homily, the priest or deacon asks the individuals for their intentions. The couple exchange vows, the priest or deacon blesses the ring(s) and the actual marriage ceremony is complete. The couple also receives a special marriage blessing.

# Order

The Church traces the sacrament of order back to the sending out of the twelve (Mark 3:13–19; Matt 10:1–5; Luke 6: 12–16) and the sending of the seventy (Luke 10:1), as well as the commissioning of Peter as the foundation of the Church (Matt 16:18) and the commissioning of the disciples (Matt 28:16–20). After the death and resurrection of Jesus, his followers received new power and greater responsibilities with the coming of the Spirit on Pentecost (Acts 2:14; 3:1–10). Peter, as already noted, assumed leadership within this Church, as did Paul and many others. The references to the laying on of hands in 2 Timothy 1:6 and 1 Timothy 5:22 show how this Jewish ritual became incorporated into the early Church as a means of conveying the Holy Spirit to those candidates who assumed a new office and ministerial responsibility in the Church.

The New Testament recognizes several grades of ministry coexisting (1 Cor 12:28; Eph 4:11). The twelve is the most limited order, followed by apostles. The terms *bishop* and *presbyter,* although at times used interchangeably, also express a determined order, as does *deacon.* The New Testament also speaks of prophets, pastors, teachers, evangelists and administrators. In the middle of the third century the church historian Eusebius remarks that the Church of Rome had a bishop, forty-six presbyters, seven deacons, seven subdeacons, forty-two acolytes and fifty-two exorcists, readers and porters. In the Middle Ages theologians and church practice divided the orders into two groups—major orders: subdeacon,

deacon, priest and bishop; and minor orders: porter, lector, exorcist and acolyte. Since the Second Vatican Council the sacrament has been accepted with three grades: episcopacy, priesthood and diaconate. Despite these grades, the Catholic Church teaches one sacrament of order.

The Council of Trent defined order as a sacrament instituted by Jesus, and it imparts the special gift of the Holy Spirit to aid in the fulfillment of the responsibilities assumed. God gives the Spirit through Jesus as an individual assumes a leadership role in the Church in behalf of others. In the Roman Catholic Church only men who promise celibacy may be ordained. Only duly ordained bishops may ordain to the priesthood and diaconate, and only bishops may ordain to the episcopacy. The ordination of priests and bishops maintains an unbroken line from apostolic times to the present day.

The earliest reference to an ordination takes place in the early third century, and from the following century several rites survive. In the Middle Ages the gospel book given to the deacon formed part of the rite, and the giving over of chalice and paten, used in reception of the Eucharist, became the ordinary rite of priesthood ordination. Pope Pius XII formally declared that the actual rite of ordination to the three grades of order is the laying on of hands.

## The Rite of Ordination

In the ordination to the deaconate the ordaining bishop confers the order within the celebration of the Eucharist. The bishop lays his hands on the head of the candidate and then says the ordination prayer. After the deacon has been vested in a stole, the bishop hands him the book of the gospels with a charge to live what he proclaims.

In ordination to the priesthood, the priests present join the bishop in the laying on of hands, followed by the ordination prayer. The bishop then anoints the hands of the candidate with oil, again sacred chrism, and gives him both paten and chalice containing the bread and wine offered by the people. The ordained then assumes the vestments of the priesthood and joins the bishop in the celebration of the Eucharist.

The ordination of a bishop requires two other ordaining bishops. While the three bishops recite the prayer of ordination the gospel book is held over the head of the candidate. The principal ordaining bishop then anoints the head of the candidate, delivers the book of the gospels to him, puts a ring on his finger and a mitre on his head and gives a pastoral staff. The newly ordained bishop then joins the other bishops in the celebration of the Eucharist.

## The Sacraments

The Catholic Church in its sacramental system uses myth, ritual and symbol to express the concern of the Church for its members at moments critical for salvation. At birth the Church welcomes the newly born into the Church. In the critical period of adolescence the Church expresses the hope and prayer for the young in confirmation. When people fail and sin, in the moment of a sinner's repentance the Church declares not only forgiveness but also the assurance that the Church loves and cherishes the penitent. Since people need nourishment in life, the Church offers spiritual nourishment with daily guidance in the celebration of the Eucharist. When illness befalls a person, reminding the sick person of personal mortality and the need for comfort, the Church responds with an anointing with oil along with prayers for health and for God's grace to complete the person's final journey. When people commit to each other in marriage, the Church expresses its love and concern in matrimony, and when a person assumes office in the Church, it promises the assistance of the Holy Spirit. In the celebration of the sacraments the Church expresses itself bringing people to God to worship and God to people to bless.

### TOPICS FOR DISCUSSION AND STUDY

1. Why is worshiping God important?
2. Worship promises contact with the divine. Explain.
3. Why is ritual important in life?

4. What are the different ways in which people worship God?
5. Worship involves mystery. Explain.
6. Did the reform of the liturgy in Vatican II help or hinder the contemporary Church, or both? What are some of the benefits and what are some of the problems?
7. What happens in the liturgy in your local church, both theologically and practically?
8. Does good liturgy really make any difference?

# Works Consulted

Adam, Adolf. *Foundations of Liturgy: An Introduction to Its History and Practice.* Collegeville, Minn.: Liturgical Press, 1992.

Bausch, William J. *A New Look at the Sacraments.* Mystic, Conn.: Twenty-Third Publications, 1998.

Beguerie, Philippe and Claude Duchesneau. "The Sacraments in the History of the Church." In *Contemporary Catholic Theology.* Trowbridge, U.K.: Cromwell Press, 1998, 484–99.

Cooke, Bernard J. *Ministry to Word and Sacraments.* Philadelphia: Fortress, 1980.

Guzie, Tad. "From Symbol to Sacrament." *Contemporary Catholic Theology.* Trowbridge, U.K.: Cromwell Press, 1998, 434–44.

Kavanagh, Aidan. "Liturgy (Sacrosanctum Concilium)." In *Contemporary Catholic Theology.* Trowbridge, U.K.: Cromwell Press, 1998, 445–51.

Kilmartin, Edward. *Christian Liturgy.* New York: Sheed and Ward, 1988.

———. "Sacraments as Liturgy of the Church." *Theological Studies* 50 (1989): 527–47.

Martos, Joseph. "The Development of the Catholic Sacraments." *Contemporary Catholic Theology.* Trowbridge, U.K.: Cromwell Press, 1998, 453–83.

Mason, Herbert, et al. *Myth, Symbol and Reality.* Notre Dame, Ind.: University of Notre Dame Press, 1980.

O'Grady, John F. *The Roman Catholic Church: Its Origin and Nature.* Mahwah, N.J.: Paulist Press, 1997.

Rahner, Karl. *The Church and the Sacraments.* New York: Herder and Herder, 1963.

Strathman, H., and R. Meyer. *"Leitourgeo, leitourgia, leitourgos, lei-tourgikos."* *Theological Dictionary of the New Testament.* Grand Rapids: Eerdmans, 1964, vol. 4, 215–31.

Vorgrimler, Herbert. *Sacramental Theology.* Collegeville, Minn.: Liturgical Press, 1992.

# CHAPTER 8:
# MEDIATION—MARY
# AND THE SAINTS

Catholics have always venerated Mary, the virgin of Nazareth and Mother of the Lord. Almost alone among the Christian churches the Catholic traditions relating to Mary have continued to magnify her role not only in salvation history but in the life of the Church. Traditional Catholic piety includes the rosary, novenas to Mary and sacramentals such as the miraculous medal, the brown scapular and the green scapular. Catholic shrines to Mary dot the landscape of every major city or town in Europe and other parts of the Western world. Apparitions of Mary to faithful believers, especially children, abound, from Lourdes to Fatima to Medjugorje to Conyers, Georgia, to an image on the glass wall of a building in Tampa, Florida. In fact, however, Christians know very little about Mary, the virgin of Nazareth and mother of the Lord Jesus.

## Mary in the New Testament

Mark, Matthew and Luke mention her by name, but no one else in the New Testament calls her Mary. The earliest reference to the mother of Jesus in Galatians 4:4 merely remarks that Jesus was born of a woman. In the common tradition of Mark, Matthew and Luke, Mark and Matthew identify Jesus as Mary's son (Mark 6:3; Matt 13:55). In the parallel place in Luke the author omits any reference to Mary (Luke 4:22). Later in Mark, although not mentioned by name, the author refers to the mother of Jesus and his family and seems to imply that they think he is out of his mind (Mark 3:18–21). Some ten verses later Mark comments that the true family of Jesus, including his mother, are those who do the will of God (Mark 3:31–35). In the parallel place in Luke (8:19–21) the author, rather than separate Jesus from his natural family, implies that the mother and family of Jesus are his disciples. The physical family of Jesus is his true family, however, not because of blood ties but because they hear the Word of God. Luke confirms this position in Acts 1:14, where Mary the mother of Jesus and his brothers are among the 120 brethren who constituted the believing community after the resurrection. This reference is the last specific mention of Mary in the New Testament.

## Mary in Matthew and Luke

Luke makes more mention of Mary than does any other evangelist. Mary figures prominently in the infancy narratives in chapters 1 and 2 of Luke. With the differences apparent when one compares Matthew's story with Luke's, some early Christians concluded that Joseph told Matthew the story and Mary told Luke the story. No definitive evidence exists to support such a theory. Both Matthew and Luke composed their birth stories long after the ministry and resurrection of Jesus, and both use many Old Testament traditions to explain the divine origin of Jesus. Both Matthew and Luke teach the virginal conception of Jesus. The thought of a virginal conception, however, did not come from any family remembrances but from a combination of historical fact and theological reflection, including a rethinking of several Old Testament passages. Historically speaking, it could have been public knowledge that Jesus was born within the nine-month period after his parents came to live as husband and wife. This knowledge seems presupposed in the account of Matthew and implied in the account of Luke. Early Christians, having a choice between believing that Jesus was illegitimate or that Jesus was born through some special intervention of the power of God, chose the latter. They reflected on the belief that Jesus was God's special son, born free from sin, and concluded that Jesus was born of a virgin who conceived through the power of the Holy Spirit.

## Mary in Luke

Luke records the teaching of Jesus that his mother and brothers are those who hear the Word of God and keep it. In the annunciation to Mary of the birth of Jesus Luke dramatizes Mary precisely in the manner in which Jesus spoke of his family: Mary heard the Word of God and believed—"Be it done unto me according to your word" (Luke 1:38). Alone among the Synoptics, the Gospel of Luke records another reference to the mother of Jesus. In Luke 11:27–28 a woman from the crowd remarks: "Blessed is the womb that bore you and the breasts that gave you nourishment." But he said, "Rather blessed are those who hear the word of God and keep it." Like the woman in the crowd, Elizabeth also praises the physical motherhood of Mary: "Blessed are you among women and blessed is the fruit of your womb" (Luke 1:42) "...and blessed is she who believed that the word of the Lord to her would be fulfilled" (Luke 1:45). Luke's presentation of Mary comes not from the actual historical period of the birth of Jesus but from the traditions of the mother of Jesus from his ministry. Luke also records the visit of Mary to Elizabeth, and since his presentation of Mary goes back to the ministry of Jesus, the portrayal of Mary as a woman of kindness and compassion, like her quality as a woman of faith, must also go back to early church traditions about the mother of Jesus. Mary is the faithful believer in the Word of God and the kind and compassionate woman who responds quickly to those in need.

## Mary in the Gospel of John

In the Fourth Gospel the mother of Jesus appears in two scenes not recorded in the Synoptics: at the marriage feast of Cana and at the foot of the cross. In neither instance does the evangelist call her by name. Instead he refers to the mother of Jesus and uses the title "woman." Both scenes are unusual and appear only in this gospel.

The Synoptics make no mention of mighty miracles in Galilee except for a few instances in which the sick are healed (Mark 6:5). The miracle at Cana itself differs from other recorded miracles of Jesus. The context is family. Jesus works the miracle of abounding wine for the convenience of his mother's friends. Even the conversation between Jesus and his mother is strange, almost defying logical explanation. Jesus seems to refuse the request with his remark: "Woman, what does this concern of yours have to do with me? My hour has not come" (John 2:4). Yet Mary acts as if he has agreed when she says to the waiters: "Do whatever he tells you" (John 2:5). Then Jesus takes care of the matter.

Perhaps this scene depicts the same tendency in the Synoptics with regard to family. Jesus does not concede to the wishes of his mother because of family ties, but then Mary acts as a believer and Jesus works a miracle. Here the author of this gospel depicts Mary as one who does not completely understand and yet trusts that Jesus will do what she wishes and will act as the kind and compassionate savior who responds to people in any need. This story actually contains Old Testament parallels concerning the coming of the messiah. The advent of the messiah will be like a wonderful wedding banquet in which wine will flow in abundance. Jesus is the real bridegroom rather than the one who married, and his mother represents all those faithful believers who accept Jesus as the anointed one of God.

At the foot of the cross his hour has come (John 13:1), and again the woman appears, without any mention of her name. Instead, the author uses the title mother of Jesus. Also at the foot of the cross stands the Beloved Disciple. Both are historical figures, but both are also symbolic. The other gospels make no mention of any male disciple at the cross. They note, rather, that all the male disciples had fled (Mark 14:53). The other gospels have women present but at a distance (Mark 15:40; Matt 27:55–56; Luke 23:49). Mark and Matthew call the women by name without ever mentioning whether one of them was the mother of Jesus. By contrast, the Fourth Gospel has two individuals at the foot of the cross who are not named but are given titles, both with a symbolic value for which the synoptic tradition leaves little room.

> When Jesus saw his mother and the disciple whom he loved standing near he said to his mother, "Woman behold your son." Then he said to the disciple, "Behold your mother."
>
> (John 19:26–27)

Jesus makes his mother the mother of the Beloved Disciple and therefore the Beloved Disciple becomes the brother of Jesus. Like the Synoptics, the Gospel of John rejects any claim to Jesus based on blood. Mary is truly his mother because of her faith and her discipleship. At the foot of the cross stand the two perfect believers, Jesus' mother and the Beloved Disciple. They receive his Spirit (John 19:30) and witness the blood and water issuing from his side (John 19:34).

## Christian Tradition

Christian tradition depicts Mary as "mother" not only because of a physical relationship to Jesus but especially because of her fidelity to the Word of God both as received and expressed in her son. The incarnation of the Word of God continually demands updating to respond to the needs of changing history. Otherwise the incarnation becomes something that happened rather than something that still happens. Thus Christians have always attempted to modernize Jesus, whether dressing him up in renaissance attire in Florentine art or in the colorful costumes of the Broadway play *Godspell*. Of course, people know more about Jesus in the gospel than about Mary. Changing our image of Jesus too greatly can cause anxiety, but since we know little about Mary, Christians can continually update her. Mary symbolizes whatever any believer wants, provided she remains the mother of Jesus, the disciple and believer par excellence. Fulton J. Sheen made her Our Lady of Television, which inspired a statue. In the Middle Ages Mary was the fair lady of the knights, the symbol of chaste love. Even the American bishops have hailed her as the model of the liberated woman. In each case the Church has made a contemporary image to invoke the ideal of Christian discipleship. Mary is the symbol through which the Church continues to discover meaning for different ages and different peoples. This explains how and why the

Catholic Church has always clung to its devotion to Mary. She remains always the faithful follower of Jesus, the kind and compassionate woman and mother anxious to respond to the needs of her children, calling each of them to follow her son. Mary heard the Word of the Lord and followed it.

# Mary Ever Virgin

Most Christians believe that Jesus was conceived of the Virgin Mary through the power of the Holy Spirit. Catholics and some other Christians believe that Mary remained ever virgin. After the birth of Jesus, Mary and Joseph did not have any sexual relations, and Jesus did not have any brothers and sisters. Many Protestants believe that after the birth of Jesus Mary and Joseph lived as normal husband and wife and thus Jesus had both brothers and sisters. The New Testament itself causes the difference in belief.

James is called the brother of the Lord in Galatians 1:19. Mark, Matthew and Luke make reference to the brothers of the Jesus:

> Is this not the carpenter the son of Mary and brother of James, Joses, Jude and Simon and are not his sisters here with us?
>
> (Mark 6:5)

> Is this not the carpenter's son? Is not his mother called Mary? And are not his brothers James and Joseph and Simon and Judas? Are not all his sisters with us?
>
> (Matt 13:55)

> Then his mother and his brothers came to him but they could not reach him for the crowd.
>
> (Luke 8:19)

Later Christian tradition tried to make the brothers of Jesus another expression for the twelve apostles. Acts 1:13–14, however, clearly distinguishes the twelve from Jesus' "brothers." Luke names eleven apostles and then adds: "...together with the women and Mary the Mother of Jesus and with his brothers" (Acts 1:14). Several New Testament authors use the ordinary Greek words for brother and sister and seem to teach that Jesus had brothers and sisters. Several explanations are possible:

1. Jesus had blood brothers and sisters. After the birth of Jesus, Mary and Joseph lived as ordinary husband and wife.
2. The second-century apocryphal gospel, the Protoevangelium of James, claims that Joseph was an old man and widower when he married Mary and that he had children from a previous marriage.
3. The Greek words for brother and sister are translations from Aramaic or Hebrew, and these languages do not have the specifically nuanced words for blood brothers or sisters, cousins or half-brothers, or even members of the same tribe.

Catholics believe that Jesus did not have brothers and sisters and that Mary remained ever virgin. Most Protestants interpret the language of the New Testament literally. Unfortunately the New Testament does not give a definitive answer. Some Protestants accuse the Catholic Church of maintaining the virginity of Mary after the birth of Jesus to denigrate marriage and emphasize the superiority of virginity and celibacy. Catholics in turn accuse Protestants of denying an early tradition, even if not contained clearly in the New Testament, and of failing to appreciate the New Testament virtue of virginity. Unfortunately the New Testament takes the blame for something it never started. No New Testament author ever states directly whether the brothers and sisters of Jesus so named are the children of Mary. Protestant and Catholic traditions differ. Catholics should respect Protestants who accept the New Testament literally. Protestants should respect Catholics who accept early church tradition.

## The Immaculate Conception

Catholics also believe that Mary was conceived without sin. Often Christians and even Catholics confuse the virginal conception with the immaculate conception. Virginal conception refers to the conception of Jesus. The immaculate conception refers to the conception of Mary. Original Sin means that people are born into an evil environment and are affected by this environment. If original sin further means that people contribute to this evil environment by personal sin and people are not fully attuned to God's presence, then no Christian should find it hard to believe that Mary did not experience original sin. Although born into a sinful environment Mary was neither affected by this evil nor did Mary contribute to the evil in the environment by personal sin. Moreover, since the New Testament depicts her as a woman of faith who heard the Word of God and kept it, then God entered into Mary fully. Her being was attuned to God. Mary's whole person was graced. Although not in Scripture Catholics have concluded this from thinking and praying about the meaning of the mother of the Lord. In 1830 Mary appeared to St. Catherine Labouré from whom the Church has received the miraculous medal. During these apparitions Mary told Catherine of her title: the immaculate conception. This took place more than twenty years before the Church officially declared Mary immaculately conceived. The prayer around the medal has become a favorite for Catholics: "O Mary conceived without sin, pray for us who have recourse to you."

Pope Pius IX declared the dogma of the immaculate conception in 1854. Four years later Mary appeared to St. Bernadette at Lourdes and said to the little girl: "I am the Immaculate Conception." When Bernadette relayed this message to the local priest he could not understand how a poor uneducated girl could know such recent dogmatic declarations by the Church. Catholics willingly acknowledge the privileged position of the mother of Jesus and affirm their faith that Mary lived and died without being influenced by sin.

## The Assumption

Catholics also believe that God assumed Mary into heaven. Even here, however, confusion remains. The declaration of Pope Pius XII in 1950 never states that Mary did not die. It does not assume that those who gathered for her funeral saw her being taken bodily into heaven. Christians believe that all the faithful will be raised from the dead through the power of God in the end-time. Christians profess belief in the resurrection of the dead every time they recite the creed. The fullness of salvation must involve the bodily or the physical, for to be human is to have a body, to be material. If all are destined to rise from the dead, whatever that may practically mean, why not have Mary as the first after Jesus to be raised bodily? Although this also has no firm basis in Scripture, since Mary was and remains the perfect disciple, why not afford to her what will be the common fate of all believers? The Catholic Church also professes belief in this privilege afforded to the mother of the Lord.

## Marian Apparitions

In 415 C.E. Bishop Scutarius built the first cathedral in Le Puy, France, dedicated to Mary. The bishop was convinced that Mary appeared there on the top of a pagan arch. With permission from Rome he built a cathedral and even included the arch. Since that time devout Catholics have made pilgrimages to many shrines in honor of Our Lady in dozens of places through the world. The Shrines of Our Lady of La Salette, Our Lady of Lourdes, Our Lady of Knock, Our Lady of Fatima, Our Lady of Guadalupe and many others attract numerous pilgrims each year. The Church has approved some but not all. But what does approval mean? Pius X remarked:

> In passing judgment on pious traditions…the church uses the greatest prudence….Even then she does not guarantee the truth of the fact narrated. She simply does not forbid belief. On this matter the Sacred Congregation of Rites, thirty years ago, decreed as follows: "These apparitions [La Salette and Lourdes] have neither been approved nor condemned by the Holy See. It has simply allowed that they be devoutly believed by purely human faith, according to the tradition which they relate."[16]

Catholics are free to make whatever pilgrimage they wish to whatever shrine they wish. Private revelations never supersede the revelation of Jesus. Often they support the teachings of Jesus.

When they seem contrary to biblical and Catholic faith, they can surely not help anyone. When they are in accord with biblical and Catholic faith, they can give guidance and support to a pre-existing faith.

## Marian Sacramentals

Catholics will always revere the mother of Jesus. As his mother, Mary never replaces Jesus. Catholics do not worship Mary. Like all Christians, Catholics worship God alone and him whom God has sent, Jesus Christ. Medals, statues, rosaries, scapulars and novenas honoring Mary exist only as sacramentals. They remind people of the love of God through Jesus and the love of Mary the mother of Jesus for all disciples. If rings or pieces of jewelry can remind people of loved ones, other objects can remind people of Mary, of Jesus and of the one God of all. The Church invokes God's blessing upon such objects with words such as the following:

> Our help is in the name of the Lord, who made heaven and earth. May this statue (rosary, medal, scapular) remind all those who see it (and use it) of God's love for all through the gift of Jesus and the gift of Mary his mother and our mother. I bless it in the name of the Father and of the Son and of the Holy Spirit. Amen.[17]

## The Saints

Jesus mediates God to all Christians. Mary also mediates. Just as Mary offered her son to shepherds, representing all outcasts, and to the Magi, representing all nations, so Mary offers her son Jesus to all peoples of all times. Since God willed to enter into human history, so people within that history bring God to others and others to God. Without taking anything away from Jesus as the one true mediator, Mary and the saints can also mediate God to others. Holy men and women have always functioned as mediators and today living holy men and women continue the tradition. If the living mediate God so can those who have preceded this present generation in faith.

## Ordinary Lives

Too many people take much of life for granted. They overlook mysteries, fail to see everyday miracles and miss aspects of life that can offer greater meaning to anyone's life. What is in a name? A rose is a rose is a rose, or is it? Michael, Brian, Patrick, Karen, Noreen, Diane, Elaine, Suzanne, Cornelia—all are names and more than names. They belong to individual people today and have been carried through life by millions of others no longer alive. Most people live ordinary lives and never become outstanding people or great believers or famous artists or even martyrs or recognized saints. But most people bear a name that was once borne by such a person. Sharing a name in common with a great person may make more conceivable the possibility of living a great life.

## All Saints Day

The Catholic tradition celebrates saints. Many days are dedicated to the memory of holy men and women, and one day each year the Catholic Church celebrates the feast of All Saints. November 1 belongs to everyone. The Church celebrates the great believers of the past, the great men and women who bore the same name that people carry today and in their lives showed a love of God and neighbor that has brought them into the household of saints. Even if their greatness went unrecognized while they lived, their faith sufficed for future generations to recall them as a blessing.

Catholics look back into history and know that for two thousand years great men and women have accepted and believed and lived the gospel of Jesus Christ. Numerous men and women and children found purpose and meaning in Jesus and tried to practice a love of God and neighbor. Most lived ordinary lives, like people of today. They entered this world, grew up, some married, others did not, and they died. But in that ordinary life they lived something extraordinary. Their earthly lives may have passed away, but something essential to their being remains.

Many Marys have lived. Not just Mary the mother of Jesus but a Mary who raised her children alone after her husband died and a Mary who dedicated herself to helping the poor. The name Theresa belongs to a mystic, a young Carmelite nun who died early in life and to an Albanian woman whom the world recognized as a saint. Everyone Christian can look into the past to discover great people who carried the same name as they do and lesser people who had the same names but as people of faith belonged to the household of God. Each lived not far from the reign of God and the gospel of Jesus.

## Everyday Saints

Holy men and women have mediated God to others, and we call them saints whether so declared by the Church or recognized by the people whom they influenced. People in the past as well as today have felt the flame of the gospel. The good news of victory ignited their hearts by its power and warmth. Then these same people passed on the flame to the hearts of others. The Catholic Church celebrates these people on November 1 for all, and individually on many days throughout the year. Saints lived real lives and continue to do so.

The veneration and respect for saints in the Catholic Church reminds its members of the glorious tradition that has preceded them. People of the past have contributed to the lives of people today. These earlier believers gave something to the next generation, who in turn passed it on to the generation following it. The Catholic Church proclaims and glories in this noble heritage.

Names given in baptism or confirmation remind people today of the believers great and small who made this world a better place by their being alive, and in some cases in their dying. The honor and veneration given to Mary the mother of Jesus and the saints makes believers better people, for it reminds anyone who will pay attention to the wonderful possibilities given to every

Christian. One mediator and many mediations through men and woman and children for almost two thousand years are part of the Catholic heritage and tradition.

The Catholic tradition celebrates holy men and women. Statues, icons and images of saints adorn churches and many Catholic homes. Usually a priest will bless these images using the prayers from the *Book of Blessings*. The prayers capture the reasons for having such images. Looking at the images of those who faithfully followed the Lord reminds all who see them to seek the reign of God, learn from them how to follow the gospel and gratefully acknowledge communion with those who intercede ceaselessly for all of God's family.

## TOPICS FOR STUDY AND DISCUSSION

1. People need mediators. Christians believe in the one mediator, Jesus Christ. Catholics believe in this one mediator in many mediations.
2. Why do you think the New Testament says so little about Mary?
3. What aspects of New Testament comments on Mary do you like?
4. What are your thoughts on the family of Jesus? Are his true family those who believe?
5. The controversy on the brothers and sisters of Jesus continues. What are your thoughts on this matter?
6. The Catholic Church teaches that Mary was conceived without original sin. What does this mean to you?
7. How can belief in the assumption of Mary give hope to followers of Jesus?
8. Do you like devotion to the saints? How can this help ordinary people?
9. How can Catholics better celebrate the feast of All Saints on November 1?

# Works Consulted

Brown, Raymond, ed. *Mary in the New Testament.* Philadelphia: Fortress, 1978.

———. *The Birth of the Messiah.* New York: Doubleday, 1993.

Cunningham, Lawrence. "A Decade of Research on the Saints: 1980–1990." *Theological Studies* 53 (1992): 517–33.

———. *The Meaning of Saints.* New York: Harper and Row, 1980.

———. "Saints and Martyrs." *Theological Studies* 60 (1999): 529–37.

Johnson, Elizabeth. "A Community of Holy People in a Sacred World." *New Theology Review* 12 (1999): 17–26.

———. *Friends of God and Prophets: A Feminist Theological Reading of the Communion of Saints.* New York: Continuum, 1998.

———. "Mary and the Female Face of God." *Theological Studies* 50 (1989): 500–26.

Meier, John. *A Marginal Jew.* Vol. 1. New York: Doubleday, 1991, 316–32.

Pelikan, Jarislav. *Mary through the Centuries.* New Haven: Yale University Press, 1996.

Schillebeeckx, Edward. *Mary Mother of the Redeemer.* New York: Sheed and Ward, 1964.

# CHAPTER 9:
# PRAYER AND DEVOTIONS

For some, personal prayer seems to have fallen on hard times. Many people do not find it easy to pray. Some have given up the practice as something left over from a previous era and no longer necessary in a scientific age. Yet recently many scientific studies have shown that prayer not only helps the person who prays but also the person for whom the prayers are offered. Medical schools have begun to add some education on the role of spirituality and prayer in the healing of the sick person. The New Age movement has attracted millions of Americans to reconsider the value of prayer, meditation and contemplation. In a church in France, before a stand of candles, hangs the following prayer:

> Dear God, I want to pray but don't know how
> I have too much to do and too little time to do it.
> So I'll leave this little candle here to remind you of me
> And remind me of you. Amen.

Traditionally, prayer is defined as the lifting of the mind and heart to God, or simply as speaking with God. This description centers on prayer as a conversation, a communication, a sharing with and listening to God. But how can anyone speak to God and lift up the mind and heart if that person lives unaware of God's nearness? The Old Testament offers the foundation for all prayer, for all times, in its awareness of the presence of the God interested in every aspect of human life.

# Prayer in the Old Testament

Ancient religions often viewed prayer as magic, a control that people had on the gods. Perform rituals, repeat so many incantations, and the god had to respond. The writers and teachers of the Old Testament constantly tried to overcome any trace of magic in their prayers. Israel founded its prayer on the experience of the presence of God as powerful and gracious and good. The God of Israel had promised the people after the call of Abraham, "I will be with you and bless you" (Gen 26:3). The God of the patriarchs could not be controlled. People may try, but they will fail. The almighty one lives in transcendence above all efforts by people to control and lives with those who respond to the presence of God in faith.

God remained faithful even in the midst of human infidelity. God looked into the hearts of people to find "a contrite and humble heart" (Ps 51:19). The Jewish people knew that they could not control their God and that the God who was present to them was powerful and merciful. They knew their failures and sins and constantly experienced the forgiving presence of God. No matter what people did, God would remain true to the promises of old.

Prayer in the Old Testament had three dimensions. First, it constituted a memory of the past: God has delivered the people from the bondage of Egypt. Second, it focused on the present: God will not forget the covenant. Finally, it articulated an expectation of a future, final and definitive presence of their saving God: "See your king comes to you" (Zech 9:11). They knew their God had been faithful to them in the past, which gave them encouragement to pray in the present as they awaited a final presence in the future.

The devout Jew based prayer on a profound sense of the personal presence and guidance of God. God was not absent from any aspect of life but lived with the Jewish people as closely as life itself. The faithful Jew turned to God for assistance in every aspect of life, even to the point of praying that God would come and destroy his enemies. "May all be put to shame and fall back that hate Zion. May they be like grass on the housetops which withers before it is plucked" (Ps 129:5). God lived with the people and forever maintained fidelity to the promises of old. God blessed the people and so the individual believer turned to God in every need.

Temple prayer, liturgy, ritual and sacrifice evoked both the awareness of the presence of God and the holiness of the people in response to God's nearness. This basic assurance gives unity to all the prayers of the Old Testament, even as the prayer takes on many forms as people, individually and collectively, respond to the presence of God. The community celebrated the providence of God:

> Happy are you who hear the Lord and walk in his ways.
> For you shall eat the fruit of your handiwork.
> Happy shall you be and favored.
>
> (Ps 128:1–2)

> Behold as the eyes of the servants are on the hands of their masters,
> As the eyes of a maid are on the hands of her mistress,
> So are our eyes on the Lord, our Lord till he has pity on us.
>
> (Ps 123:2)

The psalms offer numerous examples of the community at prayer, and in each case the community experiences the nearness of God with confidence in the goodness and mercy of God. Conscious of the majesty of God, the Jewish people turned to God and felt assured that God would answer their prayer.

Israel did not engage in magic. They did not try to control God. Sometimes God said, yes and other times God said no. But since God promised to bless them, the people had confidence in God. They prayed because they knew God was present to them and interested in their personal and collective lives. They prayed for whatever they wanted. God placed no limits on their prayer. They praised God, thanked God, asked God and even quietly relaxed in the presence of God, knowing that God was near to them.

## Prayer in the New Testament

Jesus taught his disciples to pray. Frequently they would withdraw together to pray to God but it seems that more frequently Jesus prayed alone. Jesus prayed in conjunction with the principal events of his ministry: his baptism, the selection of his apostles, his acts of healing, at the last supper, in the garden and finally from the cross. Evidently Jesus felt the need to lift his mind and heart to his God, to speak to God whom he also called Abba.

Each gospel portrays an intimate relationship between Jesus and God. He felt at ease when he prayed and evidently could feel free to pray for anything, even for deliverance from what he foresaw as a painful death (Mark 14:36). Most often, however, Jesus prayed for others (John 17:15): a lesson for his followers.

As a Jew, Jesus knew God had been faithful in the past and would be faithful in the present and in the future. God had blessed him and so Jesus could die with confidence for he could entrust himself into the hands of his loving God: "Father, into your hands I commend my spirit"(Luke 23:46).

## The Our Father

When Jesus taught his followers to pray he told them also to call God Abba, father. In the Lord's Prayer he instructed them to begin by praising God for goodness with a hope for the recognition of the presence of God by all people. This prayer, the model of all prayer, continues with praying for all daily needs, then asking forgiveness and promising to offer forgiveness to others and finally begging God to preserve the people from getting in over their heads (Matt 6:9–13; Luke 11:2–4).

The Our Father is fundamentally the prayer of a child. When the child wants something the child praises the parent and then asks for something. The Our Father does just that. But then the prayer seems to switch its perspective at the end and becomes more the prayer of a parent for a child: "Don't let the child get into situations which he or she cannot handle and keep them from evil people."

Sometimes people say this prayer so often that the meaning gets lost. Saying the prayer beginning with the last petition calls to mind the meaning of the whole prayer:

> God, preserve me from bad people.
> (Too easily they bring out the evil in me.)
> Do not let me get in situations too much for me.
> I promise to forgive those who have offended me.
> For I too need forgiveness.
> Help me each day with all that I need for the day to live.
> I pray that all will recognize your presence on earth.
> And respond to your call,
> For you are the holy one of all and
> You I can call Abba, as Jesus did, Father.[18]

All prayer, whether individual or within the community, presupposes the belief in the nearness of God and in the presence of God through Jesus. Over the centuries the Catholic Church has developed many types of prayer apart from the official prayer of the sacraments and the official prayer of the church, the Prayer of the Hours. Priests and religious and many laypeople daily recite established prayers and readings. These members of the Church pray constantly for the whole Church. For many other Catholics the Church has developed devotions to assist in praying always.

## Devotions

Much has happened in the Catholic Church in the past thirty years. Vatican Council II brought rapid changes, with everyone expected to adjust quickly, as printing presses turned out directives and Vatican II documents appeared along with the innumerable commentaries and explanations. It was time for a change. Pope John XXIII recognized that fact in 1962. Paul VI concurred. Looking back over the past thirty years, we see how much has changed in such a short period of time. Some however look back with longing for an earlier time in the Church. They especially miss the church devotions of that earlier period.

The celebration of the Eucharist remains the most important activity in the life of the Church and never should be overlooked or forgotten. As the central ritual of Christianity, the Eucharist should always remain central in everyone's devotion. Mass, however, does not eliminate the need for other expressions of faith. Believers require other ways to express their love for God in ritual and prayer.

The Catholic Church has in its history novenas, missions, holy hours, forty hours devotions, first friday devotions, first saturday devotions and special prayers or rituals honoring Mary in May and October. Along with these expressions of faith the Church also has Bible devotions, stations of the cross and benediction. None of these can ever replace the central ritual of the sacraments, but for many each (or some) of these devotions can help in the journey of faith.

## Communal Devotions

Many of these devotions are private and personal. They can also become expressions of the faith of a group. Someone can obtain a copy of a novena or a book of prayers for May and October and offer them privately or collectively. Others say prayers while walking around the church observing the fourteen stations of the cross, either privately or with a group of people. People can pray together. In prayer people can turn to God with confidence. The faith of one person affects the faith of the other. When life brings problems, people need the encouragement and support that praying together can bring. Prayer in common helps people to draw closer to God and closer to living the gospel of Jesus. Group prayer offers that support. In a confused world and an often-troubled Church, people praying together help one another and offer guidance and support.

Pluralism characterizes American society. It also influences the Catholic Church. People with different backgrounds have different needs. When such people pray together it can be expected that there will be various expressions of that prayer. The rosary is a private devotion but can also be said in a group. Novenas seem better when prayed in a church with others. Holy hours are designed for group participation, but an individual can benefit from them. The stations of the cross is a powerful devotion, especially during Lent and particularly on Good Friday, when people follow in thought and prayer the path of Jesus as he walked through the city to his death. Focusing upon each station helps people today to relive the role of the bystanders, paying attention to the suffering of Jesus. The following of the stations helps believers to rethink their own reaction, even indifference, to the suffering of the Lord and to remember how easily people can change from proclaiming "Hosanna" to crying "Crucify." The stations belong to both past and present each time people follow the path. This devotion appeals to all types of people. Old and young, liberal or conservative can benefit, for the stations cause a person to think of his or her own pain and suffering and how he or she might accept that pain and integrate that suffering into the ordinary aspects of daily life.

## Other Devotions

Over the course of centuries the Catholic Church has developed other devotions in addition to the sacramental system. While these devotions can never take the place of the sacraments, they can often assist an individual in maintaining a close relationship to God, to the Lord Jesus and to those who have proceeded in faith. Aided by the presence of the Holy Spirit, many individual Catholics have propagated certain devotions that have become popular over the course of centuries. Many are associated with Mary, such as the rosary or novenas that honor her under one of her many titles.

## The Rosary

The rosary acts as a mantra. The repetition of the same prayers allows the individual to become enveloped in the prayer, allowing the prayer to wash over the person, giving a sense of peace and harmony. Many people use the rosary as a means of slowing down the body, especially in preparation for sleep. The fifteen mysteries of the rosary bring the repetition of the prayers within the context of the ministry of Jesus and the life of the Blessed Virgin Mary. Healing of mind and body often takes place as the person uses the rosary to raise the mind and heart in prayer.

## Novenas

Novenas usually consist of nine days of the same prayer to Mary or to one of the saints. Sometimes the novena is "perpetual," meaning that it takes place every week. In many parishes people gather weekly to honor Mary through the miraculous medal novena. The repetition expresses the anthropological need to perform some activity several times in this way, honoring the one to whom the prayers are directed. Novenas to St. Anthony or to St. Anne, the mother of Mary, are usually yearly events. Novenas also allow socializing within the Catholic community. Usually they take place in the evening when individuals can steal away for half an hour to be in church with other Catholics who also see the need for some regular prayer over and above the celebration of the Eucharist. This period away from home also gives individuals an opportunity to spend some time with their fellow believers.

## Benediction

Other devotions include benediction of the blessed sacrament when the consecrated host is placed on the altar. After appropriate prayers the blessed sacrament is incensed and then the presider blesses the congregation with the consecrated host. Some individuals also spend a holy hour in the presence of the blessed sacrament on the first Friday of each month. In addition to benediction some churches also have forty hours of devotion on a yearly basis when believers honor the blessed sacrament with appropriate prayers over several days.

# Spirituality and Mysticism

All of the devotions, all of the prayers, all of the rituals and symbols contribute to a person's spirituality. Recently in the United States many individuals from the various religious traditions and denominations within Christianity have become interested in developing a personal spirituality. The charismatic renewal unites all Christians in a commitment to Jesus through the power of the Holy Spirit. Frequently individuals from various Christian churches gather to pray in the power of the Spirit and experience the presence of the Holy Spirit among them.

The New Age movement demonstrates that people need some sense of God in their lives, whatever their image of God might be. For some, God is like a cosmic father or mother. Others see God as the ground of being or the primordial energy or force for good in the universe. Still others envision God as the all-encompassing spirit or the powerful one who is present to all people. Meditation and contemplation promise some union with God, bringing to the person a sense of well-being and belonging.

The interest in Eastern mysticism has continued to influence Christianity and Catholicism. Pope John Paul II has singled out other methods of prayer in other religions, which help all believers to penetrate more deeply the mystery of God.

Within the Catholic tradition the interest in spirituality has in fact just returned to earlier traditions. "Too late have I loved thee, ancient beauty?"[19] said Augustine in the fourth century. Many Catholics have rediscovered their roots and have begun taking their faith seriously. The great traditions of St. Teresa of Avila, St. John of the Cross, Meister Eckhart, Julian of Norwich and the classic anonymous work *The Cloud of Unknowing* have all received renewed interest within the Catholic Church. Prayer, devotions, spirituality and mysticism all belong to Catholic traditions, and all help the individual in his or her relationship with God.

## TOPICS FOR STUDY AND DISCUSSION

1. What does prayer mean to you personally?
2. What are your thoughts on the prayer when lighting a candle?

3. What aspects of Old Testament prayer appeal to you? Do you like the thought of past, present and future?

4. Jesus prays often in the New Testament. Why do you think he does so?

5. Do you have any personal prayer devotions? What value might they have today for people?

6. What can the stations of the cross contribute to Christian spirituality?

7. Do some research on various Marian devotions: the origins, the prayers said and the particular theology involved.

8. Does the New Age movement add anything to Catholic traditions?

9. What are your ideas on New Age spirituality?

# Works Consulted

Fischer, Heribert. "Mysticism." *Sacramentum Mundi.* New York: Herder and Herder, 1967–69, vol. 4, 136–52.

Houlden, J. L. "Lord's Prayer." *Anchor Bible Dictionary.* New York: Doubleday, 1992, vol. 4, 356–62.

O'Grady, John F. *Models of Jesus Revisited.* Mahwah, N.J.: Paulist Press, 1994, part 3, chap. 5.

Schillebeeckx, Edward. *Jesus: An Experiment in Christology.* New York: Seabury, 1979.

Smith, C. W. F. "Prayer." *Interpreter's Dictionary of the Bible.* New York: Abingdon, 1962, vol. 3, 857–67.

Sudbrack, Josef. "Prayer." *Sacramentum Mundi.* New York: Herder and Herder, 1967–69, vol. 5, 74–81.

# SECTION III:
# CATHOLIC LIFE

# CHAPTER 10:
# ORIGINAL SIN

"The devil made me do it." "If it were not for Adam and Eve, how different life would be!" Did the devil really make anyone do anything? Would life be so different apart from Adam and Eve? Most Christians believe that what Adam and Eve did has affected the human race ever since. Today Christianity teaches that every man, woman and child somehow feels the effects of the sin of Adam and Eve recorded in the Bible. Catholics believe strongly in the existence of original sin whether or not they all share a common understanding of the term.

The meaning of the Christian doctrine of original sin has undergone considerable development over the centuries. Certainly the basic meaning has not changed, but the explanations of what happened and to whom it happened have changed considerably. Most Catholics today do not believe in creationism. Even Pope John Paul II, thinks that evolution is the better hypothesis. If the world did evolve, then what does the story of Adam and Eve mean to the contemporary believer, especially the contemporary Catholic? To what extent is the story of creation found in these early chapters of the Book of Genesis fact and to what extent is it myth?

Since the meaning of original sin has its roots in the Jewish as well as Christian tradition, understanding the early chapters of Genesis is a necessary foundation to the Christian perception of this condition. Original sin also has been a part of the history of Christianity and somehow original sin must make sense today consonant with the general condition of the human race.

## Original Sin in the Bible

Any effort to base original sin in the Bible causes hesitation. The Bible does not contain the term, which itself implies an understanding more rooted in Christian history than in biblical origins. The Bible certainly emphasizes the force of evil and sin in the world, not only in regard to the sins of individuals but as an element in the whole history of salvation. But the Bible concentrates, especially in the New Testament, on the superabundance of God's goodness and grace, and not on the condition that demands redemptive activity. An analysis of both Old and New Testaments presumes that grace, God's presence, comes first.

## Sin in the Old Testament

The third chapter of Genesis presents the classical text in regard to the origin and power of sin:

> The woman saw that the tree was good for food, pleasing to the eyes, and desirable for gaining wisdom. So she took some of its fruit and ate it; and she also gave some to her husband, who was with her, and he ate it. Then the eyes of both of them were opened, and they realized that they were naked; so they sewed fig leaves together and made loincloths for themselves. (Gen 3:6–7)

The serpent tempted the woman; she and the man transgressed the command of God; God questioned them, then sentenced and expelled them from the garden. Everyone knows the familiar story. The theologian, however, asks what does this story mean?

## Human Temptations

Recent exegesis and theology conclude that the third chapter of Genesis presents a condition of temptation and infidelity that exists not just for Adam and Eve but for all people in the presence of their God. The people of Israel always felt drawn to the fertility cults of their neighbors and failed frequently in their commitment to God. God had entered into a covenant with the people of Israel in which God promised to be their God on the condition that the people of Israel worshiped this one God alone and accepted their dependence on this same God. In the story of Genesis, man and woman stand for the people of Israel, tempted frequently to ignore the commitment to God and instead follow the claims of the serpent. In Canaanite religion, the serpent symbolized life and fertility. People also frequently refuse to accept their dependence on God by desiring to decide for themselves what is good and what is evil. The text concludes with the results of Adam and Eve's action. Disillusionment sets in, and man and woman receive less than what they had expected. Instead of independence and life, they experience servitude and death. The serpent, the false god, never fulfills his promises.

The author of Genesis took some ideas from his own ambit and used them in a polemical way to indicate the reality of Israel's temptation as well as the continual state of decision in which Israel found itself. At the same time, the text serves as a warning for Israel. All that they think they will find in forgetting their commitment to God will not be realized. In fact they will suffer.

The chapter probably comes from the court of David. King David would have liked to have decided for himself what was right and wrong, as would have most of his contemporaries. His people also would have been tempted to worship the false gods of Canaan. The story deals with both temptations: false autonomy and false gods.

## Adam and Eve and People Today

If this chapter of Genesis mirrors Israel at the time of David, it also mirrors humankind in general. False autonomy and false gods have dotted the landscape for as long as the human race has existed. But do these chapters of Genesis have any real, historical relationship to the actual origin of the human condition? Karl Rahner uses the concept of historical etiology to view these chapters of

Genesis. A relationship exists between the events as narrated and the circumstances of humankind's origins.

Etiology studies causes. The present situation can be understood by examining the contemporary scene and positing causes for present conditions and past contributing factors. If people are tempted to deny their relationship to God today through a false sense of independence and worship false gods, then such might have been the cause of humanity's initial failure in its commitment to God.

Psychologists speak of the first five years in a child's life as greatly influential and determinative of the entire life of the individual. How a person lives today depends on how he or she lived as a child. The theologian examines Genesis in much the same light. What influences humankind now also influenced humankind in the past.

## Genesis: Past and Future

The writer of Genesis experienced evil, sin and division in his world and wondered how they originated. He knew the hatred and evil that characterized his society; he knew how people seek to destroy one another, to exploit the weak and the poor and to fail to live up to their God. He saw as well the accomplishments and the good qualities of the human race and concluded that things need not have been the way they are. He posited at the origin of human history the same refusal to accept dependence on God as occurred in his own society. Every person feels alienated within the self and alienated from other men and women and from God. Instead of living according to a commitment to God, people turned to a false sense of independence that has characterized their lives ever since. What the human race has become depends on what it was at the beginning. People transgress now as they did at the origin of history. The false sense of autonomy becomes compounded in the acceptance and worship of false gods. Genesis 2 and 3 teach all of this, and the same two temptations remain true for people today, who still want to decide for themselves what is right or wrong and constantly worship false gods.

# The Spread of Evil and Sin

The rest of Genesis continues with stark examples and variations on the theme of evil in the world, such as,

1. Fratricide:

> Cain said to his brother Abel, "Let us go out in the field." When they were in the field, Cain attacked his brother Abel and killed him.
>
> (Gen 4:8)

2. The law of blood:

> If Cain is avenged sevenfold, then Lamech seventy-sevenfold.
>
> (Gen 4:24) .

3. The general corruption that preceded the flood:

> When the Lord saw how great was man's wickedness on earth, and how no desire that his heart conceived was ever anything but evil, he regretted that he had made man on the earth, and his heart was grieved. So the Lord said: "I will wipe out from the earth the men whom I have created, and not only the men, but also the beasts and the creeping things and the birds of the air, for I am sorry that I made them." But Noah found favor with the Lord.
>
> (Gen 6:5–13)

The rest of the Old Testament presents a general condition of evil and sin: "Behold I was brought forth in iniquity and in sin did my mother conceive me" (Ps 50:5). "Enter not into judgment with your servant, for before you no living man is just" (Ps 143:2). "Can mortal man be righteous before God?" (Job 4:17). "I am a man of unclean lips and I dwell in the midst of a people with unclean lips" (Isa 6:5).

Only rarely does the Old Testament refer to Adam and Eve outside of Genesis. The sin of Adam never formed a central element of the faith of Israel. But the Bible readily accepted the condition of evil and sin in which all people live. Israel believed that every person is a sinner from origin, and although the Bible does not relate this sinful condition to the sin of Adam, at least the Bible refers the condition of evil and sin to the sins of the ancient fathers of Israel. The Old Testament accepts this condition of evil as part of human experience and at least one individual, the author of Genesis 2 and 3, related evil and sin to human origins.

## Sin in the New Testament

The teaching of the New Testament continues the Old Testament teaching concerning the power of evil and sin in the world. People live in a condition of perdition or nonsalvation, or in the shadow of darkness that are overcome only in Christ. Sin and evil has affected people in the past and continue to affect people today.

## Darkness and Evil in John

The author of the Fourth Gospel begins his prologue with the Word coming into a world of darkness. Whenever the author speaks of darkness, he seems to present it as a condition of humankind:

> The judgment of condemnation is this: the light came into the world, but men loved darkness rather than light because their deeds were wicked. Everyone who practices evil hates the light; he does not come near it for fear his deeds will be exposed. But he who acts in truth comes into the light, to make clear that his deeds are done in God.
>
> (John 3:19–21)

> Jesus spoke to them once again: "I am the light of the world. No follower of mine shall ever walk in darkness; no, he shall possess the light of life."
>
> (John 8:12)

He further emphasizes his theme when he presents the cure of the blind man in chapter 9. With characteristic irony those who are supposed to see (Jewish leaders) are in the darkness. The blind man in reality sees and walks in the light. The author subtly presents the same theme in the departure of Judas from the supper room: "...and it was night" (John 13:30). The idea appears also in the Epistles of John:

> Here, then is the message we have heard from him and announce to you: that God is light; in him there is no darkness, we are liars and do not act in truth. But if we walk in light, as he is in the light, we have fellowship with one another, and the blood of his Son Jesus cleanses us from all sin.
>
> (1 John 1:5–7)

The author presupposes a general condition of darkness that all people experience and in which all people live. This darkness opposes God who is light. If people choose to follow Christ then they no longer walk in darkness, evil and sin. John makes no reference to the origin of this darkness in humanity and the world, but presumes its presence. The darkness explains the obduracy of the Jews in their failure to accept Jesus, as well as the difficulty of believing in Jesus which all people share in common. In the midst of darkness Jesus promises life to those who will throw off the power of darkness and walk in the path that he has brightened. This theme in John corresponds to the basic theme of evil in the Old Testament.

## The Condition of Nonsalvation in Paul

Paul presents a similar idea using different images. In the Epistle to the Romans, Paul opens his letter with a presentation of the universal need for salvation. Pagans and Jews are found in a condition of alienation from God (Rom 1–3) and in need of the justice of Christ. The Epistle to the Ephesians contains similar Pauline teaching: "We are all sons of wrath" (Eph 2:3). Paul concludes in Romans that: "All have turned aside, together they have gone wrong, no one does good, not even one" (Rom 3:12). Paul sees all humankind under the condition of nonsalvation and in need of the one saving power of Christ. In Romans 5:12, Paul joins the power of evil under whose dominion humanity lives with individual sin and intertwines their effects.

Therefore, just as through one man sin entered the world and with sin death, death thus coming to all men inasmuch as all sinned.

Paul relates the presence of evil and death in the world to the actual contribution of all people to this condition by their personal sin. Both death and sin appear as independent powers that determine the existence of the individual. In the presence of such powers the individual sins and must answer for the sin. Paul will not excuse a single individual by recourse to Adam. Satan and Adam do not make people sin. People do it on their own.

In Christian tradition Augustine and others interpreted this verse differently. The last clause in the verse is causal in modern translations: "because" or "since" or "inasmuch as." Augustine interpreted this verse as a relative clause so that he accepted the translation: "...death spread to all men in whom all men sinned." All participated in the sin of Adam and so all are involved in the sin of Adam. This verse became the classical text giving a foundation for the teaching on original sin. Philologically the translation by Augustine cannot stand. The clause is causal and has no philological relationship to the traditional teaching on original sin. Paul, however, wished to establish here the relationship between Adam and the personal sins of all people. People today manifest the sin that entered the world through Adam. Any notion of a hereditary sin transmitted from one generation to another must be excluded from this verse, but Paul clearly taught a relationship between the sin of Adam and its ratification by personal sin.

## Pauline Thought on Sin

Paul offers clear ideas on evil and sin, which form the foundation for the Christian tradition on original sin:

1. Sin is a power in the world. In Romans 5:12–21 Paul teaches that sin present in the world accounts for death. People feel the affect, the influence and power of sin and suffer from its presence.

2. Sin is culpable. Throughout his epistles Paul reminds his readers that they are responsible for the sin in their lives and exhorts them to live according to the grace given to them. If they do not live who they are, they must suffer the consequences (Rom 1–3, etc.)

3. All people live in a condition of nonsalvation. Jews and Gentiles live under the same wrath of God in need of salvation through Christ. All people experience the power of sin and death.

4. This condition precedes free decision. People enter this world as sinners and contribute to the personal condition of nonsalvation by personal sin. Every individual is born in the state of captivity by sin and in need of liberation through Christ (Eph 2:1–5).

5. Sin entered the world through one individual. Paul compares the salvation of all people through one man, Jesus, to the origin of sin in one man, Adam (1 Cor 5:21). Like the theologians of the Old Testament, for Paul sin also needed a beginning.

6. Finally Paul emphasizes salvation and not damnation. Paul did not offer a clear picture of sin and alienation from God because he intended rather to offer an awareness of the salvation that had already taken place in Christ. This salvation in Christ signifies a superabundance of grace as the gift of God to all people. Since salvation depends on the need of salvation, Paul teaches that the human race lived under the condition of alienation from God. But the alienation remains secondary for Paul. He always accents the positive, grace and salvation, rather than the negative, sin and damnation.

## The Bible and Sin

Certainly the Bible does not offer a systematic presentation of original sin. Questions and problems, whether of Augustine's time or the twenty-first century, must not be read into a document coming from centuries earlier. The Bible asserts the presence of evil in the world and seeks to explain this presence in the light of human understanding of the human race and the world at the time of the composition of the books of the Bible. Later generations can offer their own explanation of the origin of evil and sin in the world without becoming detrimental to the Bible's teaching. Each age has its contribution to make to an understanding of evil and sin. Provided Christians maintain their belief in humanity's need for salvation and the origin of moral evil in the human race itself, any effort to delve deeper into the reality of sin and evil can be welcomed.

The Bible teaches the sinful condition of the human race and its need for God. The Bible knows that people contribute to the power of evil and sin in the world by personal sin. The Bible also knows that in the midst of evil and sin God has manifested the power of goodness and mercy in the sending of Jesus. Jesus Christ broke the control and power of sin and evil. With these foundations theologians have formulated ever more precise understandings of the relationship between the power of evil, personal sin and people's alienation from God.

## Original Sin in the History of Theology

Augustine often receives the title of "father of the teaching on original sin." Certainly the thought of the bishop of Hippo influenced later theologians in their understanding of original sin. But Augustine did not invent original sin. The reality of sin in the world and the need for salvation through Christ formed a constant element in early Christian theology. Believers in the first centuries and the early fathers could not be faithful to Scripture without some understanding of the power of evil and sin. The early Greek fathers, however, interpreted the presence of evil and sin in a more functional sense as a presupposition of the redemption. In opposition to a Greek dualism in which one good god constantly battles with a bad god and in which matter is evil and spirit is good, the early Greek fathers emphasized the goodness of human nature and, in particular, the goodness of matter created by the one good God. They did not teach a human self-sufficiency, even though they extolled the possibilities given to people. Usually they avoided much thought on evil and sin. Following the lead of Paul, these early theologians concentrated on the meaning of redemption through Jesus. Also, in the early Church baptism was routinely administered to adults as well as infants. Such a practice would point out the power of personal sin rather than the power of evil in the world. Irenaeus, Cyprian, Origen and other early church theologians wrote of original sin before Augustine in the fourth century. But it was the position of Augustine, responding to the controversy surrounding Pelagius, that brought the teaching on original sin to a fuller understanding. Western theology developed the teaching on original sin more so than did Eastern theology.

## Pelagius

Pelagius was a monk from Britain who came to Rome during the fourth century to study the Bible. During the barbarian invasion of Rome he migrated to North Africa and began teaching his interpretation of the meaning of sin and of Christian existence. Shortly afterward he left for Palestine, while his disciple Coelestius stayed behind in North Africa. Coelestius propagated the teaching of Pelagius, but with certain exaggerations that drew severe criticism from other theologians. The Synod of Carthage in 418 condemned the teachings of Pelagius. This condemnation was then approved by Pope Zosimus, from which came the dictum: *"Roma locuta est, causa finita est."* (Rome has spoken, the cause is finished.)

Rome had resolved the controversy on the level of church teaching. The same was not true on the level of theology. Today, scholars can reconstruct the thought of Pelagius only with difficulty, since his teaching is known only through the works of his opponents. The difficulty of distinguishing the more moderate view of Pelagius from the more extreme views of some of his disciples only adds to the problem. As a rigorist Pelagius reacted strongly to what he considered the corruption of the Roman Church. He emphasized the power of evil and sin and the need to accept personal responsibility. People can do good or evil. Too easily people choose evil. God has given individuals free will, which remains God's great gift to the human race. This liberty gives the person an opportunity to live by choice according to the example of Jesus and to make progress in the spiritual life. Pelagius argued that people need to know their possibilities. They often must be prodded into achieving what is possible for them.

Much of the teaching of Pelagius falls well within the limits of traditional Catholic theology. Unfortunately, some of the conclusions drawn from his teaching are not in accord with Catholic tradition. Too often Pelagius seemed to have interpreted the work of Christ as being only exemplary. The way he interpreted the death and resurrection of Jesus seemed to overlook the power of redemption, which brings liberation from evil and sin. Pelagius did not like the understanding that baptism was necessary to infants for the remission of sin. He was not opposed to infant baptism, only to the understanding of sin that had come to underlie the practice. How could an infant be guilty of sin? This particular idea drew the criticism of Augustine and the other North African bishops.

In Augustine's view, Pelagius taught that Adam would have died whether or not he had sinned. The sin of Adam harmed only himself and did not affect the human race. Infants are in the same condition as Adam was before he had sinned. Baptism is a consecratory rite of the Church. Whether Pelagius taught these ideas as presented by Augustine remains unclear. Any theology needs explanation, and when the explanations come from opponents everyone should wonder if they are accurately representing the intention of the original author. The controversy proved tragic not only for Pelagius, but also for Augustine. In such heated controversies, exaggerations often result instead of clearheaded thinking.

## Augustine

Augustine of Hippo always placed the teaching of the Church first. He jumped into the Pelagian controversy with a fierceness that consumed much of his energy. The Church rewarded his efforts by accepting his influence on church teaching for the following 1700 years. In dialectic the best resolution combines the best of the two positions. Such was not the case of the dialectic between Pelagius and Augustine. Augustine and his thought prevailed and the thought of Pelagius lies in shadows. The Catholic Church teaches fundamentally what Augustine taught on original sin. The teaching of Augustine however, cannot be totally identified with the teaching of the Catholic Church. Many of his ideas come from his personal experience and have never been officially accepted by the Catholic Church even if they have been accepted by subsequent theologians and even found their way into catechisms. The Catholic Church has not officially accepted the teaching of Augustine on predestination, on the relationship between original sin and concupiscence and the fate of infants who die without baptism. However, the fundamental affirmation by Augustine that all people are sinners and need redemption from the power of evil and sin through Jesus Christ prevails to this day.

## The Council of Trent

The Council of Trent treated original sin in its fourth session and sought to reaffirm the conclusions of previous councils. The bishops and theologians of this council also sought to add their own ideas according to the needs of the time of the Reformation. Above all it wanted to avoid any accusation of being Pelagian in its outlook. The conclusions were neither completely clear nor thorough. The differences in teaching by the reformers did not help the task of the council. Zwingli held a position close to that of Pelagius. This came from a different exegetical interpretation of Roman 5:12 by the humanists, especially Erasmus of Rotterdam. The reformers did not interpret this verse the way Augustine interpreted it, but rather related the sin of Adam to the personal sin of believers. Based on this interpretation, Zwingli insisted that culpability could be present only in an actualization of original sin through personal sin. Luther insisted on the corruption of humanity. Luther saw original sin as a habit that remained even in the baptized.

## The Canons of Trent

The first two canons of Trent on original sin form a unity. The first treats the sin of Adam and the second deals with the result of his sin for posterity. Adam lost the state of sanctity and justice in which he was created. The consequences of this for Adam were the anger of God, death and captivity under the power of the devil. The sin of Adam also has consequences for his posterity. Death is the common lot for all people. Original sin is transmitted to all. Adam lost justice and sanctity for all others. All experience the result of the sin of Adam. Original sin is rooted in a single source and is transmitted through propagation rather than imitation. Infants, even those of Christian parents, contract Original Sin and should be baptized. This baptism is a true remission of sin and not just a consecratory rite.

The canons of Trent makes evident the problem of original sin. The state of alienation from God preexists any personal decision or action. People are born in need of the grace of Jesus Christ. People confirm their sinfulness by personal sin. When Trent describes particular aspects of original sin such as its universality, the meaning and mode of transmission, the fact that it has one origin, it uses many terms rooted in the theology of the day. Further development in an understanding of anthropology and especially of human evolution necessitates a restudy of the meaning of original sin while preserving the basic meaning of the teaching of the Catholic Church.

## The Essence of Original Sin

In the history of theology various theologians have offered their theories on the essence of original sin. Augustine taught that the essence of original sin is concupiscence, with the corresponding inclination to evil. Original sin connotes a positive reality, a certain sickness of the soul. Anselm of Canterbury rejected the theory of Augustine since baptism was supposed to take away original sin yet did not take away concupiscence. To

Anselm original sin meant a lack of true justice. People do not have what they should have: the grace of God.

Thomas Aquinas offered a combination to these ideas. He taught formally that original sin is the lack of grace. Materially, original sin means the disorientation of powers within a person. People find themselves in disharmony within themselves, with others, with God and inclined to evil through concupiscence. How can original sin be part of human experience and yet not something personal, caused by personal decision? How can original sin be voluntary if no person voluntarily committed this sin? Aquinas speaks of terminative voluntariety. Just as the human will decides to commit murder but the hand actually fires the gun, so Adam as head of the human family influences all of his posterity. Thomas Aquinas includes generation, since what results from human generation lacks the grace of God's presence. Since original sin belongs to human nature, and a concrete human person arises only through human generation, so people transmit original sin through generation.

In the light of contemporary biology, psychology and human evolution, how valid are all these theories? Today most Catholics retain some remnant of these classical theories even as they question creationism and wonder how people can be guilty of something they never did. The classical theory admits that somehow all are born with original sin. Baptism takes away original sin but not the inclination to evil. Infants who died without baptism went to Limbo as a place of natural happiness. Somehow original sin involves generation. This has the implication that sexual relations are at least shameful, if not venially sinful, even for Christian parents.

## Contemporary Thought

Though usually a virtue, simplicity does not help in understanding original sin. The meaning of original sin must include the teaching of the Bible, both Old and New Testaments, the insights of classical theology, the official teaching of the Church and the knowledge gained through the behavioral sciences in recent years. Evolution, monogenism (the origin of the human race from one couple) or polygenism (the origin of the human race from many couples), free will, the power of evil in the world, personal sin and a lack of grace or the presence of God must somehow fit together and make sense. Original Sin creates complexity and not simplicity.

## Central Affirmation

The Bible teaches that original sin is functional. Christianity focuses on redemption, not sin. But redemption and salvation make sense only if people need redemption and salvation. People need to be saved from themselves, need to overcome the disharmony in their relationships, need to be freed from powerlessness in the face of evil and sin and need to have a purpose in life. From time to time, most people have experienced alienation in the worst sense of that word: Many are full of cynicism, estranged from others, pessimistic and searching for meaning. People need salvation, need to experience the peace and harmony that only God gives. People need redemption, need to be assured that evil will not ultimately triumph, that in spite of all the setbacks and problems the future will be better than the past and present. Original sin means people begin where they are: situated in an evil world, in need of healing of divisions within and without and in need of much direction.

The second element in this central affirmation includes the Christian belief that things need not have been this way. The condition of alienation should not be identified with creation by God. Only a sadistic God would create the human race with the sense of alienation and sin and suffering that has characterized human history. Whatever one says about original sin must include this central affirmation: Things need not have been this way.

# The Sin of the World, Personal Sin, Lack of Grace

The human condition includes the state or situation in which all people find themselves, the individual's contribution to evil by personal sin and the lack of a proper relationship to God. Original sin involves all three. Each relates to the other but each also exists independently, at least in thought.

## Sin of the World

People have solidarity in evil and sin. Evil exists as a powerful force surrounding everyone. Scripture often portrays the world as evil. John in particular used the term "world" in a pejorative light (John 1:10; 12:31; 14:19). Such a force exists, and individuals contribute to the power of evil each day by personal sin. How can one explain this reality that seems to be more than just the sum total of personal sin? The situation into which a person is born is not just that of goodness, and this evil in the human condition influences not only every human decision but also the very existence of the human race. The analysis of the situation clarifies the sinful condition of the human race.

The human condition or situation can be examined actively and passively. Actively taken, the evil environment exists outside of any person. Passively, the evil situation exists intrinsic to the person and affects the person. Both aspects interrelate. No one can exist artificially separated from the environment. If evil permeates the environment, then the person feels its effect and the situation does not remain extrinsic to the person, but becomes intrinsic. The sin of the world means more than the human condition since the human condition also includes the power of goodness in the environment. The sin of the world constitutes a powerful, complex force of evil that surrounds and permeates the human race, even if not completely. When an individual sins personally, he or she contributes to the evil in the environment, which in turn extends its influence now more powerfully than before on all the people in the environment. The circle continues and grows stronger.

## Personal Sin

When the Bible speaks of the condition of nonsalvation it especially considers personal sins. Paul in Romans 1 through 3 treats of the sins of the pagans and Jews. In Ephesians, the context also treats personal sin, and even in Romans 5:12 personal sin manifests and concretizes the sin already present in the world. People tend to destroy one another, to make others suffer. Everyone at one time or another commits the sins of pride, envy, anger, greed, lust, laziness and gluttony. People know as much about the capital sins as they do about the birds of the air and the flowers in the field. On a corporate level, war, crime, exploitation and the destruction of life appear on the pages of every newspaper in the world on a daily basis. Mutual destruction seems part of the human story.

## Lack of Grace

The actual absence of grace, the presence of God in the individual, marks the third element to be integrated in any consideration of original sin. God created the human race in the image and likeness of God. Both male and female take the place of God in creation and participate in the creative power of God. People can manifest the divine qualities of kindness, compassion, mercy and fidelity. Every person can speak the Word of God and pronounce it in their very being and not just by words. God has created people for this purpose, and when a person lives without the presence of God everyone and everything loses. What God calls a person to be is not realized. The powerful presence of God in a person's life integrates and unites all the disparate elements of the complex human personality. God's presence helps to actualize human possibilities. Grace resolves the conflict between nature and person, bringing a necessary healing. Original sin implies a lack of something that should be present. The determination of an individual, which draws the person to God, should be realized and fulfilled. When not fulfilled, the person suffers severe consequences. God freely called the human race into a relationship that was beyond the ordinary human potential. God freely gave, but since people said no, individuals experience a deprivation of a perfection that should be part of every human life. A person should respond to God on the level of personal communication because God has spoken to the individual on this level. The lack of due grace signifies that a person has refused to respond, has denied the call to communicate with the divine on a personal level. Original sin cannot be understood apart from an alienation from God as well as an alienation from other people and lack of personal harmony. Grace, the self-offer of God to a human being, is not present and it should be present.

The individual lives in a sinful world influenced by the evil that surrounds everyone. As a result of this lack of grace and the influence of the situation and environment, the person contributes to the evil in the world by personal sin. The terrible vicious circle grows in force and control. Once sin entered the world, it spread until all were under its influence.

## The Plan of God and Original Sin

God has always acted through mediators. God comes in a human fashion, in creation and through humans, the highest of creatures. God mediates the great gift of self and grace through humanity. God wanted people to mediate the presence of God to others. But instead of passing on from one generation to another the presence of God in grace and mediating this presence through compassion, kindness, mercy and fidelity, people could mediate only what they had, a mixed bag of good and bad.

No one knows whether the first conscious human act was a rejection of God through the rejection of another person, but Catholic faith teaches that it was human beings who introduced moral evil into this world. Once evil was present, parents could mediate to their children only the sinful condition and not a grace-filled condition. Parents bring children into this sinful world and they quickly learn of the power of evil. Children come into existence not filled with the presence of God but in need of personal acceptance of God in their individual lives. Parents generate children and offer them what the parents have: a share in a sinful world and a sinful life. Certainly parents also offer their children the goodness they have but never without the presence of evil and sin. How quickly children learn to hurt, and much more easily, it seems, than to love.

## The Origin of Evil and Sin

Genesis offers insights into present times as well as into the history of the human race. All experience the temptation to live separated from God, seeking a false autonomy, wanting to decide for themselves what is right or wrong. Instead of taking into consideration other people and even God, individuals like to live separate lives in which the individual makes decisions based on what he or she thinks is good for herself or himself. False gods also litter the human landscape. Genesis teaches that such has been the human condition for a long time. Somewhere in the distant past, the human race started the strife that has characterized human life ever since. Evil entered this world when an individual person turned against another person. This period of history lies beyond the scope of analysis. Perhaps in the movement from consciousness to self-consciousness the first human act was one that sought to destroy another person. From that moment the evil spread until all came under its influence. Whether the origin of the human race involved one couple or many, it wasn't very long afterward before people started to destroy one another. From that moment the power of evil waxed strong and has continued to grow.

Perhaps evil and sin were inevitable. If a person can choose between good and evil then the time would surely come when someone would choose evil. The universality of original sin may have taken some time to be realized, but in the history of humankind it probably was inevitable and quickly became the condition for all.

## The Future of the Human Race

God has decided that the future of the human race is God. Goodness is the destiny of humankind. Once people thought the stories of Genesis dealt with the past. Perhaps they deal instead with the future. Jesus of Nazareth broke the vicious circle of evil begetting evil and sin begetting sin. Jesus came into this evil world but was not influenced by the evil and sin in his environment. Jesus never lived without the presence of God. Jesus was the Word of God incarnate. Jesus was the human face of God. Through him people can contribute to the reversal of the evil process. Instead of being influenced by evil and contributing to evil and sin, Jesus, free from sin, repaid evil with good. He broke the sinful circle. The control and power of evil could be diminished because of Jesus Christ. The human race needed someone to reverse the process and make it possible to reintegrate the person in the light of God. Jesus accomplished this. Jesus established the good future for the human race in which the power of evil and sin will be overcome by the power of goodness. Paradise may never have existed in the past but it will in the future.

## Original Sin and Baptism

Catholic tradition has always associated baptism with original sin. Baptism however should never be viewed as a magical washing of some sickness of the soul. Rather, baptism introduces the baptized into the church community. By this personal commitment to the Lord Jesus, the individual baptized makes a commitment not only to Jesus but also to overcome evil and sin. Baptism finds its completion not in the end of the ritual but when the baptized has reached the term of baptism in death. Baptism as an ongoing sacrament calls the individual to overcome evil and accept the holiness offered by God through Jesus. Baptism encourages the baptized to contribute to the holy community, the Church. The baptized look to the future when the holy community will be united with all things and all people under the one Lordship of Christ in the presence of the one God of all.

Baptism expresses faith and makes a person holy since the person accepts freely the offering of God's presence in grace. Once baptized, the person allows the grace of God to permeate the entire human personality so that with time, and finally in death, every aspect of the human person feels the influence of the presence of God.

In the Catholic tradition the newly developed Rite of Christian Initiation of Adults refers to adult baptism as normative. The adult expresses faith and willingly joins the Christian community. But baptism should never be limited to adults. Catholic tradition has always baptized infants going back to the earliest days of the Church. Children need the influence of the Christian community while growing up. When they come to a personal acceptance of Jesus they need to have had the guidance and help that only the Church can give. Baptism begins the process for the infant and reaches a plateau of personal acceptance when the individual is capable of making his or her own faith commitment, first expressed for the infant through parents, godparents, family and friends. Baptism finds a final resolution in death when the baptized chooses freely and completely and irrevocably God, the power of goodness and the destiny for the human race.

Original sin is real, a powerful force in all people. But original sin has been relativized by Jesus. The human person may be born without God but with a strong orientation to God, since everyone is created in the image and likeness of God, destined to share in the glory of God through Jesus. Original sin may be real but must also fit into the broader picture of the person blessed in creation and destined for God. Grace demands personal acceptance in freedom, but the individual has the assistance of the holy church community of which the baptized person has become a member. No one ever lives totally deprived of God, even people who enter this world without grace and come into a sinful world. Original sin marks the entrance of moral evil or sin into the world, which need not have been so even if inevitable. Original sin as present to people includes the sinful world in which all live and to which all contribute by personal sin and the absence of harmony within people who lack the full presence of God to integrate their lives. Original sin universally affects the human race.

But original sin has fundamentally been overcome because of the redemptive life, death and resurrection of Jesus Christ.

## Paradise

One of the most remarkable and lasting features of the popular story in Genesis is the vividness of the description of the Garden of Eden. God was present to Adam and Eve and they lived in peace and harmony with all of creation. This couple lived an idyllic life with all pain and suffering conveniently excluded. The story, however, should not be taken at face value but should be studied for its meaning. The image of the garden teaches that Adam and Eve truly experienced the presence of God. They reigned over all creation and were superior to all other animals. Genesis does not explain how the human race received this relationship and how long it lasted, other than to say that God did it all.

As people struggle today to understand human origins and even individual origins, the Bible teaches that the grace of God reaches a person where the person is, in the actual situation of one's life. Grace includes a human capacity for faith and love. And God gives grace for the pilgrimage toward God, a journey that lasts for generations and millennia. Genesis speaks of the beginning of humanity, and so the author depicted God's presence as an initial growing and expanding familiarity with God.

### TOPICS FOR DISCUSSION AND STUDY

1. The story of Adam and Eve in Genesis needs rethinking in the light of evolution and theological development. What do you think?
2. People still face the same two temptations: the desire to decide for oneself what is good or bad and the attraction to false gods.
3. Evil permeates this world, and all people are affected by it.
4. People experience a lack of harmony within themselves, with others and with God. How can this help to explain original sin?

5. What elements in the history of the theology of original sin cause you the greatest confusion?
6. Does evolution make sense? How does this theory affect theology?
7. Why does baptism end only when a person has died? What does it mean for parents?
8. Should the Catholic Church teach more about original sin?

# Works Consulted

Alszeghy, Zoltan. "What Did Trent Define about Original Sin?" *Gregorianum* 52 (1971): 57–65. *Theology Digest* 5 (1967): 197ff.

Blenkinsopp, Joseph. *The Pentateuch.* New York: Doubleday, 1992.

Connor, James, "Original Sin: Contemporary Approaches." *Theological Studies* 29 (1968): 215–40.

Duffy, Stephen. "Our Hearts of Darkness: Original Sin Revisited." *Theological Studies* 49 (1988): 597–622.

Duquoc, C. "New Approaches to Original Sin." *Cross Currents* 28 (1978): 189–200.

Haag, C. *Is Original Sin in Scripture?* New York: Sheed and Ward, 1969.

McDermott, Brian. "The Theology of Original Sin: Recent Developments." *Theological Studies* 38 (1977): 511–24.

O'Grady, John F. *Christian Anthropology.* Mahwah, N.J.: Paulist Press, 1976.

———. *Pillars of Paul's Gospel: Galatians and Romans.* Mahwah, N.J.: Paulist Press, 1992.

Padovano, Anthony. "Original Sin and Christian Anthropology." *Catholic Theological Society of America Proceedings* 22 (1967): 93–133.

Rahner, Karl. *Foundations of Christian Faith.* New York: Crossroad, 1978, 111–15.

———. *Hominization.* New York: Herder and Herder, 1965.

———. "Original Sin." *Sacramentum Mundi.* New York: Herder and Herder, 1967–69, vol. 4.

———. The *Teaching of The Catholic Church.* Cork: Mercier, 1966.

Rondet, Henri. "Pelagianism." *Sacramentum Mundi.* New York: Herder and Herder, 1967–69, vol. 4, 383–85.

Sabourin, Leopold. "Original Sin and Freudian Myths." *Biblical Theology Bulletin* 4 (1974): 323–31.

———. "Original Sin Reappraised." *Biblical Theology Bulletin,* 3 (1973): 51–81.

Schoonenberg, Piet. *Man and Sin.* Notre Dame, Ind.: University of Notre Dame Press, 1965.

# CHAPTER 11:
# GRACE IN THE
# CATHOLIC TRADITION

Catholic theology has used the word *grace* in many different ways and with varied meanings. People prayed for the grace of a happy death. The sacraments bestowed grace upon an individual and this grace differed according to the various sacraments. Actual grace was a helping grace. Sanctifying grace made people holy. Actual grace, sacramental grace, sanctifying grace, habitual grace: the Catholic Church used all of these terms to express a reality that involved God and people. Simply, grace is God present to and in a person. Since God's presence varies according to each person and to the needs of the moment, this presence can take on different nuances and dimensions.

Grace involves the mystery that is God and the mystery that is the human person. *Mystery* does not mean something that no one can ever know anything about, but rather a reality that can never be fully known. *Mystery* means knowing something but not everything. Since both God and the human being exist as mysteries, grace will be the unfolding or the revealing of the mystery of God in relationship to the mystery of the human person.

When God enters into a relationship with a person, the person changes. The individual becomes different; a newness of being occurs. This new dimension includes God present and active in the individual, and the true meaning of the person becomes evident not only to the individual, but also to others. God's presence sanctifies and justifies people. They become holy and live in the presence of God. Although many terms and descriptions were used in Catholic theology, grace denotes God's presence in the life of a believer.

## Grace in the New Testament

The plurality of terms used in the New Testament refers to the same reality under different aspects. *Charis* (grace or charity or love), *doxa* (glory), *agape* (love), *zoe* (life) and *phos* (light)—each refers in some way to the presence of God in the life of a person and how that presence changes the individual. The mystery of grace is neither simply the mystery of God in self nor simply the mystery of humans, but the mystery of the communication and communion between God and the human race. The different expressions indicate more or less fully the plurality of the aspects of this one mystery. Certain expressions designate grace as a reality in God in the sense of being well-pleased *(eudoxia)*, the salvific will of God *(prothesis)* or gratuitous grace and mercy *(elesos)*. Some of these expressions, such as *charis* and *agape*, express the new reality in the individual believer.

Other expressions such as *zoe* and *phos* indicate the communication of God to people according to different phases. Certain terms indicate more grace inasmuch as the communion has taken place: *koinonia* (fellowship or communion); *enoikein* (to live in); or *menein* (to remain). Still other expressions imply a determined action of God, such as justification and sanctification, so that from this action of God a determined effect takes place in a person. The person is holy and just.

A dialectic exists between the present state and the final or eschatological state (Rom 8:22–25), and a polarity persists between the indicative and the imperative (Rom 13:1–14; Gal 3:27) as far as the new condition of a person in grace. What a person experiences now will be perfected in the future, and what has taken place demands a corresponding lifestyle. People should live who they have become through God's gift. This new existence for a person, to be "in grace" (Gal 5:2), brings a new mode of acting (Rom 6:4; 13:13; Gal 5:16). Grace involves a process as a person moves from sin and darkness, under the power of evil, to the new existence: eternal life, living in the light, in the Spirit, with God's freedom. Original sin emphasized the evil and the negative. Grace emphasizes the positive and the power of goodness given to all by God.

The writings of John and Paul in the New Testament offer the most thorough treatment on grace, but they use different terminology. From the many texts of Paul, two give particular insight into the meaning of grace: Romans 5:1-11 and Romans 8:12-17.

> Therefore since we are justified by faith we have peace with God through Our Lord Jesus Christ. Through him we have obtained access to this grace in which we stand, and we rejoice in our hope of sharing the glory of God. More than that, we rejoice in our sufferings, knowing that suffering produces endurance and endurance produces character, and character produces hope, and hope does not disappoint us because God's love has been poured into our hearts through the Holy Spirit which has been given to us.
>
> (Rom 5:1-5)

The passage can be divided in two parts: Verses 1 through 3 treat the salvation that individual believers receive when justified, while 4 and 5 center on the power of the love of God.

**Verse 1:** "...we are justified by faith...." (Cf. Rom 4:25—Christ rose for our justification). Our new condition is justified by faith (Rom 3:21-30). This condition is further described in the following verses. The interpretation depends on whether the verb is exhortative or indicative. If indicative, then the new state is described as a state of peace with the Father through Christ. *Eirene,* or peace, in the full biblical sense means the experience of salvation or right order with God. The concept presupposes the Hebrew idea of *shalom* (Isa 52:7) which means "to be blessed with everything." Either people have peace or are exhorted to accept this peace.

**Verse 2:** "...we have obtained access to this grace in which we stand and we rejoice in our hope of sharing the glory of God." Glory in the Old Testament refers to manifestations of God's power and goodness. The power and goodness of God has been given to those justified and so they can deal with any problem. God has power over all and God in great goodness has invited people into a communion.

**Verses 3–4.** Some of the tribulations flow from persecution. Others are just ordinary human troubles. In human estimation, they indicate frustrations, dangers and human loss. Believers consider them as nothing. In a justified person they are received in a positive sense, inasmuch as the person accepts them with a note of active perseverance, looking to a future that will be better.

**Verse 5.** Hope is not overcome because God has given the Spirit. This reality of the Spirit indicates the love of God. The firm certitude of hope of the believer is founded not only in trial and tribulations, but also on the reality of the Spirit, which rests on the certitude of the love of God:

> While we were still weak, at the right time Christ died for the ungodly. Why one would hardly die for a righteous man—though perhaps for a good man one will dare even to die. But God shows his love for us in that while we were yet sinners Christ died for us. Since, therefore, we are now justified by his blood, much more shall we be saved by him from the wrath of God. For if while we were enemies we were reconciled to God by the death of his Son, much more now that we are reconciled, shall we be saved by his life. Not only so, but we also rejoice in God through Our Lord Jesus Christ, through whom we have now received our reconciliation.
>
> (Rom 5:6–11ff.)

**Verses 6–11** rest on the understanding of *agape* (love) in RSV verse 5. God's love works powerfully. The human condition includes helplessness and ungodliness. When helpless, Christ died for all, who also were ungodly. Paul remarks that even for a just person one would scarcely die. But then he modifies this affirmation; perhaps for a good person one might die. But God has manifested love for all since Christ died for all sinners.

**Verse 9** concludes with a reference to the foundation: If the love of God has already perfected such an unheard of work, future salvation becomes possible for all. All will be saved from any future wrath through the blood of Christ.

**Verses 10 and 11** note that if as enemies people have been reconciled with God through the death of the Son, much more will all be reconciled, inasmuch as they have part with the glorious Christ. Through Jesus people are reconciled, and so people can rejoice in what they have received.

> So then, brethren, we are debtors, not to the flesh, to live according to the flesh—for if you live according to the flesh you will die, but if by the Spirit you put to death the deeds of the flesh you will live. For all who are led by the Spirit of God are children of God. For you did not receive a spirit of slavery to fall back into fear but you have received the spirit of sonship. When we cry "Abba, Father" it is the Spirit himself bearing witness to our spirit that we are children of God, and if children then heirs, heirs of God and fellow heirs with Christ, provided we suffer with him in order that we may also be glorified with him.
>
> (Rom 8:12–17)

In the preceding verses Paul distinguishes the two spheres of flesh and spirit. People can live in two ways, in the sphere of the flesh or the sphere of the spirit (8:1, 5). In 8:12–17 Paul acknowledges the more complex distinction, inasmuch as those who are in the sphere of the spirit battle with the sphere of the flesh.

**Verse 12** begins in the form of a personal admonition that if believers are in the sphere of the spirit they are not debtors to the flesh and do not live by its standards. The form is negative but it supposes a positive sense. Believers are debtors but to the Spirit.

**Verse 13** expresses the foundation for the admonition: The life according to the flesh is death, while the life according to the Spirit is life. The text emphasizes the active and dynamic aspects of the new life. To pertain to the sphere of the Spirit is not only a gift of God that a person receives (Rom 8:1–11), but the person ought to respond so that in one's personal life the works of the flesh are dead, giving place to the Spirit.

**Verse 14** teaches that those who act in the Spirit of God are children of God. The new state invites believers to live as members of the family of God.

**Verse 15.** The Spirit who works in believers is not the spirit of servitude in fear, as was the condition outside and before Christ. The Spirit of filiation, a juridical term in Greek, which expresses the act of adoption, characterizes this new life. The term thus indicates at the same time a new and singular relation of the person to God and the distinction from the filiation of Christ, who is a natural Son of God. In this sphere of the Spirit and in the power of this Spirit, people cry: "Abba, Father." Praying to God as Abba here probably does not refer specifically to the Lord's Prayer but to an ecstatic acclamation such as Lord Jesus! (1 Cor 12:3). The believers, placed in the sphere of the Spirit, with all intensity and with the love of God, can call, "Abba," and such an exclamation has its foundation in the reality itself that believers are sons and daughters of God.

**Verse 16.** The Spirit renders testimony to the human spirit that all are children of God. The accurate meaning of the term *pneuma* (spirit), which occurs twice here, cannot be easily determined. *Pneuma hemon* indicates "our spirit" inasmuch as the person already lives in the sphere of the Spirit of God. The text certainly expresses an element of vital experience, joined with the new condition. Grace as a reality does not transcend consciousness, but profoundly determines human consciousness and gives people the living experience that they are children of God, holy and justified.

**Verse 17.** Paul concludes his argument: "...if children, then heirs..." (Gal 3:15–4:7) to the inheritance that God gives and that believers receive in Christ. Since they have suffered with Christ, so with him they will share in the final glory.

## Paul's Theology of Grace

The new condition overcomes the previous condition: that of sin, infirmity, ungodliness, servitude, fear and the state of hostility toward God. Previously they had lived according to the flesh, and in this condition people were worthy of the present and final wrath of God. Grace signifies liberation from all of this.

The saving work of Christ makes this possible with special reference to the cross. God justifies, sanctifies and reconciles the person of faith. The love of God causes this new condition, made according to a divine, not a human, measure. God loves a person even if that person is a sinner.

The new condition and state of salvation bring peace with God through Christ. Grace creates the ambit of the new life in which believers live. This new state implies divine filiation, which is an adoptive filiation, and an existence in the sphere of the Spirit who makes all certain of the love of God and who gives a living awareness of being children of God, supporting and sustaining hope for the future.

The new state is an intermediary state, which holds at the same time a dialectic between "already" and "not yet," and between the indicative and the imperative, what has happened and what should happen. Thus the new condition, far from a tranquil possession, involves a struggle of Christians against the influence of the power of the flesh. This new state also includes tribulations. Thus the Christian has the same lot as that of Christ: to suffer with him and to glory with him. Hope remains essential to this life. Since people find themselves in the family of God, they are directed to the possession of a future inheritance from Jesus and promised by God.

## Ephesians

Whether Paul wrote Ephesians or not, the general theology of grace included in this letter supports and continues the thought contained in Romans. Ephesians 2:1–21 treats of the manifestation of divine power in the faithful believers. Ephesians 2:1–10 develops the theme that those who were dead in sin are vivified and are gathered together with Christ. Ephesians 2:1–3 describes the preceding state of Gentile Christians. Ephesians 2:4–7 and 8–10 treat the new condition of Christians in relationship to God and to Jewish Christians.

> For by grace you have been saved through faith; and this is not your own doing; it is the gift of God.
>
> (Eph 2:8)

> But now in Christ Jesus you who were once far off have been brought near in the blood of Christ. For he is our peace who has made us both one...and might reconcile us both to God in one body through the cross.
>
> (Eph 2:13,16)

These verses present the human condition of sin and servitude before Christ. People lived under the power of death, manifested in the desire of the flesh and worthy of the wrath of God. Now, Christians both from the Jews and from the Gentiles have a new existence in Christ. Thus they are new creatures. They are reconciled with God and with one another. They now are one communion.

The ultimate reason for salvation rests in the mercy, love and grace of God. Salvation signifies that God calls all that are dead to life with Christ and gives all new life in Christ, who gathers all together. Baptism accomplishes this new life. The purpose of the action of God brings the praise of God's grace. In this life Christians are the sign of grace for the future. The new existence includes as an imperative to walk according to the ways of God. Good works are necessary so that grace will be visible.

## The Gospels

The preaching and the mode of acting of Christ expresses God's grace. The kingdom of God and certain parables show how the grace of God works and affects people. Jesus announces the kingdom as near, and this kingdom means salvation. Now the hour of salvation is present in which he announces the joyful news and in which the mercy of God approaches all people through the work of Christ. The announcement of the kingdom of God includes the news of the grace of God, which comes to people in the work of Jesus.

The "parables of the lost" in the fifteenth chapter of Luke illustrate the saving will of God (Luke 15:4-7, the lost sheep; Luke 15:8-10, the lost coin; and Luke 15:11-32, the lost son). In the parable of the great dinner, in particular the Lucan form (Luke 14:16-24), grace transcends national boundaries since all are called to the dinner. The parable of the servant whose debt is forgiven (Matt 18:23–35) also offers insights into the meaning of grace.

In addition to these parables, the scriptural renderings of the healing of the sick (Mark 2:1–12), the remission of sins (Mark 2:5) and the call of sinners (Luke 7: 36–50; 19:10) as well as the suffering servant of God theme in the Gospel of Mark all show the presence of God's grace. All these indicate that grace and the kindness of God have appeared in the world in the person and works of Jesus.

## The Gospel of John

The author of the Gospel of John celebrates life given to all that believe. Paul speaks of grace and John speaks of life. The prologue affirms that the Word became flesh. This manifestation of the Word of God in flesh brings life (John 14:6; 6:35, 48, 51; 10:10; 3:15). As the Father always gave life to the Son, so now God the Father gives life to Jesus and through Jesus to others (5:26; 1 John 5:11). The world, which was in darkness, now having its origin in the Logos, has life and light (1:4). The darkness of which John speaks should not be viewed as an ontological dualistic sense, but a historical sense. The world is in darkness because it closes itself in relationship to true life and the Word of God. In Jesus the true light has appeared. Hence people find themselves in crisis whether they remain in darkness or receive and come to the light in faith (3:15; 5:24; 6:40, 47; 10:28).

Eternal life in this gospel is *now*. Physical death is then relativized inasmuch as the believers have already been transferred from death to life (John 5:24). The realism of John is seen in the notion of the vine and the branches, which illustrates the vital unity between Christ and believers (John 15:1–11). God has created the human race (1 John 2:29; 1 John 3:1), and so John can speak of the seed of God that remains in us (1 John 3:9; 5:1). Since origin has been derived from God this filiation should not be understood as only moral or only eschatological because God makes believers children of God, a reality present now in all the baptized. They are born in the Spirit (John 3:5). The

Spirit signifies truly that God remains (1 John 3:24; 4:13), but the final and eschatological aspect is not totally lacking, as seen in John 17:24 and 1 John 3:2. The gift of eternal life joins the determined imperative in the love of neighbor (1 John 3:14; 4:12; John 14:21; 15:10; 1 John 3:24).

## The Glory of God

The theme of the glory of God *(doxa theou)* of the New Testament refers to the glory *(kabod)* of the Old Testament, which expresses and manifests the intimate nature of God. The glory of God demonstrates God's power and goodness. God has power over all other gods, even over Pharaoh. God shows goodness in leading an enslaved people into freedom. Throughout the Old Testament the goodness and power of God takes on practical dimensions. They experience compassion, kindness, forgiveness and fidelity. The people praise God together and individually for seeing and sharing in the glory of God.

## The Glory of God in John

In the New Testament the glory of God takes on another theological dimension. Jesus is the glory of God. In the person of the Lord incarnate (John 1:14), as well as in his miracles (John 2:11), people see the glory of God. The passion and death of Jesus in John become the glorification of the Son through the Father (John 12:28; 17:4). The followers of Jesus sometimes see the glory, which Jesus had from the beginning (John 17:24). Glory also designates a future reality (1 John 3; 2). In the prologue, verse 13 expresses how people can see the glory of God: "We have seen his glory, glory of the only Son of God, full of grace and truth." The Old Testament sense of God expressing glory through power and goodness finds a fuller expression in the covenantal virtues of *hesed* and *emeth*. The first can best be translated by three English words: "kindness," "compassion" and "mercy," and the second can best translated as "fidelity." The translators of the Old Testament into Greek used the Greek words *charis* and *alaethia* to translate these Hebrew words and in English they become "grace" and "truth." In Jesus people see the glory of God, for they see the kindness, compassion, mercy and fidelity of God. They, in turn, express these same qualities, for they are graced in Jesus.

## The Glory of God in Paul

More than John, Paul considers the theme of glory in connection with the whole history of salvation. Originally, glory concerns the Father, who is Father of glory (Eph 1:17) and to whom belongs the fullness of glory (Eph 3:16; Rom 9:23). God manifested this glory in creation (1 Cor 11:7; Rom 1:18–23). On account of sin (which at root is the refusal to give glory and thanks), the world loses and people live as sinners. No longer can they recognize that transparency in creation and life which manifests the glory of God (Rom 1:23). The human condition as sinful lacks the glory of God (Rom 3:23), and in this condition all of creation has its part (Rom 8:19–21).

In the central consideration of Paul stands the affirmation that in Christ the glory of God has again appeared. This manifestation in Christ is prepared for in the Old Testament (Rom 9:4; 2 Cor 3:7–11). The full revelation takes place in Christ who is the Lord of glory (1 Cor 2:8), and in his appearance shines the glory of God (2 Cor 4:6). This glory in Christ shines also in the apostles of the gospel (2 Cor 4:4). In the preaching of Jesus, people will find the wisdom of God, which orders all to glory (1 Cor 2:6ff.).

In the plan of eternal predestination, God has destined the human race to glory (Rom 9:23; 1 Cor 2:7; Eph 1:6) expected as an eschatological gift (Rom 5:2; Phil 2:13), implying the assimilation to the glorious body of Christ (Phil 3:21). The whole of creation will participate in this redemption (Rom 8:21). The reality, already present in faith (Eph 3:16), gives power to all and implies tribulations and suffering with Christ (Rom 8:17; 2 Cor 4:16). Paul then conceives the process as dynamic, leading to the final and eschatological glory.

Glory and grace demand thanksgiving in faith (Rom 4:20). If the fault of pagans consists in their refusal to glorify God (Rom

1:21), Christians have as a specific task to give glory not only in worship (Rom 15:9) but also in the reality of the Christian life (1 Cor 6:20; Rom 2:7,10).

## The New Condition: Participation in the Divine Nature

The author of 2 Peter affirms clearly that people will share in the divine nature:

> He has granted to us his precious and great promises that through these you may escape from the corruption that is in the world because of passion, and become partakers of the divine nature.
>
> (2 Pet 1:4)

The divine power gives everything for human life. People accept these gifts through accepting their vocation in life: revealing the glory and the power of God. Participation in the divine nature appears as a gift of God and includes the aversion from sin. The formula itself indicates that believers have a share in the life of God (1 John 1:13). The expression itself also refers to the eschatological and final consummation when God is all in all, and all are in God.

## The New Personal Relationship to God

Since the communication of divine life comes from the Father through the Son in the Spirit, then the personal relationship to God involves all three. The new state of justification signifies the new presence of the Trinity in people. According to 1 Corinthians 3:16, people are temples of the living God who dwells within. The same is affirmed of the Spirit (Rom 8:11; Phil 1:14). John affirms that followers are in Jesus and vice versa (John 14:20). Because of the union between Jesus and the Father, the Father and Son come and make their home within (John 14:23).

*Koinonia* (fellowship or communion) expresses the same reality that believers have with Christ (1 Cor 1:9) and the spirit (2 Cor 13:13; Phil 2:1). The announcement of salvation ought also to enlighten the readers of the epistles that they have *koinonia* with the early witnesses, with those who saw and heard and touched the Word of life. Through the same faith they have *koinonia* with God the Father. *Koinonia* is communion according to the same faith, which is communion by reason of the life received through faith. Communion with the Father is possible only through the Son (John 5:12). To indicate the same reality, John uses the formula to be one in God and to remain in God (John 2:5; 4:13). These formulae certainly express a certain intimate personal relationship between people and God, which implies a communion of life.

The dialectic between "already" and "not yet" also refers to the affirmation of the communion with God, since the perfection of that communion remains in the future (John 3:2; 2:25). The same persists for the dialectic between the indicative and the imperative. The indicative admits of present communion with God. The imperative implies a communion ever to be perfected. The communion with God has some demands. According to (John 1:6) to walk in darkness is incompatible with *koinonia*. The love of neighbor particularly flows from the condition of communion with God (John 2:9–11; 4:11 ff.; 14:23).

## Personal Relations to Each Member of the Trinity

The new relation in grace brings a personal relation to the Father. People can call God Father, or Abba (Rom 8:14), because of the free communication in Christ through the Spirit. Because of this free communication people really are children (1 John 3:1) and heirs (Rom 8:17; Gal 4:7) of God, having part in the inheritance of Christ (Rom 8:17).

Grace also implies a personal relation to the Son, to Jesus Christ. Paul notes that believers have put on Christ (Gal 3:27; Rom 13:14) in baptism. The formula in Christ in a general way implies that believers exist in a new sphere of life opposed to the sphere of the flesh, which brings with it an intimate relationship to the glorious Christ. Thus the expression "to be in Christ" reminds people that they live in an environment in which they experience the personal influence of the glorious Christ, which begins in baptism, when followers become clothed in him.

Believers also experience the presence of the Holy Spirit. The Spirit of God dwells in all who believe (Rom 8:9). This same Spirit will give life to mortal bodies (Rom 8:11). The presence of the Spirit in everyone brings a variety of gifts (1 Cor 12:4), and to each is given a measure of the Spirit for the common good (1 Cor 12:7). The presence of the Spirit within a follower of Jesus makes that person God's temple (1 Cor 3:16), and this same Spirit gives people of faith freedom. "Where the Spirit of the Lord is there is freedom" (2 Cor 3:17).

The new life of the person of faith contains inexhaustible richness, so that the author of Ephesians can pray:

> I do not cease to give thanks for you, remembering you in my prayers that the God of our Lord Jesus Christ, the Father of glory may give you a Spirit of wisdom and revelation in the knowledge of him having the eyes of your hearts enlightened that you may know what is the hope to which he has called you, what are the riches of his glorious inheritance in the saints, and what is the immeasurable greatness of his power in us who believe....
>
> (Eph 1:16–19)

God's self-communication of God's life both as given and as accepted brings God's free and personal favor. God enters into a relationship with a creature and communicates a love that will forever remain unmerited. No one can lay claim on such a love. God freely offers and the person freely receives. People accept this free self-communication through Jesus in a dialogical partnership. Such a dialogue presupposes that the human person has been so constituted to enter into this dialogue. The Bible supports this belief with its teaching that God created both male and female in God's image and likeness (Gen 1:26). God's presence remains unmerited, and yet the human being desires this relationship, for God has so created the human race.

Grace in the Catholic tradition means the presence of God actually experienced by a person in differing degrees in different moments of life. Life itself is a sign of God's presence, or God's grace. People can also bring both this presence and the awareness of this presence in another's life. In moments critical for salvation, the Church expresses its love for the individual, and God enters into a special relationship by means of the Church and its sacramental system. Moments of peace and contentment and happiness and joy and fulfillment remind the faithful believers of how near God remains. Whether in good times or in bad, the presence of God never departs from one who believes. People can stand in the presence of God because God has so declared in Jesus. People are sanctified, made holy to share in the household of the saints through their faith in Jesus. God's grace suffices for life, for grace means God's holy presence in every moment of life. And when life is finished, the presence of God begun in faith finds completion when the individual gives himself or herself into the loving hands of the one who created. Then and only then do people fully experience God's loving presence, God's grace.

## TOPICS FOR DISCUSSION AND STUDY

1. What does the word *grace* mean to you? Has your understanding changed as a result of this chapter?
2. God communicates to people. God is present to people. How should this affect Christians?
3. What appeals to you in Paul's theology of Grace?
4. Why is glory so important in the Bible?
5. People can stand in the presence of God because God has so declared.
6. Every believer is holy and has a personal relationship to God: Father, Son and Holy Spirit. How should this affect a person's self image?
7. God's presence changes as a person changes. Yes? No?
8. Peace, contentment and happiness remind a believer of God's presence.

# Works Consulted

Coffey, David. "The Theandric Nature of Grace." *Theological Studies* 60 (1999): 405–31.

Collins, Raymond. *Letters That Paul Did Not Write.* Wilmington, Del.: Michael Glazier, 1988.

Davis, Charles. *God's Grace in History.* London: Fontana, 1967.

Fransen Peter. "Augustine, Pelagius and the Controversy on the Doctrine of Grace." *Louvain Studies* 12 (1987): 172–81.

———. *Divine Grace and Man.* New York: Mentor Omega, 1965.

Mertens, Herman-Emiel. "Nature and Grace in Twentieth-Century Catholic Theology." *Louvain Studies* 16 (1991): 242–62.

O'Grady, John F. *According to John.* Mahwah, N.J.: Paulist Press, 1999.

———. *Pillars of Paul's Gospel: Galatians and Romans.* Mahwah, N.J.: Paulist Press, 1992.

Purcell, Michael. "Gloria Dei, Homo Vigilans: Waking Up to Grace in Rahner and Levinas." *Louvain Studies* 21(1996): 229–60.

Rahner, Karl. "Concerning the Relationship between Nature and Grace." *Theological Investigations.* London: Darton, Longman and Todd, 1966, vol. 1, 297–318.

———. *Foundations of Christian Faith.* New York: Crossroad, 1978, section 4.

———. et al. "Grace." *Sacramentum Mundi.* New York: Herder and Herder, vol. 2, 1967–69, 409–27.

Roy, Louis, and W. Meissner. "Toward a Psychology of Grace." *Theological Studies* 57 (1996): 322–37.

Segundo, Juan. *Grace: The Human Condition.* New York: Orbis, 1973.

Shogren, Gary. "Grace." *Anchor Bible Dictionary*. New York: Doubleday, 1992, vol. 2, 1086–88.

Vandervelde, George. "The Grammar of Grace: Karl Rahner as a Watershed in Contemporary Theology." *Theological Studies* 49 (1988): 445–59.

# CHAPTER 12:
# DEATH AND
# ESCHATOLOGY

No one has returned from the dead in spite of the near-death experiences documented by many. Near-death does not mean death. Even the light so frequently spoken of in such experiences can be explained through physical and chemical reactions in the human body. No one really knows what dying is like. People know more about pain and suffering and sickness. Some people even have had moments of out-of-body experiences, but no one has died and returned to tell about it. Even doctors have trouble declaring when true death has occurred. Previous definitions of death such as the cessation of breathing do not hold today. Even brain death is not universally understood to indicate the irrevocable end of life.

Dying involves a process. In fact, both the writer and the reader of this book are now dying. Every member of the human race is terminal. The only variable is how long one has to wait before the final outcome of the terminal illness called living. The process of death may last weeks or months or even years before a person finally dies. Others die quickly. An unexpected heart attack, and then it is over. With the approach of death some physical functions shut down quickly while others last longer. Genetics has much to do with this phenomenon. A good sturdy heart may remain pumping even as the other major organs are no longer able to absorb life-giving oxygen.

# Thinking about Death

Most people do not want to think about dying and death. They believe that such thoughts are morbid and belong on the top shelf in a big box in the back of the closet. They do not want to even think of pulling death out into the realm of reflection until it intrudes. Then they try to get rid of it quickly before it contaminates life. Because people do not know how to deal with death, they just decide not to think about it.

Some philosophers, psychologists, theologians and even pundits say that dying is part of living. But people know life: the good and the bad. They know what they like about life and what they dislike. People know little about dying and see no useful result in relating it to life. Like Scarlet O'Hara, many people say: "I'll think about it tomorrow."

Life means getting up and living. Life means loving and playing and enjoyment and satisfaction, even working. Life also means being sick or misunderstood, and earthquakes and famine and cancer; but that is not real life. Real life is good health and a zestful enjoyment of the good things life has to offer. Living means challenges and hopes and accomplishments and relationships and pleasure and contentment and, in general, "feeling good." Everyone knows what living means. Real living is living well. Forget about the pain and surely avoid the whole question of dying and death.

But death comes and too quickly. The body shuts down. It just will not work anymore. Then the person is gone, has passed on, passed away, and now only the memories remain. In the Capuchin Church in Rome, near the fashionable Via Veneto, some ambitious monk many years past gathered all the bones of the dead monks and made macabre displays of skulls, tibia, ulnas and all the rest. Some even more thoughtful monk placed a notice for all those who enter there to read: "What you are I once was; what I am you will be!" Death comes to all, sooner for some than for others. In a society mesmerized by youth, vitality and life, thinking about dying and death may not be fashionable but such thoughts may give some insights into living.

## Death and the Arts and Sciences

The Catholic Church teaches people how to live and to die. Such a subject involves more than just biology and psychology. Dying and death join the arts and sciences together. Every human discipline is affected by dying and death. Just think of Mozart and his requiem, Picasso and *Guernica*. Think about the philosophers and the theologians, as well as the internists, cardiologists, transplant surgeons and pathologists. Think of the poetry and works of art that deal with dying and death: *Romeo and Juliet* and the *Dying Gaul* in the museum in Rome. Dying and death do not discriminate in the realm of human knowledge. Death has intruded everywhere in human understanding, and yet death remains so little understood.

Some wise people both encourage and personally engage in the often painful exploration of death. Before his tragic death, while negotiating peace in Africa, the late secretary general of the United Nations, Dag Hammarskjöld, remarked: "In the last analysis, it is our conception of death which decides our answers to all the questions that life puts to us."[20] The philosopher George Santayana also reflected on death: "To see life, and to value it from the point of view of death is to see and value it truly....It is far better to live in the light of the tragic fact, rather than to forget or deny it, and build everything on a fundamental lie."[21] Putting off thinking about death helps no one. On the other hand, seeing all of reality in the light of death invites a morbid outlook that stifles everything. People must think about death but not so much as to forget about life.

## Age and Achievement, Life and Death

In a country that celebrates youth so much, chronological age has always been distinguished from psychological age. Death, too, often becomes associated with old age rather than with life. Accomplishments have also been associated with youth instead of life. Plato wrote *The Laws,* one of his finest dialogues, when he was about eighty years of age. Michelangelo completed the *Pièta* in his twenties but was over seventy when commissioned to design the magnificent St. Peter's in Rome. Benjamin Franklin became a diplomat in his seventies, invented bifocals at seventy-nine, functioned as governor of Pennsylvania and helped frame the Constitution during his eighties and made an appeal to Congress for the abolition of slavery at the age of eighty-four. At seventy-five Thomas Jefferson began drawing the plans for the buildings of the University of Virginia as well as developing its curriculum. In his self-composed epitaph he regarded these activities more important than being president.

In this century Winston Churchill became prime minster of Great Britain at sixty-six and was again elected to this high office at the age of seventy-seven. Pope John XXIII, one of the most forward-looking of modern popes, did not assume office until he was seventy-seven. Ronald Reagan became president when he was seventy-one and served for eight years. Longfellow wrote: "Nothing is too late 'til the tired heart shall cease to palpitate."[22] But eventually life is over and it matters little how many years have passed. But even then, outrage often accompanies this demise rather than quiet acceptance.

> Do not go gentle into that good night
> Old age should burn and rave at close of day;
> Rage, rage against the dying of the light....
> Dylan Thomas[23]

People do not want to die. They still think of what might be accomplished and, following in the examples of those mentioned above, much might still lie ahead of them. But try as one may, eventually death calls, and everyone must respond.

What does the Catholic Church teach about dying? What does the Church teach about the afterlife: judgment, heaven and hell? What do the Scriptures say about the future of the individual and the human race? Are all people saved? What do good works mean and how do they contribute to a good afterlife? What does the Bible say about the future? What does the Old Testament teach and what does Jesus and the New Testament teach?

## Eschatology: The Last Things

Most people do not know the word *eschatology*. Catholics usually know the meaning of the phrase "last things": death, judgment, heaven and hell. To these four the Catholic Church adds purgatory. Eschatology deals with the last things but not in the sense of an hypothesis of science nor of a philosophical and historical prognosis. *Eschaton* in Greek means "the end." *Eschatology* concerns the end of individuals, the human race and the world, and includes what Jesus has revealed of this future ending.

Recent theologians have emphasized not just the future but the presence of the future NOW. The Second Vatican Council and its document on the Church, *Lumen Gentium,* viewed the Church as journeying to its union with the heavenly Church (chapter 7). The future is present. Accepting a future demands making a decision now. Many accept the present aspect of eschatology while others will emphasize the future aspect. Actually, eschatology deals with the end of life and the end of the universe, but also with the present, for the future affects life today. Believers understand the future in the light of the Word of God. Eschatology also addresses the elements of daily faith, which leads individuals to understand daily life.

## Eschatology of the Old Testament

The Catholic Church accepts the Old Testament as part of its tradition but goes far beyond the Old Testament in its understanding of the future. The people of Israel saw the future belonging to the community and not the individual. The individual lived on in his or her children and in good deeds. For most of the history of Israel no future life existed for the individual. The exile in Babylon in the sixth century contributed to the understanding of the future by adding a new dimension: The individual believer and not the nation became the religious unit. Contact with Greek philosophy in the second century before Christ also added to the understanding of the future in Judaism.

But for most of the Israelites of the past and for many contemporary Jews, no afterlife exists. This is it and this is all. The future concerns the triumph of Israel and the judgment against the Gentiles. The future prosperity of the people of Israel overwhelms any future for the individual.

## Places of the Departed

The Old Testament speaks of heaven but in an unclear fashion: "You will guide me with your counsel and afterward you will receive me to glory. Whom have I in heaven but you and there is nothing on earth I desire but you" (Ps 73:25). Heaven belongs to God and not necessarily to people, even those of great faith. People die and go to Sheol, a shadowy type of existence. If people are 100 percent alive at the age of twenty-five, then the rest of life brings a diminishment until the person barely lives. These people move from earth to Sheol.

Hope of resurrection to new life appears rarely in the Old Testament (Isa 26:19), and then only with reference to the holy people and the messianic kingdom. It was a prevailing view that all Gentiles were to be destroyed (Isa 34–35) or that all who were hostile to Israel were to be destroyed, while the others were to rest in a shadowy state.

In general the future belonged to the community, the people of Israel, and not the individual. When, at the end of the Old Testament period, the Book of Wisdom speaks of a future life for the individual, such teaching comes more from the influence of Greek philosophy than from the traditions of Israel. In the view expressed in the Book of Wisdom, people never completely die. They move from true living to a shadowy existence in Sheol. The righteous have a longer life than the unrighteous. This, and not future reward or punishment, distinguishes the good from the bad.

## The Future in the New Testament

The New Testament continues the teaching of the Old Testament with certain significant additions. Final salvation for the people will come and the God of Israel will triumph, but this will also include final salvation for the individual. Christianity recognized Jesus as the Messiah, and so the last times were here *now*. The Church lived as the eschatological community. The time of salvation is present, but there will still be definitive salvation to come when salvation will become visible.

The eschatological event took place in Christ. The kingdom of God exists now even as the Church anticipates a future kingdom. A future resurrection of the body, the renovation of the universe and the final conquest of evil will come in the future. But all of these have a beginning in Christ and his event because he himself is risen and lives now with the Father, even as he will come again. Jesus is exalted and ready to come to manifest the definitive conquest of the kingdom (Col 3:1–4).

The divine action present in Christ means mercy toward the world and all people—the poor, despised and forgotten (Luke 4:18; 6:20; Matt 5:3; Mark 2:17; Luke 15:11–32). The individual must decide for or against Jesus. Once made, the decision remains definitive. In Jesus Christ, God has offered the final merciful manifestation for all people. The future also contains God's judgment (Matt 25:31–46; Luke 17:22–37), which has begun now (John 5:24). God will be merciful to those who have faith and have loved. Known now only in faith, the future exists under a veil in efficacious signs (Mark 4:11; Luke 10:21). Eventually it will be manifested openly (Matt 24:27; Luke 17:24; Mark 13:24–26).

Present life determines the future. Future life depends on the present. The present situation offers the opportunity for the eschatological decisive situation (Matt 10:32; Mark 8:38; Luke 13:1–5). The urgent present situation foreshadowing the final eschatological event causes anxiety (Mark 1:15; Luke 10:9). Therefore be vigilant (Mark 13:32). The admonition to do penance and prepare and witness at the same time offers a promise that brings hope, which is secure.

# Eschatology in Other Writings
# of the New Testament and in the Early Church

The early Church passed on what Jesus announced, interpreted his teachings and amplified them. In Acts the Spirit helped people to understand the sayings of Jesus. The Church sensed itself as the community of the Messiah living with them, the new people of God enjoying the eschatological times (Acts 2:15–38, 46; 10:34–43). These signs manifested more clearly the presence of the eschatological fulfillment, but the Church realized that this was not complete. More was yet to come (Acts 3:20).

Paul teaches the same eschatology: present but yet to come. Justification and salvation have already taken place, but definitive salvation remains in the future. The powers of darkness are already overcome, but only in the future will this be fully manifested. The giving of the Holy Spirit characterizes Christian existence. The Spirit brings the eschatological existence and the new creature (2 Cor 5:17; Gal 6:15). Life now contains tears and darkness. Flesh fights against the spirit (Rom 8:12; Gal 5:16, 25). As a gift from the life and resurrection of Christ, the Spirit dwells in the Christian (1 Cor 15:45–50) and, on the other hand, only in the resurrection of the body will it be fully manifested (Rom 8:9–11). Christians in the Holy Spirit no longer pertain to this age of evil, but they will expect a full liberation to come (Rom 12:2; 1 Cor 7:29–31).

The parousia or second coming figures prominently in Paul's preaching. The body will rise, different from the earthly body but identified with the same person (1 Cor 15:39–48). Then the whole universe will receive glorification (Rom 8:20). The end comes from God and pertains to the final age and not to the history of this age. No one can imagine it and Scripture gives no definitive description.

The Gospel of John has its own eschatology, which emphasizes the present. The author takes the terms and ideas of the future and applies them to the present. Death, judgment and eternal life have begun *now* (John 5:24; 17:3). The author places the future in a mystical mode in the present but he also accepts a future aspect that completes what has already begun

(John 5:28; 6:39, 54; 12:48). Having accepted Jesus in faith, the believer lives in Christ. They are where Christ is and vice versa (John 14:3; 17:24).

## Death in the Old Testament

In the early writings of the Old Testament the necessity of dying seems apparent. To be human means to die. But often these same writers disagreed on why people had to die. Since God created humanity and everything else, whether people live by themselves or of themselves, their lives are totally dependent on the will of God giving life or taking it away (Gen 2:7; 3:19; Ps 90:3; 104:29; 146:4; Job 34:15; Eccl 12:7). Human life follows the way of all earthly things (Job 23:14; 1 Kings 2:2; Job 16:22). People progress and die like the grass in the fields (Isa 40:6; Ps 103:15). In such texts death appears to the Jews as something to be lamented, but yet part of the lot of all (2 Sam 14:14; Sir 14:17; Job 7:9; Ps 89:49). Death follows life and life is better (Prov 3:16; Job 2:4; Eccl 9:4).

Eventually the Jews receive and accept death as coming from the hands of God, the Lord of life and death (1 Sam 2:6; 12:15–24; Ps 39:14; 90:10; Eccl 3:2; Job 14:5). People viewed a long life as a reward and grace from God, given for a life well lived (Deut 5:16; 16:20; 30:15–19; Ezek 3:21).

## The Problem of an Early Death

But what of death in the prime of life (Isa 38:10–20; Ps 55:24; 102:25; Jer 17:11)? Some saw an unprovided death as a penalty from God for sins. Others tried to move away from an untimely death as a penalty, but in general most writings of the Old Testament viewed an early death as a sure sign of God's wrath (Ps 55:24; Job 15:32; 22:16; Jer 17:11). Since no great reward existed in the afterlife, everyone wanted to live as long as possible.

# Origin of Death

Reading all of the books of the Old Testament shows a development in understanding the origin of death. The simple answer is that a person is a creature, and so death is inevitable. But this can scarcely be the final reason. Little by little, the writers of the Old Testament related universal death to sin. The author of Genesis in particular related sin to death (Gen 6:3). Although death was seen as a possibility apart from sin, nevertheless it did not enter the world until sin entered (Gen 3:16). In Genesis 3:14–20 sin explains the depravation and destruction of life. Pain, misfortune, imperfections and sickness signify that death already exists and permeates the whole of human life, and all on account of sin. Death as the consequence of sin and as seen in relationship to the sin in paradise can be found in Deuteronomy 25:24 and Wisdom 2:23. Both passages refer to Satan, who seduced Adam and Eve and brought death to all.

# The Abode of the Dead

Sheol, a state or place after death, has already been described. The Old Testament uses other terms for the place of the dead: a tomb or a pit (Isa 14:15; 29:4; Ezek 26:20; Job 7:21; 17:16; Ps 22:16) or the bowels of the earth (Dan 12:2). God has created the human person as a transitory being but with a certain element of permanence even after death. Life becomes greatly diminished after death but is never completely taken away. Even the biblical image of being gathered to one's fathers, or to one's people, indicates this shadowy type of existence (Gen 25:8; 35:29).

Sheol exists as a specific location under the earth (Num 16:33; Deut 32:22; Isa 14:9; Ps 55:16). The Book of Job placed Sheol under the waters that surround the land (Job 6:5). To die means to descend to Sheol (Gen 37:35; Ezek 31:15; Ps 55:15), the place of all the dead (Job 23:14; 30:23; Ps 89:49; Sir 8:7). No distinction exists between the good and the bad in Sheol. All experience the same since all live in the absence of God, and God has forgotten them (Ps 88:1–6). They live far from God and cannot praise God

(Isa 38:18; Ps 6:5). Sheol exists a long way off, both in this world and yet separated from it (Isa 14:15; 38:10; Ezek 32:23; Job 38:17). It is a place from which no one may return (2 Sam 12:23; Job 7:9; 16:22; Eccl 12:5).

But God has power even over Sheol. God can save from Sheol (1 Sam 2:6; Ps 30:3; Amos 9:2; Job 38:7). The Book of Wisdom seems to indicate different lots in Sheol. In Wisdom 4:7 the just are in peace but not the unjust (Wis 4:19). This of course may be due to Greek influence rather than Israelite faith.

The books of the Maccabees offer a certain faith in a final restoration (2 Macc 7:9, 11, 14, 23). The persecutors will not rise (2 Macc 7:14). Isaiah 26:18 and Daniel 12:2 mention the resurrection of the dead, but Jewish interpretation has disputed the precise meaning of all of these passages. Since the Jews do not accept the Book of Wisdom nor the books of the Maccabees as part of their sacred collection, these cannot be used to promote a belief that the Israelite theology accepted an afterlife.

In summary, the theology of the Old Testament does not offer a clear doctrine either on death or the fate of a person after death. Nor do the writers ever speak of the separation of body and soul. Death is a fact of the total person, and death is present in life *now* and not only in the end.

## Death in the New Testament

The opinions and ideas on death presented by Jesus were influenced by the understanding of death that prevailed in the cultural and religious environment of his time. The death and resurrection of Christ clearly altered this thinking, but Jewish thought remained its framework. The New Testament presupposes the Old Testament and rarely repeated it. But the New Testament writers viewed death in light of the evolution of later Judaism as well as the death and resurrection of Jesus. At the time of Christ some already believed in a future eschatological time that would bring liberation even from death. At least a part of humanity conceived the possibility of a resurrection. The coming of the definitive kingdom of God, or the Messiah, would bring life itself. Earthly death would then be not a definitive but only a relative death (Rev 2:11; 20:6).

## Synoptic Gospels

The Synoptic Gospels present a conscious and clear faith in the resurrection of Christ. Such a resurrection brought a promise of resurrection for others. Death becomes changed. The advent of the kingdom of God brings the advent of life eternal and the only true life. Those to whom the gospel was preached lived previously in darkness and death and sin, and they had come to eternal life through faith. Conversion from sin brought a conversion to life (Luke 15:24). The whole of Christian life involves the necessity of dying and bearing the cross, but now Christ has changed this to include a promise of eternal life. So all of life involves the acceptance of death (Matt 10:39; 16:25; Mark 8:35; Luke 9:24; 17:33) changed now into the gateway to eternal life.

## Paul

Paul offers a profound theology of death, unlike the Synoptic Gospels, which provide only some considerations without a unified presentation. But even in this theology Paul does not treat death in itself but rather as it relates to the mystery of Christ. What he writes of life and death and sin always involved the declaring and preaching of the mystery of God in Christ.

The people of Adam are destined for death. People are naturally earthly and carnal (1 Cor 15:42–49). Paul explains this fact by considering it from a perspective of the history of humanity. Death enters the world on account of sin (Rom 5:12–21; 1 Cor 15:21). As in Judaism, Paul connects death with the sin of the first parents and relates death to individual sinfulness (Rom 5:12). Paul does not consider death in itself or as natural to the human race, but rather as the consequence of the historical fact of sin. Sin had destroyed the harmony and friendship of humanity with God. All live under the power of sin and death, which Paul sees almost as a personal power (Rom 5:12–16; 7:8; Gal

3:23). All the powers of this world adhere to the power of death or even become identified with it (2 Cor 7:10; 1 Cor 15:26). Death is the last evil.

People are carnal and therefore mortal (Rom 6:16; 8:11; 2 Cor 4:11). But this does not mean that all remain under the power of death. Only those who are carnal, who sin and remain in their sinfulness against God and who are therefore not spiritual, fall under the continual power of death. The resurrection of Christ accomplished the definitive death of sin (Rom 7:14; 8:3 Gal 6:7) and brings to life all who believe.

Paul considers death under different aspects. To the issue of physical death he always adds a theological and eschatological aspect. Death never exists as something indifferent. Either death is a transit to eternal life or it is a permanent and absolute separation from God. But God has power over death. Although every person must go through death because of sin, nevertheless the person of faith has hope in God. So death, even though inevitable, brings with it a hope in eternal life (Rom 8:18). The divine action of liberation from death has already taken place in Christ. Jesus was subject to the power of death in his whole life, but he conquered death. This made it possible for all to do likewise (Rom 6:9; 8:3; 2 Cor 5:21; Gal 3:13). The death of Christ in obedience to the Father conquers and destroys the power of death. The full manifestation of this final victory will take place on the last day (1 Cor 15:28).

## Paul's Theology of Death

1. Death and sin are intimately connected.
2. Paul viewed death neither as a merely natural process nor as a philosophical premise, but rather as it related to the actual history of salvation.
3. Death for Paul becomes a religious event. Death exists because of sin, and a person needs the mercy of God to be liberated from death. This is accomplished through the obedient death of Christ.

4. Death exists now, present in the world and in the life of the individual as a power.
5. Death will be destroyed in the end but some will remain in the definitive death.

Paul in his writings acknowledged the problem of the present and the future. Jesus had already accomplished victory over death, but the definitive full victory remains in the future. This belief pervaded the teaching of Paul and determined his whole understanding of the present Christian situation. His chief points include:

1. The preaching of Christ demanded a clear decision. Those who believed had life; those who did not embrace death (2 Cor 2:14). Death results from the failure to believe. Death means that a person lacks definitive salvation (Rom 1:32; 6:16; 8:2; 2 Cor 3:7; Rom 9:22; 1 Cor 1:18).
2. Only those who believe can overcome the power of death. No one can do this without reference to Christ, who conquered death. The Christian died with Christ and already lives with him (Rom 6).
3. The believer experiences this death with Christ in baptism (Rom 6). The former person dies—and dies to sin (Rom 6:1) and to the law (Rom 7:6; Gal 2:19) and to the flesh (Gal 5:24; Rom 7:24) and to self (2 Cor 5:15) and to the world (Gal 6:14). Such texts emphasize the personal contribution. The individual must do something with Christ. The communion with Christ in death through baptism means the believer passes from a carnal existence to a spiritual existence.
4. The power of death still remains somewhat present in the life of a Christian, but in different ways and occasions (Rom 8:11, 18, 23). The life of Christ demands a personal acceptance and a death to self (Rom 8:35; 2 Cor 6:9). So dying with Christ is also a comfort and consolation (2 Cor 1:4; 4:7). To die is the same as to sleep in the Lord (1 Cor 15:18), and desired by the Christian so that the believer can be with Christ (Phil 1:23). The victory of Christ over death and all powers will be totally manifested only on the last day (1 Cor 15:26, 44 ff.).

# John

The Gospel of John uses different terminology but contains the same basic view of the doctrine of death as the writings of Paul. The person without Christ is dead. Sin and darkness in particular express the sense of death as seen by Paul. Death involves disbelief (John 1:9–11; 1 John 1:8), and so sin leads to death (John 8:21; 1 John 5:6). Death dominates where neither faith nor charity exists. The mission of Jesus liberates the world and destroys death. His followers continue this same mission (John 13:24). For through his death Jesus takes away sin and death (John 1:23; 1 John 2:2; 3:5; 4:9). John insists on the presence of eternal life: "...who believes has already passed from death to life" (John 5:24). And who observes the Word of Jesus will not die (John 8:51). The resurrection of Lazarus demonstrates the great victory over death (John 11:25). Such a life joins a life in charity in the present. Who hates his brother is a murderer (1 John 3:15) and is in death because he does not have life in him. One who loves has life (1 John 3:14).

# A Theology of Death as an Event of the Person

Death brings the personal *eschaton,* the end of the individual living humanly on this earth. But no one can be considered as only an individual. Death also involves the *eschaton* of the whole of humanity and of the universe. Since all live as children of the universe, a single death affects everyone and everything. Scripture clearly presents death as an eschatological fact of humanity and the universe. And since death as the end already now exists, death determines life and the universe itself. The end of all affects both the beginning of all and the living out of all and so the end of all.

The death of everything can be considered as biological, physiological, medical, philosophical and theological. All living things must die. As a natural fact death affects every living creature. At the same time, death occurs to all as both necessary and universal. All living things die reluctantly. Even plants and animals resist to the end the dying process. No living being has within itself a reason for dying. Why should living things die? Why can they not preserve the life and the potentials they have received?

From a natural standpoint, the human person possesses the highest level of life and the most to lose when faced with death. This belief immediately raises the question: What specifically differentiates human death from that of other life-forms? Somehow human death must differ from plant and animal death, whether considered biologically, philosophically, phenomenologically or theologically. People know they will die. Animals and plants do not. The thought of death affects the whole of human life. Death never seems so natural that people just accept it because they understand it. Rather it seems to contradict human reason. People want to live without end. So the necessity of dying and the lack of full understanding confound human reason and make death a theme frequently avoided, while at the same time the subject for inexhaustive treatment.

Theology considers the human person as a religious being existing in the presence of God. Thus death becomes a definitive eschatological fact in human life leading to God. Theology must explain what the meaning of the decisive event of human life in the presence of God means. Otherwise the final sense of death gets lost in the actual dying.

## The Person Dies at Death

Describing death as the separation of body and soul satisfies few. People want to understand more than that. Theology sees death as an event of human life, and somehow death relates to sin. So death must be understood as a personal act and event accepted and perfected in a personal way. Otherwise death becomes something external to the person. Since the person dies in death, then after death the human being no longer lives as a human being. The person functions as a natural unity of matter and spirit. Nothing in a person exists that is not both material and spiritual. This remains true even if someone says that the body makes a person mortal and the spirit makes a person immortal. The human being is not one or the other but both.

The Catholic Church teaches that the soul is immortal and exists as the principle or spirit in a person. But this does not mean that the person does not die in death since the person is more than spirit. Saying that the soul lives after death also cannot mean that the human being lives after death. If death destroys the unity of the person as body and spirit then the person dies, although the soul or spirit remains in existence. A human person must never be seen as a disembodied soul.

## Death Is Not Nonexistence

Any attempt to understand death reveals the total lack of precision in our terminology about death. Existence is composed of life, body and spirit. To describe nonlife or nonexistence does not begin to comprehend its significance. Certainly death brings the end of human life, but death should never be accepted as merely nonexistence. But then, what is death? The use of the term *person* can help to clarify this. Does death so destroy the person so that the person no longer transcends or goes beyond death? No. The person is not destroyed so that it no longer exists. Death means something personal, an event of the person. Death is something that the person does and must do. In death the person dies but does not cease to have a personal existence. Death diminishes the existence of the person in one sense and completes that existence in another. The person in death ought to give up the self totally so that in the moment of death he or she does have it in his or her power to dispose of self through a decision that makes the future unchangeable. The person never loses total existence.

## The Personification of Death

Motion pictures and novels often personify death. Such fantasies often cause more confusion than clarity. Death does not exist as a personal power, in the sense that God and people are personal powers. Death should not be viewed from a material standpoint. Nor is death a natural force existing in itself. Death is a direction or tension in every living thing. The New Testament personifies life, since the Gospel of John says that Jesus is life. But the same thing is not possible with death. In spite of the human tendency to personify what people do not know, death can never be identified with the devil or Satan. So death should be accepted as an event within the duration of human existence, an event that God places in life as author and in which the person has his or her own part.

## Death and the Giving of Self

Scripture recognizes only the death caused by sin. This involves accepting death as a natural aspect of humanity. Death belongs to creatureliness but also involves sin. Many authors both Catholic and Protestant (Karl Barth, Emil Brunner, P. Althaus, Karl Rahner and Ladislas Boris) think that, based on Scripture and philosophy, death pertains to the primordial order. Death comes to humanity from God as Creator, since humanity through death manifests both the distinction and the distance between God and people and the absolute dependence of humanity on God. In death God manifests ultimate power over humanity. In receiving and accepting death from God, people subject themselves to the power of God and honor God, whom they recognize as their Creator.

In the dying process, death as a moment of personal decision definitively and finally issues in a transition from a state of probation in life to full acceptance by God. The person moves from the possibility of accepting personal existence from God to the definitive state through the acceptance of the meaning of the person as related to God and a confirmation on the part of God. Death demands the willing giving over of personal possession and one's proper existence. Death extracts the terrible and irrational and horrible and painful giving up with the consciousness of no longer existing within an earthly sphere and with the experience and consciousness of the loss of oneself superseded by the hope of acceptance by God.

In death God definitively confirms the decision of the individual. But why did God demand a painful giving over of self? God offered the human race the blessing of a life well lived. The end could have been a giving in love, and it need not have been an unwilling and painful surrender. But the human race, perhaps inevitably, brought upon itself darkness and separation in death by choosing darkness and separation in life. An evil environment and personal sin hinder the free giving in love to another, and so these same human conditions hinder the final giving of love to another in dying.

## Death and Sin

The Bible offers some insight into the matter of death but never complete understanding. Even the Bible presents death as something terrible and horrible and irrational. And the Bible retains the note of personal decision in death. If Scripture somehow relates death to sin, this can be accepted even if death belongs naturally to all life. Death, the Bible teaches, exists because of a sinful act of Adam. Death now belongs to life as the consequence of an antecedent event in the history of humanity before God, which introduced sin. Death remains natural but now death has some overtones, which need not have been present.

Death includes the transition to a definitive state of decision. This transition becomes necessary because of creatureliness and the human personality. Because God freely created human beings and gave them freedom to choose, a person can accept that gift of life or can refuse it. God forces no one. What the individual determines through free decision, God accepts. But why should this be fully accomplished only in death? God could give new and fuller life without death. There seems no reason to have the painful necessity of death. Nor should anyone argue that God wishes to fill the person more abundantly only after that individual has gone through a painful giving up of self. This would be the same as saying that the person has to sin so that God can be merciful. Such a concept does not fully understand the notion of God as love.

Death as an event in the life of the person, as the Bible teaches, can be understood fully only with reference to sin. Death participates in the mystery of evil. People do not always understand that death should not be seen as primarily a penalty arbitrarily inflicted on people. Death should rather be seen primarily in relationship to sin, which is the refusal to live with God. The solidarity of humanity in sin relates to the solidarity of humanity in death. Original sin introduced the painful and terrible experience of death.

Death comes into the world on account of sin. This should be recognized by all who see the full historical dimension of humanity and its relationship to God. Humanity exists now affected by sin: the evil environment, personal sin and the lack of harmony within the self, with others and with God. The individual adds personal decision to sin and to death, and at death this lived decision becomes definitive. People die as they have lived.

## Death in the Light of the Death and Resurrection of Christ

Jesus united in himself the sinful flesh of humanity, admitting and recognizing the presence of sin, and destroyed the power of sin and then of death. As Son of God and human, Jesus accepted and perfected death, since he gave himself over to God the Father in his dying. He died as he lived: the faithful, loving and obedient Son of God. He disposed of himself totally as Son in the love of God. This contrasts with the alienation that humanity experienced face to face with God. Jesus experienced all the terrible effects of sin in his death—the darkness, the separation and isolation—and in dying gave himself totally to the Father in love.

Christians have been affected by this death so that they can see death as a totality present in life. Death also sums up the personal relationship to God. People must make their personal decision, the disposal of their lives as a definitive decision. The anxiety and trepidation still remains: Will this be a total giving over and will God accept it? In death the individual experiences both the necessity for the giving of self and the need for faith in giving and knowing that God accepts. Only in Christ can a person have the possibility of giving and the certitude of the acceptance of the person by God in death. Death as the *eschaton* of the person as sinner takes its meaning only from the life and death of Christ. Through and in Jesus believers know the experience of that total loss of self in the hour of death, which becomes the sign and the sacrament of the acceptance on the part of God. None can hope for full life except through belief that in the death in Christ, God has accepted all human life. Human death now conforms to the death of Jesus. So after the death of Jesus everyone can die in Christ by accepting the meaning of Jesus, but always in the obscurity of faith.

People can prepare for death. Since death brings the end, then death permeates life now. For believers baptism makes the death of Christ a reality. The Eucharist also relates to this death of believers because it celebrates the mystery of the death and resurrection of Christ and also the death of all that celebrate his presence. The Eucharist invites the giving of self in love and in the form of the sacrifice of life made in the mind and life of the Lord. This however will be fully manifested only in the full coming of the victorious Christ in the *eschaton* of the universe. So in the Eucharist Christians have the pledge of future glory and faith that death will be overcome. But all of this presupposes the self-disposal of self in life and then in death.

## Death Present in Life

Death as the *eschaton* of the person exists truly present in individual human history and in the history of all of humanity. Death is present in every moment when an individual makes a value judgment and especially in dying to oneself, which is the giving of self in life. Since no one knows the moment when death, the final and definitive value judgment, will come, people must pay attention to those moments in life when the other is accepted and loved and not just the self.

Single decisions of love and concern for others always involve decisions for the future. The decision here and now reflects the future and prepares for the final decision. Death sums up the life of the individual in the presence of God as the supreme value. In this the final decision takes place, but only in the sense that as the person lives, so the person will die.

## TOPICS FOR DISCUSSION AND STUDY

1. Why don't people like to think about death?
2. American culture celebrates youth. Why does this limit the culture?
3. Is belief in an afterlife necessary for religion?
4. What are your reactions to the general Jewish belief that a person lives on in children and in good deeds?
5. How can understanding original sin help us to understand death?
6. Is death present in every value judgment?
7. Are you afraid of dying?
8. What comforts you in studying death in the context of the death of Jesus?

# Works Consulted

Aune, D. E. "Eschatology (Early Christian)." *Anchor Bible Dictionary*. New York: Doubleday, 1992, vol. 2, 594–609.

Boris, Ladislaus. *The Mystery of Death*. New York: Herder and Herder, 1965.

Doss, Richard. *The Last Enemy: A Christian Understanding of Death*. New York: Harper and Row, 1974.

Gulley, Norman R. "Death." *Anchor Bible Dictionary*. New York: Doubleday, 1992, vol. 2, 108–11.

Kung, Hans. *Eternal Life? Life After Death as a Medical, Philosophical and Theological Problem*. New York: Doubleday, 1984.

Lewis, Theodore J. "Abode of the Dead." *Anchor Bible Dictionary*. New York: Doubleday, 1992, vol. 2, 101–5.

Nickelsberg, George W. E. "Eschatology (Early Jewish)." *Anchor Bible Dictionary*. New York: Doubleday, 1992, vol. 2, 579–94.

Nuland, Sherwin. *How We Die*. New York: Knopf, 1994.

Petersen, David L. "Eschatology (OT)." *Anchor Bible Dictionary*. New York: Doubleday, 1992, vol. 2, 575–79.

Phan, Peter C. *Eternity in Time: A Study of Karl Rahner's Eschatology*. Selinsgrove, Pa.: Susquehanna University Press, 1988.

Rahner, Karl. *On the Theology of Death*. New York: Herder and Herder, 1961.

Reddish, Mitchell G. "Heaven." *Anchor Bible Dictionary*. New York: Doubleday, 1992, vol. 3, 90–91.

Sachs, John. "Apocatastasis in Patristic Theology." *Theological Studies* 54 (1993): 617–40.

———. "Current Eschatology: Universal Salvation and the Problem of Hell." *Theological Studies* 52 (1991): 227–54.

# CHAPTER 13:
# HEAVEN, PURGATORY
# AND HELL

People want to know about heaven. Does it exist? Do all go to heaven? What is heaven like? Does going to heaven depend on what you have done in life? Like most questions about the future, no one really knows all the answers. The Bible gives some help, but even in the Scriptures, different and often conflicting images arise.

The form of this world will pass away (1 Cor 7:31). Some passages in the Bible see the end as catastrophic (Matt 24:35; Rev 21:10). In the Bible *heaven* and *earth* are terms that encompass the whole of the universe and indicate that somehow a complete transformation of the world as we now know it will take place. At present the universe suffers and struggles. Yet eventually all will be liberated (Rom 8:19).

## The Renewed Universe

The renewed universe involves not only all life-forms but also every aspect of creation. Just as the human race needs other living things in the present world, so will relationships with other living beings exist in the renewed universe. Creation, however, requires liberation from the exploitation that the human race has too often visited upon it. The future holds a movement toward fulfillment and perfection for the universe as well as for the human race.

Evil surely will be destroyed (Rev 7:17). This does not mean that the earth will be destroyed. The images of a catastrophic end in Mark 13 and other apocalyptic passages in the Bible employ literary forms and should never be taken literally. Would God destroy what is good? Goodness remains, but it will be transformed. The universe itself will become accessible to the human race in all its relationships and all its intelligible content. The renewed universe will reflect God and especially God's Son (Col 1:15). Whatever happens must involve more than the spiritual because people are embodied spirits.

The coming of the Lord, the resurrection to a fullness of life and the renewal of the universe will all come together. The last things function as one single unit, with humanity perfected and evil destroyed. The world exists to foster a unity between God and humanity; thus the whole world will be united and God will be all in all (1 Cor 15:28).

## Communion with God and Others

Heaven involves a community with God and people. The individual becomes open to all others. Personal growth, however, remains possible since without growth and development heaven would be less than human. Actually heaven means the giving of oneself into the incomprehensible mystery of God. Thus heaven "becomes" through a process that involves the universe—the physical as well as the spiritual.

Do all people experience the saving presence of God? Many early church fathers thought so. The New Testament remains ambivalent (Rom 5:12–21; 1 Cor 15:22; Eph 1:10; 1 Tim 2:4; 1 John 2:2; Matt 25:31–46). The Catholic traditions include both opinions: All will be saved or some will experience damnation.

## Judgment

Traditional Catholic teaching includes a particular judgment of the individual at death and a general judgment at the end of human history. Matthew 25:31–46 contains the foundation for this traditional belief. The king separates the sheep from the goats and proclaims: "As often as you did this to the least of my brethren you did it to me" (Matt 25:45). The Gospel of John teaches that anyone who has come to the light and believes "has eternal life; he does not come into judgment but has passed from death to life" (John 5:24). The New Testament contains references to both a future and a present judgment. The decision for Jesus in faith begins the final judgment, which God fulfills in the definitive decision for God in the actual dying process. With belief in Christ the individual need not fear any future judgment. The future flows from the present life of faith.

## Purgatory

Traditionally most Catholics think of purgatory as a place or condition in the next world where the souls of those who die in the state of grace but who are not yet free from all imperfection must expiate unforgiven venial sins and endure the temporal punishment due to sins. Once purified, they can enter into heaven.

The scriptural bases for belief in purgatory are at least dubious: 2 Maccabees 12:39–45; Matthew 12:32 and 1 Corinthians 3:10–15. Historically, several synods and councils of the Church dealt with purgatory, especially Trent. These councils seem to imply that the punishment due to sin must be enacted, and the soul can be helped by prayer and good works. Although established in popular imagery, the fires of purgatory are not part of the official teaching of the Catholic Church. Most recently, the Holy Father John Paul II refers to the images of fire in purgatory and hell as just that, images, which must not be taken literally.

## The Purifying Process

The Church clearly teaches the need for a purifying process. Even the use of the word *punishment* misleads since God does not exact a vindictive penalty. Rather, a medicinal process takes place. Perhaps purgatory should be seen as a full tutoring in the love of God. In dying a person must experience the painful process of separation with the hope that the end ushers in a life with God. If a person, in life, has given of himself or herself to others, then the process of purification and of tutoring in the love of God must of necessity be less painful. The one trusting too much in self must go through the sense of pain and darkness trusting in another. The Catholic teaching on purgatory may in fact be a fuller explanation of the dying process.

But, then, how can prayers help? Since death means the passing into a definitive mode of existence, passing from time into eternity, the prayers of others in life may affect the person as he or she dies. In dying the person becomes fully free, surrounded by the love of others. The same love can affect what happened as one passed out of time.

## Hell

An individual may freely reject God. A person can refuse the saving presence of God in life and in death. Hell means this refusal. All else are images. Loss characterizes hell. Being alone, belonging to oneself epitomizes hell. Idle speculations on the actual nature of hell offer nothing. As already mentioned, hell fire should always be understood as an image that expresses the pain of loss and separation, not as actual fire.

## Biblical Teaching

The Old Testament, with its concept of Sheol, provided the foundation for the Christian understanding of hell. The spirits of the dead live on in the underworld. Whether one had been good or bad in life, the underworld was no great place. In later Old Testament theology the fire of judgment burning in the valley of Hinnom (both a place of abomination where human sacrifice took place and a city dump where the burning of refuse was constant) influenced the notion of real fire.

Jesus, like the Baptist before him, spoke of hell as a place of eternal punishment prepared for all who rejected salvation (Matt 25:41). Hell means the punishment of unbelief and the refusal to repent (Matt 5:29; 13:42). The New Testament uses images of fire (Matt 5:22) and darkness (8:12; 25:30) that surely in themselves are contradictory. Paul speaks of hell abstractly as eternal destruction and loss (2 Thess 1:9; Rom 9:22; Phil 3:19; 2 Thess 2:10). The New Testament centers on the refusal to believe rather than on any actual punishment.

Any interpretation of hell based on the Bible must be viewed from within the framework of the literary discourse that was intended to threaten its listeners. We must not presume that these biblical images constitute a factual preview of what may come in the future or what actually exists today. *Hell* is a word for the possibility of failure in life, such that some individuals can be estranged from God in every dimension of their existence.

## The Theology of Hell

The biblical texts do not concern themselves with the number of persons who have suffered estrangement from God. The Bible speaks rather of the universal salvific will of God and the redemption by Christ, which has affected all people. Individuals hope in salvation, yet are always mindful of the possibility of nonsalvation.

The eternity of hell comes from the nature of freedom. God forces no one to accept redemption and salvation. But freedom also brings with it the possibility of constant revisions of decisions. Eternity does not mean the continued duration of time but rather the definitive achievement of time and history by the individual and ultimately of the human race. If a person has reached a definitive state by free choice, then in that state the person will remain.

Like heaven, hell begins on earth in the refusal to believe. People can accept or reject the Lord Jesus. The meaning of hell involves pain—not physical pain but the pain of loss and the awareness of the possibility of an eternal contradiction. People are made for God, and if a person freely rejects God then the internal contradiction occurs. The Catholic Church teaches the possibility of definitive rejection of God on the part of an individual but does not teach whether this possibility has ever happened.

## TOPICS FOR DISCUSSION AND STUDY

1. How are people judged while alive?
2. If heaven is not a place but rather the eternal human fulfillment, what does heaven mean humanly?
3. The Church teaches the existence of purgatory. Can this be in fact the dying process?
4. Hell does not mean eternal fire but eternal separation.
5. Heaven begins on earth, already but not yet. How does this affect people?
6. Why do people not want to think about an afterlife?
7. People die as they live. Is this true?

# Works Consulted

Fortman, Edmund. *Everlasting Life after Death.* New York: Alba, 1976.

Klinger, Elmar. "Purgatory." *Sacramentum Mundi.* New York: Herder and Herder 1967–69, vol.5, 166–68.

Kreeft, Pete. *Everything You Wanted to Know about Heaven...But Never Dreamed of Asking.* San Francisco: Ignatius Press, 1990.

Lachenschmid, Robert. "Hell." *Sacramentum Mundi.* New York: Herder and Herder, 1967–69, vol. 3, 7–10.

Phan, Peter. *Responses to 101 Questions on Death and Eternal Life.* Mahwah, N.J.: Paulist Press, 1997.

Sachs, John. "Apocatastasis in Patristic Theology." *Theological Studies* 54 (1993): 617–40.

———. "Current Eschatology: Universal Salvation and the Problem of Hell." *Theological Studies* 52 (1991): 227–54.

# CHAPTER 14:
# CONSCIENCE IN
# CATHOLIC TRADITION

Catholic belief and tradition teach a primacy of individual conscience. Individuals must eventually make an accounting of their lives, and no book, law, priest, bishop, pope or anyone else can substitute for the one to whom God has given the gift of life. Certainly in the Catholic tradition individual Catholics must pay attention to laws and regulations and listen to the primary teachers, but ultimately people make their own decisions and accept the responsibility for their actions. The ultimate decision to obey any type or manifestation of authority or to accept another's ability to influence thought, opinion or behavior rests upon a personal decision of conscience. With each expression of authority and every exercise of power the encounter between two individuals or an individual and the community demands a personal acceptance through a moral decision. Any failure to apply personal conscience abdicates a responsibility primarily owed to the self, but often to the group as well, and ultimately to God.

Some people question whether conscience really exists. For centuries both scholars and individuals with no academic background have debated the existence of conscience—its origin and function and its authority. Many people are aware of psychological/spiritual reflexes, but are such experiences instinctive or are they the result of some economic necessity or a learned superego? Even if some admit conscience as an awareness of moral responsibility, do people learn it from society or family or is conscience part of the individual's experience, dependent upon some objective moral order? At least most people will admit that at times they transcend themselves and act in favor of others. This forms the basis for understanding conscience.

Conscience is neither a feeling nor a confirmed judgment. A person most fundamentally experiences the self as a moral agent transcending ordinary concerns of self-centeredness, aware of the interaction with others and drawn to making a choice. Christians might also see conscience as the most fundamental experience of the self, as a new creation in Christ Jesus. The individual believer has experienced the Spirit, which will affect not just the personal and isolated individual life but also the social and communitarian life.

## Conscience in the Old Testament

The Old Testament does not offer a systematic presentation on conscience. The idea is interwoven with authority and freedom and cannot always be clearly distinguished from them. As a result, no univocal meaning for conscience exists in the Hebrew Scriptures, but several forms of what people call conscience find expression in the Old Testament. Perhaps it would be better to view conscience in the Old Testament as related to the Hebrew word for heart, *leb*. Several uses of the word *leb* will give the reader a "feeling" for its meaning even if an accurate definition remains elusive.

> The king's heart is a stream of water in the hand of the Lord; he turns it wherever he will. Every way of a man is right in his own will. Every way of a man is right in his own eyes but the Lord weighs the heart.
>
> (Prov 21:1-2)

> Prove me O Lord and try me. Test my heart and mind.
>
> (Ps 26:2)

> Then David arose and cut off the skirt of Saul's robe. And afterward David's heart smote him because he had cut off Saul's skirt.
>
> (1 Sam 24:4-5)

> Do not give heed to all the things that men say, lest you hear
> your servant cursing you; your heart knows that many times
> you have yourself cursed others.
>
> (Qoh 7:22)

Like most ancient peoples, the Hebrews did not make a clear distinction between physical and psychic powers, and attributed psychological and spiritual functions to certain parts of the body. The heart was the chief organ of the body, the core of individual life and the ultimate source for the physical, emotional, intellectual and volatile energies. The heart enabled the individual to make contact with the religious and the divine. In the heart dwell the plans, fears, hopes and expectations of the person, and these form the character of the individual.

The heart is the wellspring of the intellectual life as well as the ethical and volitional life. Readers of the Bible can understand these aspects of Hebrew thought only when they realize that they rest upon the most fundamental tenet of the Judaic creed: the individual's relationship to God. The heart of the person is open to God and subject to God's influence. God looks in a person's heart and the heart speaks to God (Ps 27:8). God is able to harden the heart, as he did to Pharaoh in the Exodus (Exod 4:21). The Old Testament knew that the heart of humankind turned to evil as well as good, and the hope for overcoming the evil that dwelt in the heart was the hope for a divine intervention. Eventually God himself would write the law in the hearts of people (Jer 31:33). God would remove the heart of stone and exchange it for heart of flesh (Ezek 36:26; 24:7). God's people would then be completely attuned to their Creator. They would no longer need some external law to bind them to their Creator, but their very being would be receptive to the presence of God and God would dwell in their hearts.

Many examples from the Old Testament depict the heart as the seat of the volitional and moral life. If the heart forms the center of the intellectual life, then it is only a natural conclusion to see how the heart affects the decisions of the individual. The good heart is blameless (Ps 119:80) and upright (Ps 32:11). The evil heart plots wicked deeds (Prov 6:18) and may even become godless (Job 36:13). Other uses of the word *heart* in the Old Testament show the heart as the seat of both the emotions and the intellect. The complete psychic life centered on the heart, as did the physical life. But in all of these instances, the Hebrew faith recognized a close relationship between God and the believer, and the point of contact was the heart. The evil heart was so heinous because the very source of the religious and divine life had become perverted and became the contact point with evil.

The Catholic notion of conscience appears in four modes in the Old Testament:

1. Conscience is the remorse of the heart from an awareness of having done something wrong (Wis 17:10).
2. God himself can function as a conscience for the nation (Jer 11:20; Prov 21:2).
3. Prophets can act as the conscience of the nation (Ezek 11:14–21; Jer 31:31–34).
4. Centering specifically on morality, in the future, God will write the law on people's hearts. Morality will become internalized (Jer 31:33; 32:39; Ezek 37:14).

Although the understanding of conscience in Jewish thought incorporates religion as well as Greek philosophy, fundamentally the meaning reaches back to the ancient meaning of *heart:* the locus of personal contact with the divine. The primacy of individual conscience rests upon the personal relationship that exists between God and the individual. Such an appreciation gives the individual the responsibility to deal with authority and laws and regulations and power according to the dictates of personal conscience.

# The New Testament

The New Testament continues the understanding of heart as found in the Hebrew Scriptures. Jesus, in Matthew, quotes Isaiah's statement that the people's hearts are far from God (Matt 15:11). The first beatitude in Matthew emphasizes the meaning of *heart* in relationship to God but also as significant in personal decisions: "Blessed are the single-hearted, for they shall see God" (Matt 5:8). The author of First John also contributes to the understanding of heart and conscience in the New Testament.

> This is our way of knowing we are committed to the truth and are at peace before him no matter what our consciences may charge us with: for God is greater than our hearts and all is known to him. Beloved, if our consciences have nothing to charge us with, we can be sure that God is with us.
>
> (1 John 3:19–21)

The gospel writers as well as the author of First John offer insights into the Christian meaning of conscience but the full development comes from Paul. Paul starts with the Greek word *syneidesis* (conscience), which had several connotations:

1. Conscience is a human faculty and part of human nature.
2. God or gods implanted conscience in the human person.
3. Conscience relates to a person's actual deeds.
4. Paul treats specifically consequent conscience, which often causes pain, rather than antecedent conscience. This means that God has so constituted human nature that people who go beyond the moral limits established by their nature will sense the pain of conscience.

The term occurs first in 1 Corinthians 8:7, which deals with the controversy of eating food offered to idols. Paul admonishes the strong that they need not abstain, but should consider the consciences of the weak. In 1 Corinthians 10:25 Paul states that the strong are not to be fettered in their freedom by the weak. In Romans 13:5 Paul admonished his listeners to obey the state and avoid the pains of conscience. It seems that conscience for Paul has almost become a regulative principle, which raises the question of the relationship between conscience and mind or reason. In Romans 2:14–15 Paul distinguishes:

1. The law written in the heart
2. Conscience
3. Reason

> They [Gentiles] show that what the law requires is written on
> their hearts, while their conscience also bears witness and
> their conflicting thoughts accuse or perhaps excuse them
> on that day when according to my gospel, God judges the
> secrets of men by Christ Jesus.
>
> (Rom 2:15)

In Romans 14:5, however, the mind seems to have taken the
place of conscience as found in 1 Corinthians 8:10. In 1 Corinthians 10:28–29 conscience appears to pass judgment not only on
the individual but on the acts of others. Every person is endowed
with a sense of moral discernment, which enables the individual
to assess the conduct of others in the sight of God.

Paul borrowed his understanding of conscience from his
opponents at Corinth. He did not, however, always emphasize its
importance because he believed that the ultimate court of appeal
is Jesus himself. Conscience, like the person who possesses it, is
open to conflicting influences. Like the spirit of the individual,
it must be enlightened by the Spirit of Jesus. Conscience was not
a fully examined concept for Paul and, although he contributes
to its clarification, he remains inconsistent in his usage.

The word *conscience* also appears in 1 Peter, the Pastorals and
Hebrews. In 1 Peter 2:19 it may simply mean "consciousness." In
the Pastorals the author relates conscience to faith (1 Tim 1:5, 19;
3:9; 4:2). The Christian life depends upon faith and good conscience. To cast away the latter will cause the collapse of the former.
In the Pastorals, the attitude of the weak has become a menace to
the community, and in conscience the attitude should be opposed.
Some seem to think that in the Pastorals conscience has become
domesticated, due to the need for an intermediate ethic as the
believers prepare for the final coming of the Lord, now long
delayed. Such a notion fails to recognize the close relationship
between conscience and the life of faith. Christianity does not
become static as the Church settles into history. This becomes particularly evident in the use of the term *conscience* in Hebrews.

In Hebrews 9:14 conscience has an accusing function and in
Hebrews 10:22 the author speaks of a wicked conscience. In
Hebrews 9:9 the old sacrifices have no relationship to where a

person confronts God's holiness, that is, conscience or the person's heart, recalling the Old Testament concept. Throughout Hebrews the author directs conscience toward God, not in a moralistic sense but in a theological sense. The understanding of conscience in these passages, taken from Hellenism, joins the more fundamental understanding as found in the Old Testament concept of heart. The combination of both elements offers to moralists complementary ideas, which they use in offering a systematic presentation of conscience.

## Thomas Aquinas

The thirteenth-century scholar Thomas Aquinas has several important ideas to contribute to the Catholic understanding of conscience.

1. Conscience is the judgment act of reason.
2. Conscience binds because reason is the best recourse to what is right.
3. Conscience influences action by guiding prudence.
4. Thinking and reasoning well and the immanent effect of that reasoning forms conscience. Both thinking and reasoning require investigating the matter and paying attention to authority.
5. Wisdom is the virtue of conscience.

Such a development of conscience has gone far beyond the understanding of heart in the Old Testament and even beyond the New Testament. Aquinas, like Paul, was influenced by Greek philosophy, but in this case the philosopher was Aristotle. In subsequent centuries, until recently, Catholic teaching on conscience rested primarily on the thought of Thomas Aquinas.

## Contemporary Moral Theology

Contemporary moralists distinguish various levels of meaning in conscience. St. Jerome, through a faulty translation from the Greek, distinguished between *syneidesis* as an act of conscience and *synderesis* as the habit of conscience. Although no such distinction exists in the New Testament, the mistranslation effectively coined the word *synderesis,* which proves helpful for theology today. Vatican II viewed conscience as that which summons believers to love good and avoid evil. The most helpful distinctions go further and offer three distinct meanings for conscience:

1. The sense of value and personal responsibility.
2. The judgment deciding what is right and wrong.
3. The decision itself.

While this may be helpful in a careful analysis of difficult moral decisions, it seems insufficient for day-to-day application.

Karl Rahner's analysis of conscience speaks of a "moral instinct of faith," an almost intuitive knowledge of right and wrong in an individual's belief. On this basis people of faith can make judgments and moral decisions. This religious awareness seems part of the Judeo-Christian experience, traceable to the Old Testament. Part of this religious consciousness, some contemporary moralists say, is a sense of value and personal choice.

Individuals created in the image of God retain vestiges of God in their person. The individual becomes aware of the nearness of God, which in turn will influence decisions—not just the momentous moral decisions of life but the various value judgments that occur every day. When an individual has this "feel" for God, it informs the ultimate criteria for obedience. Rahner remarks that the discernment of the Spirit is fundamental to making value judgments in life. Often, individual believers have acted contrary to the established authority because their consciences, the result of both their creation by God and their personal experiences of God or the Spirit of God, enabled them to make personal decisions without reference to some external authority.

Can conscience change? Since all decisions are partial and incomplete, development can occur in personal conscience. Since the roots of conscience lie in the relationship between the individual and God and since all admit of development in this relationship, an individual's value judgments will be affected by his or her unfolding relationship with God. At times, people even have to make compromises with regard to conscience. Since not all of us are on the same relationship level with God and since none of us has a constant and complete grasp of the implications of the God relationship, conscience changes and needs continuous evaluation. As people change in their understanding of God and as this relationship develops, so will a person's conscience change.

Every individual exists within a community, with corresponding responsibilities, and every individual bears the responsibility for personal life decisions. In a Christian context the relationship that already exists with God helps the believer both personally and as a member of the community. Both develop as the person remains open to the presence of God. Always, however, individual conscience, the experience of self as a moral agent, rests on the more fundamental understanding of conscience from the Bible: the relationship to God. Such a relationship stands the individual in good stead as he or she faces the various options offered in the ordinary experience of life. No understanding of authority and in particular no exercise of power coming from the community or its representative can ever ignore the primacy of the individual conscience in a personal life.

The existence of the individual in community demands an authority, but one that must always recognize its limitations. Through personal conscience, in particular the awareness of the relationship to God, an individual responds to the presence of authority and the exercise of power. Those who exercise authority in the Church must always take into consideration the primacy of conscience just as Jesus respected the conscience of his followers. The individual in the Church recognizes the need for authority but also remains faithful to personal conscience.

## The Formation of Conscience

In Catholic tradition the formation of conscience involves both external authority and internal control. Moral decisions rest on making choices on the basis of reason, taking into consideration both who the person is and what and how the person chooses. Conscience involves character development, and for a Christian this includes the acceptance of the presence of the Holy Spirit in a person's life. A spiritual life assists in the formation of conscience, which in the Catholic tradition includes a frequent reception of the sacraments, in particular, the sacrament of penance.

A personal formation of conscience does not occur in a vacuum. The Catholic also pays attention to the teachings of the Church. Every individual needs help in seeking the truth. The Church's accumulated wisdom, along with the promise of the Spirit, offers some assurance to the individual in a quandary. The traditions of the Church, along with the rituals, images and language of the Christian community, give guidance to the individual as he or she makes the moral decisions that affect a person's life. Any serious moral decision includes an analysis of the situation, a questioning of who is involved, where and when and why and how. Evidently, alternatives exist in life, which make for moral heart-searching. The Christian seeks a formation of conscience, deeply aware of the presence of God through the Spirit of God given to all by Jesus, and aware as well of the need to live fully within the Christian community.

## Individual Conscience and Church Teaching

Contemporary American Catholics differ considerably from the Catholics who preceded them and from whom they received their Catholic upbringing. People will admit that they must always seek to do what is right and avoid what is wrong. If a person sincerely believes that he or she should do or avoid something, he or she must so act. In moral theology the Catholic Church has avoided making any infallible statements. Recently some Vatican officials seem to teach that the present pope has done so in his encyclical: *Veritatis Splendor.* No universal agreement in this matter exists, however. Every Catholic moralist will admit that the Church can never speak to the totality of the concrete situation in which a person finds himself or herself. Objective morality may exist, but only in the abstract and not in the concrete life of a person. It is the

Catholic tradition that a person must always follow his or her conscience even if it is erroneous.

Catholics must always take into consideration church teaching, and in most cases, even though open to revision and reevaluation, the teachings of the Church should be given presumptive authority. In fact on certain matters, especially matters of human sexuality and reproduction, many American Catholics differ considerably from official church teaching. These American Catholics are not laxists, nor half-hearted Catholics. They are good and decent people who adhere to their faith with a powerful commitment and yet in conscience differ from the teachings of the Church. Since ultimately they must render an account of their lives, they have to live with themselves in peace. If, after every effort to seek guidance and wisdom, they make a decision in conscience to act contrary to church teaching, they are obliged to follow their conscience, even if erroneous.

## TOPICS FOR DISCUSSION AND STUDY

1. Why is individual conscience primary in matters of morality?
2. What elements from the Old Testament help in understanding conscience?
3. What elements from the New Testament help in understanding Christian conscience?
4. How do you react to the contemporary understanding of conscience in moral theology?
5. How can one try to live with an informed conscience?
6. What happens when in conscience a person disagrees with church teaching?
7. Can the sacrament of penance help in forming conscience?

# Works Consulted

Baum, Gregory. *Theology and Society.* Mahwah, N.J.: Paulist Press, 1988.

Behm, Johannes. "Kardia (heart)." *Theological Dictionary of the New Testament.* Grand Rapids: Eerdmans, 1964, vol. 3, 605–14.

Bonsor, Jack. "Homosexual Orientation and Anthropology: Reflections on the Category 'Objective Disorder.'" *Theological Studies* 59 (1998): 60–83.

Cahill, Lisa. *Between the Sexes.* Philadelphia: Fortress, 1985.

Coleman, Gerald. "The Vatican Statement on Homosexuality." *Theological Studies* 48 (1987): 727–34.

Collins, Raymond. *Christian Morality, Biblical Foundations.* Notre Dame, Ind.: Notre Dame University Press, 1986.

Connery, John. *Abortion: The Development of the Roman Catholic Perspective.* Chicago: Loyola University Press, 1977.

Curran, Charles E. *The Catholic Moral Tradition Today.* Washington, D.C.: Georgetown University Press, 1999.

Dedek, John. *Contemporary Sexual Morality.* New York: Sheed and Ward, 1971.

Dorr, Donal. *Option for the Poor: A Hundred Years of Vatican Social Teaching.* Maryknoll, N.Y.: Orbis, 1983.

Fabry, H. J. "Leb (heart)." *Theological Dictionary of the Old Testament.* Grand Rapids: Eerdmans, 1964, vol. 4, 399–437.

Genovesi, Vincent J. *In Pursuit of Love: Catholic Morality and Human Sexuality.* Wilmington, Del.: Michael Glazier, 1987.

Greeley, Andrew. "Sex and the Single Catholic." *Sex: The Catholic Experience.* Chicago: Thomas More, 1994.

Haight, Roger. "The Mission of the Church in the Theology of the Social Gospel." *Theological Studies* 49 (1988): 477–97.

Himes, Kenneth, and James Coriden. "Pastoral Care of the Divorced and Remarried." *Theological Studies* 57 (1996): 97–123.

Hofmann, Rudolf. "Conscience." *Sacramentum Mundi.* New York: Herder and Herder, 1967–69, vol 1, 411–14.

Lawler, Michael G. *Secular Marriage, Christian Sacrament.* Mystic, Conn.: Twenty-Third Publications, 1985.

Lawler, Ronald, Joseph Boyle, and William May. *Catholic Sexual Ethics.* Huntington, Ind.: Our Sunday Visitor Press, 1985.

Mackin, Theodore. *What Is Marriage?* Mahwah, N.J.: Paulist Press, 1982.

Mac Namara, Vincent. "Approaching Christian Morality." *Contemporary Catholic Theology.* Trowbridge, U.K.: Cromwell Press, 1998, 374–88.

Maurer, Christian. "*Sundoida, suneidaesis* (Conscience)." *Theological Dictionary of the New Testament.* Grand Rapids: Eerdmans, 1964, vol. 7, 889–919.

McCarthy, Timothy G. *The Catholic Tradition: Before and After Vatican II.* Chicago: Loyola University Press, 1994.

McGoldrick, Terence. "Episcopal Conferences Worldwide on Catholic Social Teaching." *Theological Studies* 59 (1998): 22–50.

O'Callaghan, Denis F. "What's Special about Christian Morality?" *Contemporary Catholic Theology.* Trowbridge, U.K.: Cromwell Press, 1998, 369–73.

O'Connell, Timothy. "The History of Moral Theology." *Contemporary Catholic Theology.* Trowbridge, U.K.: Cromwell Press, 1998, 389–402.

————. *Principles for a Catholic Morality.* San Francisco: Harper and Row, 1990.

Orsy, Ladislas. "Magisterium: Assent and Dissent." *Theological Studies* 48 (1987): 473–97.

————. "Marriage Annulments: An Interview with Ladislas Orsy." *America* 177 (1997): 10–18.

Otten, Willemien. "Augustine on Marriage, Monasticism and the Community of the Church." *Theological Studies* 59 (1998): 385–405.

Pope, Stephen J. "The Order of Love and Recent Catholic Ethics: A Constructive Proposal." *Theological Studies* 52 (1991): 255–88.

Rahner, Karl. "The Church's Commission to Bring Salvation and the Humanization of the World." *Theological Investigations.* New York: Seabury, 1976, vol. 14, 295–313.

————. "Concerning the Relationship between Nature and Grace." *Theological Investigations.* London: Darton, Longman and Todd, 1961, vol. 1, 297–318.

————. *The Dynamic Element in the Church.* New York: Herder and Herder, 1964.

Rausch, Thomas P. "Sexual Morality and Social Justice." *Contemporary Catholic Theology.* Trowbridge, U.K.: Cromwell Press, 1998, 403–33.

Schussler-Fiorenza, Francis. *Foundational Theology.* New York: Crossroad, 1985.

Wall, Robert W. "Conscience." *Anchor Bible Dictionary.* New York: Doubleday, 1992, vol. 1, 1128–30.

# CHAPTER 15:
# CATHOLIC MORALITY

Catholic morality differs from Christian morality based upon the sources for this moral teaching. Sexual and social morality is not treated extensively in the New Testament, whether in the teachings of Jesus in the gospels or in the other later writings. Many Christian churches attempt to base their moral teaching on the New Testament alone. The Catholic Church, however, also uses the principle of natural law. While many descriptions of natural law exist, in general it can be described as reason's reflection on human experience discovering moral value. The Catholic Church believes that it can teach a morality valid for every time, place and circumstance precisely because it relies on natural law as well as scriptural tradition as a dual foundation. The natural law tradition offers moral guidance, not just to believers but to all people who honestly and critically reflect on human experience.

The Bible, however, offers some foundation for morality and even for natural law. In the Wisdom tradition the lived experience of peoples gives guidance and direction for what does or does not work humanly. In his parables Jesus uses this Wisdom approach. Paul also makes use of nature in dealing with morality. Critical reflection on lived experience in the biblical tradition can give some moral guidance, additional sources are needed. Catholic morality rests on both Scripture and the human capacity to know and choose what is right and good. But since natural law rests more on the evaluation of human conduct, it has never produced a single philosophical and moral system yielding a clear and consistent code of ethics. Neither the Bible nor natural law can offer answers for every individual in every instance.

## Sacred Scripture

> For the Son of man also came not to be served but to serve
> and to give his life as a ransom for many.
>
> (Mark 10:45)

The gospels clearly present the mission of Jesus. He was concerned with the reign of God, with people coming to faith and recognizing the presence of God in himself. Jesus taught and healed, both physically and mentally; he forgave sins and drove out evil. His life's ministry focused on responding to the needs of others, yet was always aimed at helping people to delvelop a better relationship to God. The mission of Jesus was both natural and supernatural. These two dimensions coexisted without distinction. No dichotomy separated the natural and supernatural, the sacred and the profane. The love of God permeated the love of people, and the love of people permeated the love of God. Jesus' mission certainly included moral behavior. Loving God includes loving others and living in peace and harmony with others.

To be a follower of Jesus surely includes the interpersonal and social dimensions of life. Sexual and social morality form part of the heritage of the Catholic Church. Yet the Church's positions in both these areas often cause confusion, anger and resentment among Catholics today, especially in the United States. Issues of human reproduction and intimacy as well as social justice may divide Catholics as often as they unite them. Birth control, divorce, premarital sex, homosexuality, abortion, the death penalty, war, racism and segregation, equal rights and pay for women—all are moral issues, but very few American Catholics accept without hesitation every official position of the Catholic Church on each of them.

# Sexual Morality

The Catholic Church has always taught that human sexuality is God's gift to the human race for the purposes of mutual love and bringing new life into this world. The encyclical *Casti Connubii* (1930) of Pius XI and the Pastoral Constitution on the Church in the Modern World (*[Gaudium et Spes]* nos. 47–52) emphasize the centrality of conjugal love and the positive understanding of sexual relationships in marriage. In the history of the Church, however, some theologians have conveyed an image of sex as at least unseemly, tolerated only because it brings children into the world but never to be used for pure human pleasure. The official Church, following the traditions drawn from the Bible, conveys no ambiguity about sexual pleasure. The Song of Songs celebrates the erotic love of a man and woman. Jesus, when tempted by the pleasure of food in the gospels of Matthew and Luke, responds that "Not by bread alone does a person live (Matt 4:4; Luke 4:4)." Pleasure, even sexual pleasure, is good, but it is not the end and purpose of life. In Mark and Luke Jesus does not approve of divorce. Matthew modifies this teaching by his famous exclusion clause: except on the grounds of *porneia* (*porneia* is left untranslated because no one is quite sure of the meaning of the word [Matt 5:32]). Paul sees marriage as a gift from God and allows an exception for divorce (1 Cor 7:15). Certain sexual acts, however, are condemned in the Bible—adultery: Levi 20:10; Genesis 39:9; Mark 7:22; Matthew 5:28; 1 Corinthians 6:9; fornication: Sirach 42:10; Deuteronomy 22:13–21; 1 Corinthians 5:9–11; 7:22; 1 Corinthians 12:21; Galatians 5:19; homosexual acts: Leviticus 18:22; 20:13; Romans 1:27; 1 Corinthians 6:9. The scriptural authors see such acts as incompatible with a life of faith. The Bible, however, does not offer any systematic code of sexual ethics. The general principle seems to be: live who you are, a blessed, graced, redeemed person of faith. Morality flows from the graced and redeemed person and not vice versa. Because God has loved people in the gift of Jesus, so people should live expressing who they are rather than trying to live a moral life so that God might love them.

# Augustine and Sexual Morality

Few theologians have had such a profound influence on Catholic theology as Augustine (354–430), bishop of Hippo. His teachings on the Trinity and grace have rarely been surpassed and can never be ignored. His teachings on original sin and especially on sexual morality, however, leave the reader in some confusion. Augustine often espoused a rigorist approach in the area of morality. God would not command impossible moral standards for anyone. Pius XI used this principle in condemning contraception in 1930, and John Paul II cited it in his encyclical *Veritatis Splendor* in 1993. Augustine joined this principle to his own understanding of sexual activity. After the Fall of Adam and Eve he viewed human sexuality as dominated by *libido, voluptas* and *concupiscentia*. He describes *libido* as shameful stirring of the sexual organs. Augustine says that the fluid *(semen)* of both men and women is aroused and released by *voluptas*, which is of course sinful. *Concupiscentia* seems to refer to the body's tendency toward rebellion, its refusal to obey the command of the will. The combination of the three, all stemming from the sin of Adam, causes problems in any sexual activity. Marriage and sexual intercourse are a good but only in the sense that they bring about a good, which is friendship. Augustine did not view the good of marriage to be the friendship between the couple but, rather, the procreation of children, which will bring others into friendship with God. For Augustine, God wills that humans use their sexuality for the sole purpose of conceiving a child. Since rarely can an individual limit the motivation for sexual relations solely to that of conceiving a child, Augustine's implication is that even Christian parents can sin at least venially in their expression of genital sexuality.

Following Augustine, medieval moralists taught that marital intercourse for pleasure and not for procreation was either always mortally sinful (according to the rigorists) or at least venially sinful (the opinion of other theologians). Pope Gregory the Great shared Augustine's opinion that, because of *concupiscentia*, even that genital pleasure between spouses in the act of procreation is sinful. In the seventeenth century the Holy

Office declared that every transgression on matters of sexuality was always objective serious matter constituting mortal sin. This traditional teaching on sexual morality became the accepted norm for many down to the Second Vatican Council, even if not always followed. The council, as already noted, in *Gaudium et Spes*, returned to a more biblical tradition of marriage and sexuality.

> The biblical Word of God several times urges the betrothed and the married to nourish and develop their wedlock by pure conjugal love and undivided affection....The love is an eminently human one since it is directed from one person to another through an affection of the will....This love the Lord has judged worthy of special gifts, healing, perfecting, and exalting gifts of grace and charity.
>
> (no. 49)

The sexual revolution of the sixties and seventies affected American Catholics and their thoughts on matters of sexuality. The movement from an immigrant Church to a well-educated Church also influenced what American Catholics would accept and what they would reject in personal matters of sexual morality. Today many American Catholics disagree with their Church on most issues of sexual morality, in spite of the efforts of the hierarchy to teach clearly and definitively in regulating personal sexual acts. The declarations of pope and bishops are ignored by many American Catholics even as they maintain a deep respect and commitment to Church, pope and bishops.

In 1976 the Congregation for the Doctrine of the Faith published a Declaration on Certain Questions Concerning Sexual Ethics. The document reaffirmed traditional Catholic teaching based on natural law and listed those teachings that have an absolute and immutable value (no. 4). Every genital act must be within the framework of marriage (no. 7). The document singled out masturbation, premarital sex and homosexual acts and reaffirmed the traditional understanding of all such sins as constituting serious sin. Every direct violation of this order of nature is objectively serious (no. 10). Then the document adds a pastoral note:

> It must be admitted, of course, that in sexual sins, because of
> their nature and causes, fully free consent may be readily
> lacking. Consequently prudence and caution are needed in
> passing any judgment on an individual's responsibility....
> Yet, while prudence is advisable in judging the the subjec-
> tive seriousness of an individually sinful act, it by no means
> follows that we may think no mortal sins are committed in
> matters of sex.

(no. 10)

Most American Catholics did not even know that such a declaration came from the Vatican and continued to think as previously.
For people in pastoral ministry, the document clearly taught the
seriousness of sexual sins but then added the need for pastoral
sensitivity when dealing with an individual sinner.

## Divorce, Annulments and Remarriage

Jesus opposed all divorce. At least this is the teaching found in
Mark and Luke (Mark 10:2–12; Luke 16:18). Matthew adds an
exception clause, as already noted, on the ground of *porneia*
(Matt 5:32). Paul allows for a divorce if a believer marries an
unbeliever and the unbeliever will not live in peace with the
believer (1 Cor 7:12–16). The Catholic Church also allows for
divorce and remarriage if the marriage is not consummated. The
Catholic Church admits of exceptions with regard to divorce.
Certainly being able to determine the true meaning of *porneia*
would help, but over the years the word has been translated vari-
ously as unchastity, fornication, adultery and unlawful union.
Different English Bibles use different English words to translate
this one Greek word. Whatever the meaning, it seems that the
church of Matthew recognized an exception to the apodictic saying of Jesus. In all likelihood Mark and Luke are more accurate
in passing on the teaching of Jesus than Matthew. Paul also
admits of an exception. The Catholic Church follows the tradition of Mark and Luke and opposes all divorce. The Catholic
Church also accepts the so-called Petrine privilege in which a
nonconsummated marriage can be declared null and void and

the couple can obtain a divorce and remarry. The Orthodox Church follows the more liberal interpretation and allows for divorce and re-marriage, as do most Protestant Churches.

Certainly anyone who has experienced divorce, whether personally or by a family member, knows it is a tragedy. Divorce is never good. A commitment has been violated. A relationship entered into with love has been lost and broken. But people also admit that in certain instances divorce is the lesser of two evils. Then why can't at least the innocent party remarry?

## Annulments

Many people refer to annulments as Catholic divorce. Many people also have a confused understanding of annulments. The technical term is not annulment but a declaration of nullity. The Church declares that a sacramental marriage did not exist between these two individuals and so they are free to remarry. Legally, such couples are married according to state laws and need a divorce before they may contest the validity of a sacramental marriage. The existence of the legal marriage assures the legitimacy of children, which is clearly recognized by the Church. The process of annulment or the declaration that no sacramental marriage existed in no way affects any offspring. Still, some people do not like the idea of the Church declaring that a sacramental marriage did not exist. Both within and without the Church confusion seems to reign with regard to annulments and the annulment process.

The Catholic Church believes that a marriage between two Christians includes in the covenant a relationship to God. In a truly sacramental marriage the marriage partner accepts responsibility to assist the other spouse in his or her relationship to God. The covenant brings with it certain responsibilities, which cannot be accepted lightly nor without the proper spiritual and psychological maturity. The couple also makes a permanent commitment to each other: "...until death do us part." Intention figures significantly in any marriage relationship. If the proper intention does not exist, then no sacramental marriage takes place. A marriage relationship also demands freedom and sufficient knowledge and awareness to enter into a permanent commitment. Any of these factors can figure in a judgment by a church tribunal on the nonexistence of a sacramental marriage.

## The Annulment Process

Some people erroneously think that only people of wealth and influence can obtain an annulment. Not true. Any Catholic can apply for an annulment. The process may differ slightly from diocese to diocese but in general the petitioner fills out a preliminary questionnaire. Some dioceses require an examination by a psychologist. Testimony from witnesses forms part of the application. The judgment is made by a local church tribunal, which then is sent on to another tribunal for examination. If the second tribunal disagrees with the first, the matter is sent on to Rome. Costs are kept to a minimum but may include administrative expenses, a psychological examination fee and so forth. No diocese will refuse to accept a petition if the party is truly unable to pay these minimum costs. Once the declaration of nullity has taken place, an individual is free to remarry within the Church.

In certain instances some people, unable to go through the annulment process and convinced that their first marriage is not a valid sacramental marriage, may receive guidance from a priest in confession and may receive the sacraments. All is done privately through what is known as the internal forum. The priest carries this out in the confession without any formal legal process.

There are Catholics who accept their first marriages as valid, but divorced and remarried outside the Church. The general law prohibits their reception of the sacraments. Many sincerely seek reconciliation with the Church. Can they receive the Eucharist? Some feel that they can. However, the official teaching of the Church prohibits the reception of the Eucharist by these individuals. Recently some bishops have proposed the granting of "economy." Economy is a gracious act of the Church intended to heal a wound that the law can not handle. The economy judgment anticipates the merciful judgment of the Lord Jesus in the

Church today. Such individuals may then receive communion. Rome has officially prohibited this practice.

Annulments and the annulment process involve legal issues, which protect both the individual and the church tradition. Ultimately, however, the legal process must always serve the good of the individual believers. The more Catholics understand the meaning and the process of annulments, the better they realize how the Church acts for their welfare. Certainly the process has never been perfect. Future changes can and will come. The fact that most present-day annulments were not thinkable thirty years ago indicates a change in understanding sacramental marriage in the Church.

# Contraception

The Bible says nothing about contraception even though forms of contraception existed in Egypt before and during the time of Israel. Some have attempted to use the story of Onan in Genesis 38:9–10 as a prohibition against contraception, since Onan does not allow his seed to enter into the body of Tamar. His sin, however, is not the prevention of conception but his failure to fulfil the Levirate law.

Through the centuries many theologians, for reasons that varied, condemned any practice of birth control. Some saw the gift of children as a direct blessing from God. God alone would determine the number of children. On a simply anthropological level, the high infant mortality rate made large families essential for the continuation of the race, and therefore contraception would be against nature. Most people of agrarian societies wanted many children not only for the continuation of the family and race but also for the practical necessity of working. Only in the late nineteenth century, when society changed and contraceptive practices became more common, did the issue become critical. In 1930 the meeting of Anglican bishops in Lambeth Palace approved contraceptive methods. In the same year Pius XI issued his encyclical *Casti Connubii*, condemning any form of contraception. In 1951 Pius XII approved periodic abstinence or natural family planning or the so-called rhythm method for sufficient reason.

During the 1950s, with the advent of the contraceptive pill, the question of artificial contraception was discussed with a new vigor. John XXIII established a commission to study the issue prior to the Second Vatican Council. Paul VI did not wish the issue discussed during the Second Vatican Council and expanded to sixty-nine the members of the international commission set up by his predecessor. In 1967 the commission voted 64 to 4 (Although he was a member of the commission, Archbishop Karol Wojtyla, the future John Paul II, did not attend the meeting.) in favor of changing the traditional teaching against all forms of artificial birth control. A year later Paul VI reaffirmed the traditional teaching in his encyclical *Humanae Vitae.*

The encyclical represents an authoritative but noninfallible teaching of the Church as was made explicit during the press conference in which it was released. National hierarchies in thirteen countries, including Canada but not the United States, showed a tendency to mitigate the ban by appealing to individual conscience. The unitive and procreative meanings of sexuality need to be present in the marriage relationship but not necessarily in every sexual act. This allows for the following of individual conscience. In 1980 Archbishop John Quinn, then archbishop of San Francisco, quoted a study of American Catholics during the Synod of Bishops showing that 76.5 percent of American Catholic women used some form of birth control and 94 percent of those who did used methods condemned by the Catholic Church. Pope John Paul II has reiterated on several occasions the teaching of *Humanae Vitae* condemning all forms of artificial birth control. The Catholic Church clearly teaches opposition to all forms of birth control except the rhythm or natural planning method, and most American Catholics follow their individual consciences. Nor do these Catholics seem disturbed about their disagreement with the Church on this teaching. At one time in history the practice of contraception was clearly regarded a matter for confession. Yet today many Catholics do not consider it so. They feel free to practice birth control in spite of what the Church officially teaches.

# Abortion

American Catholics generally oppose abortion. Like most Americans, they do not like it. In fact, three out of four Americans think abortion should be limited even if they do not support a constitutional amendment forbidding all abortions. This does not mean that American Catholics do not have abortions. They do, but it troubles them greatly. Abortion on demand just does not fit into the conscience of most people, especially Catholics. The desire to limit abortion, however, does not mean that all American Catholics are opposed to all abortions.

Nature clearly knows abortion. Miscarriages are nature's way of saying that something is wrong in the development of the fetus. Any woman who has had a miscarriage feels the tragedy but also knows it was for the better. The Catholic Church has never been opposed to all abortions. Ectopic pregnancies or the removal of a cancerous uterus constitute an indirect abortion and fall within the general moral guidelines of the Catholic Church. The Catholic Church opposes all direct abortions, and most Catholics agree that to directly terminate life in the womb constitutes a serious moral evil. At the same time Catholics do not know how to deal with the question of abortion in a pluralistic society. Historically many Catholic politicians will profess personal opposition to abortion while maintaining their obligation to uphold the law, which allows abortions. This has satisfied some members of the hierarchy, but not all. The issue remains unresolved.

Some may think that the Catholic Church has always opposed all abortions. Clearly such is not the case, for example, in indirect abortions. Even in the history of the Catholic Church some individual theologians permitted abortion in the earliest days of pregnancy since they did not believe that a human person existed in this early period. Thomas Aquinas thought that it took longer for the female fetus to become human than for the male fetus. During this period abortion was not considered sinful. In the study of biology, science has proved that the fertilized egg can split sometime during the first two or three weeks and thus twins are born. Also during this same period two fertilized eggs can join. One blue eye and one brown eye in a newborn testify to this biological fact. How then can anyone say that a human being exists from the first moment of conception? That would mean one human being became two, or two human beings became one. This causes additional problems for the morality of abortion. To err on the side of caution, the Catholic Church teaches that human life is present from the first moment of conception, at least potentially, and this sacred life must be protected.

On January 22, 1973, the U.S. Supreme Court handed down its landmark decision, *Roe* vs. *Wade,* legalizing abortion. Since then millions of abortions have been performed in this country. A year later the Congregation for the Doctrine of the Faith issued its Declaration on Procured Abortion, condemning all direct taking of life within the womb. In 1983 the revised Code of Canon Law ruled that anyone who obtains an abortion incurs an automatic excommunication (Canon 1398). Pope John Paul's 1995 encyclical *Evangelium Vitae* reaffirmed in the strongest terms the Church's opposition to direct abortion and called all Catholics to work to protect innocent human life.

The American Bishops have continuously fought to protect innocent human life. They set up Respect Life offices in their dioceses. Following the example of the Most Reverend Edwin B. Broderick of Albany and his pastoral letter of 1973 as well as the better known teaching of Cardinal Joseph Bernardin on the "Seamless Garment" in 1983, the bishops joined all life issues together. From womb to tomb, the Catholic Church supports, protects and nourishes all forms of human life. Life issues include euthanasia, the death penalty, incarceration, and abuse of children and the aged. Anything that lessens the quality of human life or limits its expression, including the taking of life, falls within the general concern proclaimed by the Catholic Church. Abortion, while often seen as the only life issue of the Catholic Church, actually fits within a consistent ethic of life.

## Premarital Sex

The Catholic Church has consistently taught that premarital sex is morally evil. It has declared that sexual activity should take place only within the stable union of matrimony. Today, however, many young Catholics pay no attention to this church teaching. Provided some stable relationship exists between two individuals, and that usually means an exclusive relationship, sexual activity becomes the norm. According to the opinion polls, only one out of six American Catholics think premarital sex is always wrong. Anyone who has spent any time on a college campus knows that young adults are sexually active and although they might be embarrassed by confrontation concerning their sexual activity on the part of parents or clergy, such disapproval has little effect on their behavior.

The Catholic Church teaches that sexual activity without the commitment to maintain a permanent, binding relationship often leads to deception and exploitation, especially of women. Couples living together, "trying it out" and then marrying, have a greater chance of divorce than those couples who do not live together before marriage. That statistic supports the Church's teaching. Mutual exploration of a partner's body can offer pleasure but not necessarily love. Love presupposes a willingness to do all possible for the partner to grow and develop and use personal talents. Love demands thinking of the other at least more than thinking of one's self. Love expects a continuation of love even if the one person does not understand the other. Love presumes friendship and selflessness and only then includes the erotic love binding two bodies in the mutual pleasure of each. Sexual activity should seal the love relationship rather than be the introduction to the relationship. Being intimate on a personal level rather than on a genital sexual level lasts, while the pleasure of genital expression passes quickly.

Some moralists will distinguish preceremonial sex from premarital sex. Once the commitment to marry is made, then sexual activity anticipates the ceremony. Others say that the ceremony seals the commitment. Still others will distinguish between the sexual activity of a teenager and that of a mature adult who is neither married nor blessed with the gift of celibacy. They note that the situation of two teenagers exploring each other's body in the backseat of a car differs from that of a thirty-something, who either has never married or has already experienced a painful divorce, spending a night with a good friend. The Catholic Church, however, condemns both. Young American Catholics reject this teaching with no qualms of conscience. The search to understand what is responsible behavior in sexual matters today does not easily offer black and white answers. What worked in the past no longer works today. Some think that, provided they practice safe sex, everything is good and proper. But sexual activity surely means more than this.

## Masturbation

The church teaching that every matter of sexual activity involves serious moral values includes the practice of masturbation. The attempt to frame masturbation within this traditional understanding of mortal sin in all sexual matters has probably elevated this activity to an importance that it does not deserve. Many psychologists see masturbation as part of the normal development of the adolescent. If an individual masturbates habitually, it usually indicates that sexuality has not yet been integrated into his or her personality. Masturbation often cloaks more serious problems. When persons, more frequently male although sometimes female, feel hurt, lonely, forgotten or unappreciated, they may engage in self-gratification in order to feel better. Masturbation often means something more than just personal, physical sexual pleasure. In most instances it includes some psychological dimension, which colors the act considerably.

Most Catholic moralists do not want to take the position that masturbation is a neutral sexual release. Yet, they also do not want to maintain that this activity constitutes a separation from God in mortal sin. Most people who masturbate would be embarrassed if others knew of their habit. Engaging in this type of self-gratification often leaves an individual with the feeling that something is very wrong. Such feelings are natural indicators, that the practice should not just be accepted. The experienced confessor or confidant tries to help the person to understand why he or she masturbates. Since masturbation more often is symptomatic of other issues, dealing with the cause will help the person to understand his or her own sexual nature.

## Homosexuality

Perhaps no issue of sexual morality has caused more anxiety in the Catholic Church in the past thirty years than homosexuality. Even the recent pastoral letter by the American bishops, *All Our Children*, caused opposition within the hierarchy. This letter affirms the need for parents to love their homosexual children. Yet some feared that in its first form it could be interpreted as condoning homosexual activity. Some (although certainly not most) Catholics have been influenced by certain Protestant fundamentalist preachers to think that AIDS is God's way of punishing homosexuals for their unnatural activity. Confusion persists throughout the Catholic community.

The Bible condemns homosexual activity both in the Old Testament and in the New Testament. These citations, however, may not refer to what contemporary psychologists regard as a constitutional sexual orientation. The biblical references may, rather, refer to idolatrous worship or the failure to maintain the continuity of the tribe or to heterosexuals engaging in activity contrary to their own inclinations. Some references relate to temple prostitution (Lev 18:22; 20:13; Deut 23:18). Genesis 19:48 concerns the abuse of hospitality more than homosexual activity. The New Testament refers to pederasty (1 Cor 6:9–10; 1 Tim 1:10), clearly always sinful and tragic. Paul in Romans (1:26–27) refers explicitly to homosexual relations of both men and women. Since he speaks of natural relationships, he probably did not see homosexual orientation as a firmly constituted condition. Yet there are those within the Church who will dismiss any effort to rethink these texts and insist that the Bible condemns both homosexual activity and homosexuals themselves.

Today most behavioral scientists believe that homosexuals do not choose to be gay or lesbian, even if science cannot presently determine what causes a homosexual orientation. The discovery of a so-called homosexual gene has been proven to be false, and yet most think that there is some genetic basis for this orientation, which the personal environment then supports. The dialectic of nature versus nurture plays an important part in understanding homosexuality. The debate continues.

The *Catechism of the Catholic Church* acknowledges that a homosexual orientation is not a matter of choice (2358). The Church condemns the activity and not the homosexual, even if the Congregation of the Doctrine of the faith in 1986 referred to homosexuality as a "disorder."

> Although the particular inclination of the homosexual person is not a sin, it is a more or less strong tendency toward an intrinsic moral evil; and thus the inclination itself must be seen as an objective disorder.
>
> (no. 3)

The Catholic Church also teaches that homosexuals deserve the same rights as heterosexuals. Any discrimination against homosexuals precisely because of their orientation must be considered sinful. For many Catholic homosexuals, however, this is not enough. If celibacy is a gift from God and if homosexuals did not choose their orientation and need intimacy like any heterosexual, why then is homosexual activity sinful?

Some moralists will admit that while not the norm, homosexual activity need not in every case be considered sinful. They argue that stable and lasting homosexual relationships should be encouraged, even if these relationships involve sexual activity. Others will continue to teach the need for homosexuals to practice celibacy just as the nonmarried heterosexuals must practice celibacy. No complete agreement among Catholic theologians occurs even while the Church officially condemns all homosexual genital activity.

Indiscriminate, anonymous sex, so often part of the gay community, certainly cannot be good for anyone. Yet the way society has treated homosexuals often encourages this clandestine sex. Homosexual predatory behavior can certainly never be accepted as morally good. The Catholic community continues to maintain this belief. At the same time most American heterosexual Catholics will accept the presence of homosexuals within their community and family and will abhor any discrimination against them. The day when all Catholic parents rejected their homosexual children has passed. That much is good. Like other areas of sexual activity, the Church community continues to reflect on the morality of homosexual acts, especially those within a stable and lasting union, while the official Church continues to condemn all such genital homosexual activity.

## Social Ethics

The clarity of the New Testament with regard to the mission of Jesus and even the clarity of the Church's mission in the Acts of the Apostles did not prevent confusion with regard to the social mission of the Church over the centuries. When Peter said in Acts 3:6: "I have no silver and gold but I give you what I have; in the name of Jesus Christ of Nazareth, walk," he demonstrated his concern for the man physically. Only after his cure did the man praise God (Acts 3:8).

More recently Martin Luther King remarked:

> Any religion that professes to be concerned with the souls of men and is not concerned with the slums that damn them, the economic conditions that strangle them, the social conditions that cripple them is a dry-as-dust religion. Such a religion is the kind the Marxists like to see, an opiate of the people.[24]

The mission of the Church cannot easily be divided into the spiritual and the social precisely because no person can be so divided. Both interact and mutually influence each other. "Sin is physical too."[25]

## Mission and History

The history of the Catholic Church, however, has seen a great development and often confusion in this simple understanding of mission. Even today, some see the social mission of service as substitutive. Others see it as not really part of the official mission and others still see it as a partial mission. In the light of the New Testament, all such divisions fall.

Much of theology can be understood and better explained through the study of history. The advent of Christianity as an official religion, the development of medieval theology based on the ideas of Aristotle, and the Church's adaptation of the methods of various political regimes all helped the mission of the Church to take some different turns. Instead of seeing Jesus as an itinerant preacher concerned with humanity, Jesus became the incarnation of the second person of the Blessed Trinity, with a transcendent mission. Salvation for all, became living for God now, to be happy with God forever in heaven. Eventually the mission was further reduced to living happily with God forever in heaven. If this was the mission of Jesus, then the Church had the same mission.

In medieval theology, which continued to influence theology into this century, the mission of the Church was based more on the differences between nature and supernature than on the New Testament. The Church as a perfect society, complete and autonomous, had its own end and the means to attain that end. To distinguish the Church from the other "perfect society," that is, the state, a supernatural end was emphasized. Ultimately the Church had the beatific vision as its end. Some saw one or more additional ends, namely, the exercise of the Christian religion, and the sanctification of souls, but all was directed toward the ultimate end, the beatific vision.

## Natural and Supernatural

This approach became more virulent with the development of the Enlightenment. This modern movement concentrated on the natural, the human and the rational. Since the Enlightenment rejected any supernatural revelation as the foundation for Christianity, it also rejected any supernatural goal. The Church became just one institution among many in human history with no special place or privilege. Following this period, theology, and especially the mission of the Church, concentrated sharply on the distinction between the natural and the supernatural.

Any attempt to see a social, political or economic goal as proper to the Church became suspect. Religion belonged in the Church and the clergy belonged in the sacristy.

Popes Pius XI and Pius XII both followed this strict division of the mission of the Church. As recently as *Gaudium et Spes,* the fathers of the Vatican Council wrote that Christ gave his Church "no proper mission in the political, economic or social order (no. 42)." Such an understanding of the mission of the Church seems far removed from the mission of Jesus as well as those of the early Church who both preached the kingdom that is within. Both forgave sins but also healed broken people and drove out evil.

## Various Opinions Concerning Mission

Political and liberation theology have returned to this biblical understanding of mission by refusing to separate the religious mission of the Church from its mission to contemporary society. This has earned liberation theology and political theology a large number of critics, especially among those whose theology continues to make a clear distinction between the natural and supernatural.

Underlying these different approaches are dichotomies between natural and supernatural, transcendent and immanent, preaching the gospel and raising the standards of human life. No such dichotomies existed in the Bible. Certainly some can go to extremes and claim that the gospel can never be preached until people live on a basic level of human dignity with social and economic needs fulfilled. But others can also err in claiming that Christianity can fulfill its mission with no concern for the social and economic ills of society.

## Nature and Grace

Theology in the middle of this century challenged the tradition that posed a separation between nature and grace. Henri de Lubac, in particular, but also Karl Rahner, reviewed Thomas Aquinas's understanding of nature and grace and reached conclusions that challenged the prevailing understanding. They argued that nature and grace exist integrally. Nature does not exist without the influence of grace. One historical order exists and that is a graced order. Such an approach eventually gave birth to liberation and political theology and did away with the division of the mission of the Church into a proper supernatural end and a limited natural interest.

Theologians have introduced different approaches to bring the social dimension into the religious as part of the mission of the Church. Some maintain that the mission of the Church concerns the impact of the reign of God on all dimensions of human life but that the specific social activities of the Church are subsidiary and temporary. The Church has a social mission exemplified in its maintenance of schools, hospitals, day care centers, soup kitchens and such, but it should provide such services only when secular agencies fail to offer them.

Such a position seems contrary to popular belief, acceptance and understanding. Few people think that Catholic colleges and universities exist only until the state can take them over. They belong to the mission of the Church as such. The same is true for day care centers and other social agencies. Some have argued that the Church should not own, maintain and administer such institutions but only offer chaplaincies to them. Yet a wide percentage of Catholics believe that these institutions belong to the nature of the Church.

Catholic charitable agencies within a diocese do not exist just because the state or local government is not doing enough. They are part of the mission to heal. Movements for just wages or working conditions are not part of the mission just because no one else is doing this but precisely because the mission involves driving out evil, and an environment of less-than-human living conditions is evil.

## Church Leaders, Laity and Mission

Karl Rahner in some of his writings suggests another alternative. Let the Church inspire and motivate Christians within it to accomplish what is needed for society. The official Church, especially its hierarchy, leaves the social mission to its members. The official Church has its religious mission and the layperson bears the responsibility for the secular mission. This theology underpinned the Catholic Action Movement earlier in this century.

The chief criticism of such an approach to the mission of the Church, however, is that this places a dichotomy within the Church between official church leaders and the laity. This avoids the hard question of who has the responsibility to fulfill the mission of the Church as proclaimed in the gospel. Does leadership in the Church also demand leadership in the social, political and economic order?

## Many Missions of the Church

Still others argue against seeing the mission of the Church as singular or reduced to one model. This approach avoids a dichotomy between the religious and secular, the transcendent and the immanent. The social mission becomes legitimate since it neither sees itself exclusively as the only goal of the Church's activity nor as a goal separated from the religious dimension.

This latter position differs from political or liberation theology, which seeks to link the different dimensions of the mission. Can the religious mission of the Church be distinguished completely from its social mission? Is the Church as sacrament completely distinct from the Church as servant or prophet? The answer to these questions lies in the understanding of Jesus himself. Jesus was the incarnation of the Word of God. For Catholics this is an article of faith. He was also one who offered freedom to all, cared for all aspects of human life, promised salvation now as well as in the future life and generally lived as God's human face. His mission seems clear: preach, heal, forgive sins and drive out evil forces. The social mission of Jesus was not separated from his religious mission.

# Dimensions of Salvation

An individual cannot be divided into the religious, the human, the physical, the spiritual and the psychological. World history also involves salvation history. The transcendent God has become immanent in Jesus. The sacred has always affected the profane and the profane has always influenced the sacred. When people live in peace and harmony, on a level of social and economic life that befits someone created in the image of God, these moments of earthly "salvation" anticipate the fullness of salvation to come.

Justice and freedom are God's gift to all. When people live under an unjust regime, when they are shackled by political, social or economic conditions that deprive them of their sense of freedom as children of God, then not only is God denied but the heart of the gospel is ignored. Justice, freedom and peace belong to and form part of the Christian heritage and also part of Christian responsibility.

# The Social Encyclicals

Since Leo XIII's encyclical *Rerum Novarum* (1891), on the rights of workers, the Catholic Church has officially expanded its concerns for social ethics. Forty years later, Pius XI published his encyclical *Quadragesimo Anno* introducing the concept of social justice as a directing principle or norm for public institutions and the economic order. John XXIII's first encyclical, *Mater et Magistra* (1961), continued this tradition by calling special attention to the widening gap between the rich and the poor and urging a reconstruction of social relationships. His next encyclical, *Pacem in Terris* (1963), was the first official document dealing with nuclear weapons and the responsibility of all to protect life.

The social teachings of the Vatican Council appear in two documents: *Gaudium et Spes* (1965), on the role of the Church in the world, which deals with justice as part of the mission of the Church; and *Dignitatis Humanae*, the Declaration on Religious Liberty. Both documents have had a profound effect on Catholic teaching, moving the Church from previously held positions to new interpretations of its mission as well as to a stronger commitment to issues affecting every aspect of social life.

Paul VI's encyclical *Populorum Progressio* (1967) repeated the traditional teaching on the right to private property (without presenting it as an absolute), the need for land reform, especially in developing countries, the exploitation of the poor by the rich and a critique of the profit-motive principle of capitalism. This latter caused the *Wall Street Journal* to refer to the encyclical as "warmed-over Marxism." These social encyclicals moved the Catholic Church into the market place, and no one can any longer ignore what the Church is saying about social justice.

## Justice: Constitutive of the Church

In 1971, for the first time, the official Church pronounced justice to be constitutive to the preaching of the gospel:

> Action on behalf of justice and participation in the transformation of the world appear to us as a constitutive dimension of the preaching of the gospel, or, in other words, of the Church's mission for the redemption of the human race and its liberation from every oppressive situation.
>
> *De Justitia in Mundo* (Third Synod of Bishops, no. 6)

Since that time some have had trouble with the word *constitutive.* Does it mean essential or integral? Paul VI addressed this question on September 27, 1974:

> It will be necessary to define more accurately the relationship between evangelization properly so called and the human effort toward development for which the Church's help is rightly expected, even though this is not her specific task.[26]

The Pope challenged the assembled bishops to work out the precise relationship between the spiritual mission of the Church and its social mission. The documents issued from this synod affirmed that the gospel, as well as the intimate connection between evangelization and liberation, requires the promotion of human rights. But they also added:

> ...the Church in more faithfully fulfilling the work of evangelization, will announce the total salvation of humans or rather their complete liberation, and from now on will start to bring this about.[27]

Pope Paul VI, in closing the synod, urged further study of how human liberation may be emphasized without detriment to the spiritual mission of the Church, which always remains evangelization. He seems to have wished to emphasize the primacy of evangelization but also includes in his teaching a cry for human liberation from all aspects of oppression.

## John Paul II

Pope John Paul II, in his address to the Third General Assembly of Latin American Bishops at Puebla and in his encyclicals, *Laborem Exercens* (1981), *Sollicitudo Rei Socialis* (1987) and *Centesimus Annus* (1991), further develops the Church's teaching on social justice. The present pope wants the Church to hold: "evangelization as the essential mission" and at the same time quotes the synod's affirmation that action for justice is a constitutive dimension of the Church. Following Paul VI, John Paul II links evangelization and liberation based on his understanding of theology. When people live on a less than human level socially and economically, this distortion is a false image of human nature. Human nature should be viewed under the understanding of Christology. The pope also repeatedly calls for an acceptance of the option for the poor. Every individual conscience should become sensitized to social and political justice. Surely his own experience in Nazi-occupied Poland and later under Communism has helped these ideas form in his own theological understanding. The pope criticizes capitalism, communism and socialism. Admitting the positive role of business and its allowance for human creativity in the economy, the pope believes that capitalism should never be simply presented as the goal of the developing countries. The Third World needs to circumscribe the economic dimensions of society with a juridical framework respecting the freedom rooted in ethical and religious values (*Centesimus Annus*, no. 42).

In his encyclical *Evangelium Vitae* (1995) the pope asks all people of good will to affirm life. Examples of the lack of respect for human life in today's society include the unjust distribution of resources leading to poverty, malnutrition and hunger for millions, the violence of war, the scandalous arms trade, the reckless tampering with the world's ecological balance, the spread of drugs, and the promotion of certain sexual activities that present grave risks to life (no. 10). The encyclical especially condemns efforts to limit human life at its inception and at the end of life. It also speaks out strongly against the death penalty. Cases in which society will resort to the use of the death penalty "are very rare if not practically nonexistent" (no. 56). It also condemns the experimentation on human embryos or fetuses (no. 63). The pope rejects euthanasia, suicide and assisted suicide but also respects the right of an individual to forgo aggressive medical treatment that "would only secure a precarious and burdensome prolongation of life, so long as the normal care due to the sick person in similar cases is not interrupted" (no. 65). The final chapter calls for special concern for the poor, single mothers, those needing help in overcoming addiction, the mentally ill, persons with AIDS and the disabled (nos. 87–88).

Both Paul VI and John Paul II affirm social justice as integral to the mission of the Church. Both also try to maintain the essential mission of evangelization, of preaching the reign of God. In fact they seem to have retreated from the medieval understanding of the mission of the Church to the more biblical understanding.

# Return to the New Testament

The Church still seems unsure of political theology as well as liberation theology. Yet its position appears to be evolving toward an acceptance that somehow the raising of every human being to a sense of personal worth and dignity must be part of the mission of the Church even while it preaches salvation in the midst of human damnation.

The Church must determine how justice and the concern for the social, economic and political dimensions of human life will be integrated into the actual living out of the gospel. The American Bishops have taken a lead in their statements on disarmament and the American economy. Without a concern for such dimensions of American and human society, the Church often loses credibility. At the same time, if it were to become just another social agency, the Church would lose its soul. A return to the biblical roots of mission will help the Church resolve this dialectic. Jesus preached the reign of God; he healed people both physically and psychologically and spiritually; he forgave sins and drove out evil. The Church follows his lead.

## TOPICS FOR DISCUSSION AND STUDY

1. Jesus came to serve. The Church must do likewise. How can the Church do this in your opinion?
2. Should the Church be involved with politics?
3. What are your thoughts on the mission of the Church to the world?
4. All nature is permeated by grace. If so, what are the implications of this belief?
5. What do you like about liberation theology? What do you see as some problems of this approach?
6. Do you see the value of political theology?
7. If concern for justice is constitutive of the mission of the Church, what implications should flow from this teaching?
8. Does the Church serve humanity by telling people what to do?

# Works Consulted

Baum, Gregory. *Theology and Society*. Mahwah, N.J.: Paulist Press, 1988.

Bonsor, Jack. "Homosexual Orientation and Anthropology: Reflections on the Category 'Objective Disorder.'" *Theological Studies* 59 (1998): 60–83.

Cahill, Lisa. *Between the Sexes*. Philadelphia: Fortress, 1985.

Coleman, Gerald. "The Vatican Statement on Homosexuality." *Theological Studies* 48 (1987): 727–34.

Collins, Raymond. *Christian Morality, Biblical Foundations*. Notre Dame, Ind.: Notre Dame University Press, 1986.

Connery, John. *Abortion: The Development of the Roman Catholic Perspective*. Chicago: Loyola University Press, 1977.

Curran, Charles E. *The Catholic Moral Tradition Today*. Washington, D.C.: Georgetown University Press, 1999.

Dedek, John. *Contemporary Sexual Morality*. New York: Sheed and Ward, 1971.

Dorr, Donal. *Option for the Poor: A Hundred Years of Vatican Social Teaching*. Maryknoll, N.Y.: Orbis, 1983.

Genovesi, Vincent J. *In Pursuit of Love: Catholic Morality and Human Sexuality*. Wilmington, Del.: Michael Glazier, 1987.

Greeley, Andrew. "Sex and the Single Catholic." *Sex: The Catholic Experience*. Chicago: Thomas More, 1994.

Haight, Roger. "The Mission of the Church in the Theology of the Social Gospel." *Theological Studies* 49 (1988): 477–97.

Himes, Kenneth, and James Coriden. "Pastoral Care of the Divorced and Remarried." *Theological Studies* 57 (1996): 97–123.

Lawler, Michael G. *Secular Marriage, Christian Sacrament.* Mystic, Conn.: Twenty-Third Publications, 1985.

Lawler, Ronald, Joseph Boyle, and William May. *Catholic Sexual Ethics.* Huntington, Ind.: Our Sunday Visitor Press, 1985.

Mackin, Theodore. *What Is Marriage?* Mahwah, N.J.: Paulist Press, 1982.

Mac Namara, Vincent. "Approaching Christian Morality." *Contemporary Catholic Theology.* Trowbridge, U.K.: Cromwell Press, 1998, 374–88.

McCarthy, Timothy G. *The Catholic Tradition: Before and After Vatican II.* Chicago: Loyola University Press, 1994.

McGoldrick, Terence. "Episcopal Conferences Worldwide on Catholic Social Teaching." *Theological Studies* 59 (1998): 22–50.

O'Callaghan, Denis F. "What's Special about Christian Morality?" *Contemporary Catholic Theology.* Trowbridge, U.K.: Cromwell Press, 1998, 369–73.

O'Connell, Timothy. "The History of Moral Theology." *Contemporary Catholic Theology.* Trowbridge, U.K.: Cromwell Press, 1998, 389–402.

———. *Principles for a Catholic Morality.* San Francisco: Harper and Row, 1990.

Orsy, Ladislas. "Magisterium: Assent and Dissent." *Theological Studies* 48 (1987): 473–97.

———. "Marriage Annulments: An Interview with Ladislas Orsy." *America* 177 (1997): 10–18.

Otten, Willemien. "Augustine on Marriage, Monasticism and the Community of the Church." *Theological Studies* 59 (1998): 385–405.

Pope, Stephen J. "The Order of Love and Recent Catholic Ethics: A Constructive Proposal." *Theological Studies* 52 (1991): 255–88.

Rahner, Karl. "The Church's Commission to Bring Salvation and the Humanization of the World." *Theological Investigations.* New York: Seabury, 1976, vol. 14, 295–313.

————. "Concerning the Relationship between Nature and Grace." *Theological Investigations.* London: Darton, Longman and Todd, 1961, vol. 1, 297–318.

————. *The Dynamic Element in the Church.* New York: Herder and Herder, 1964.

Rausch, Thomas P. "Sexual Morality and Social Justice." *Contemporary Catholic Theology.* Trowbridge, U.K.: Cromwell Press, 1998, 403–33.

Schussler-Fiorenza, Francis. *Foundational Theology.* New York: Crossroad, 1985.

# CONCLUSION:
# AMERICAN CATHOLICS
# AND VATICAN II

American Catholics under forty years of age know of no Church other than that which has existed since the Second Vatican Council. They take for granted that Mass will be celebrated in English with full participation by the members of the congregation. Laity are active in ministry, teach theology, work in diocesan offices and labor for peace and justice. They take central themes from the Bible as well as from tradition and Church history. American Catholics today profess their faith while exhibiting an openness to insights from other sciences. They foster a cordial ecumenical cooperation that includes an increasing number of marriages between members of different denominations within the broader Christian tradition and even many interfaith marriages.

Still, the teachings of the Second Vatican Council remain a source of tension among different parties within the American Church. Some American Catholics feel deceived or deserted by their Church. Others think that Pope John Paul II has reversed the positions of the Vatican Council and returned to a Church similar to that which existed prior to 1962. Still others think the Church should go beyond the Vatican Council to respond to the ever-changing attitudes of American Catholics. It startles many sociologists, psychologists and theologians that there can exist such a diversity of opinion within any particular age group, from the youngest to the oldest. Many younger Catholics profess an interest in particular practices, such as Mass in Latin, even though they have never experienced them as being part of the Church in their lifetime. Other Catholics in their late fifties or sixties romantically recall the Church of their youth and long for those simpler days now past. Yet other American Catholics in this same age category have become discouraged with the slow pace of change and renewal.

## Vatican II: The Dividing Point

American Catholics can be divided into three categories: pre–Vatican II, Vatican II and post–Vatican II. Usually these categories designate definite ages. Those born in the '20s and '30s grew up in "Catholic" neighborhoods, went to Catholic schools and hospitals, belonged to Catholic groups such as the Holy Name Society, the Women's Sodality and the Knights of Columbus and read Catholic newspapers and magazines. Priests and religious led this group of Catholics and convinced them that the Catholic Church was the one true church. They lived proud of their heritage, although at times with a beleaguered mentality.

The Vatican II generation came to age with the social tranquility of the Eisenhower years and the political turmoil of the 1960s. The conservatism of the '50s gave way to the liberalism of the '60s. The members of this generation witnessed their Church taking a 180-degree turn during their teenage and early adult years. English replaced Latin. The priest faced the congregation; folk music and guitars replaced Gregorian chant and the organ. Priests and nuns left religious life and married.

The post–Vatican II generation grew up in the 1970s, '80s, and '90s. This period witnessed a renewed sense of conservatism in society and government. It has seen greed become institutionalized, with a greater gap between rich and poor. This same period introduced the women's movement as well as an ever-increasing technological explosion. This group prizes its individual faith journeys and regards spirituality as more important than organized religion.

Dividing these groups into chronological ages helps but does not completely express the reality. Some in the last category feel more comfortable in the first without ever experiencing the pre–Vatican II Church. Others in the first group gladly take on some of the characteristics of the last group. Many just remain confused.

## The Changes

Vatican II cannot be reversed. Yet how the Church will function in the present millennium remains unclear. The Vatican Council, which was the culmination of decades of ferment in theological and liturgical circles, brought a series of reforms which have changed not only the way Catholics worship but also how they think. No pope or bishop nor even large groups of Catholics can pretend the Vatican Council never happened.

On October 11, 1962, more than 2,400 bishops, 102 cardinals and seven eastern patriarchs marched into the largest church in Christendom, St. Peter's in Rome, to celebrate the opening of the twenty-first ecumenical council of the Church presided over by Pope John XXIII. Following the invitation of the pope, the council fathers attempted not only to preserve the traditions but also earnestly and fearlessly dedicated themselves to the work the age demanded.

During the course of four sessions, from 1962 to 1965, first under the leadership of John XXIII and then of Paul VI, the council described the Church as the people of God *(Lumen Gentium)*, declared the Church open and respectful of other cultures *(Gaudium et Spes)* and affirmed the right of every person regardless of religious affiliation to worship God or not, according to his or her own conscience, without any interference from church or state *(Dignitatis Humanae)*. The council bishops praised the work of the Spirit of God in other religions and acknowledged a need for interreligious discussion and collaboration *(Nostra Aetate)*.

Turning to consider the inner working of the Church, the bishops asserted their identity as a college holding coresponsibility with the pope for church governance. They also claimed the Bible as a privileged source of theology and welcomed a plurality in theological methods. With full confidence in both the need and the ability of all people to find adequate expressions of worship, they called for full and active participation in the liturgy (*Sacrosanctum Concilium*).

The council brought about a rethinking of the relationship between the Vatican and the thousands of local churches around the world, each rooted in its own cultural milieu. To support the documents of the council, the members returned to the biblical roots of traditions as well as to history itself. *Inculturation* and *collegiality* became key words in the Church's effort to update itself, or, in the term used by Pope John XXIII, *aggiornamento*. The respect for different cultures shown by the council fathers encouraged an internationalization of the Roman Curia, which then promised a truly global sense of Catholicity.

The council also reconfigured the presence of the Church in the political and economic sphere. Religion was not to be relegated to the Church and sacristy but must take its place in the marketplace of daily life. If people globally sought political and economic freedom with the hope of self-improvement, then the Church supported and encouraged such efforts even if they met opposition from political regimes and economic policies.

## The Periods

The 1960s brought hope to many. The council produced a euphoria that permeated the Catholic Church, bringing a consensus among its various factions. Such hopes were characteristic of a time when people had confidence that they could in fact transform the world, wage a successful war on poverty and racism and foster world peace, love and understanding. The modern Catholic Church projected a vital spiritual presence and moral leadership just when the world faced new frontiers in science, technology and socioeconomic and political development. The '60s offered a promise gladly and enthusiastically accepted by all.

But then reality set in. President John F. Kennedy lay dead in Dallas. Within five years, Martin Luther King and Robert F. Kennedy also lay dead at the hands of assassins. Race riots, Vietnam, urban blight, the developing drug culture and a new moral code turned the hope of the future into the wake of the future. The flower children of the '60s never blossomed into the brave new world.

In July of 1968 Pope Paul VI published his encyclical *Humanae Vitae,* reaffirming the teaching that the Church considered even the occasional use of artificial birth control sinful. Previously he had appointed a commission of bishops, theologians and lay men and women to study the matter. The majority of this commission recommended a change in church policy to permit married couples to use contraceptives to regulate the size of their families. The pope reaffirmed the traditional teaching.

The reaction from clergy and laity rejecting this teaching against contraception shocked the Church, especially the officials in Rome. For good or ill, no longer would American Catholics willingly accept official church pronouncements without involvement and discussion.

The 1970s brought a hardening of positions within the Church. More traditional Catholics complained about the decline in devotions, the loss of distinctive garb by priests and especially by nuns and religious women, the massive departures from the priesthood and religious life and the diminishment of any sense of the sacred in the celebration of the Mass. Shaking hands with strangers, receiving the sacred host in one's own hands instead of on the tongue, singing popular music—for some Catholics, these changes contributed to the loss of the sacred.

More liberal Catholics blamed the intransigence of a small group of conservative Catholics for preventing a true sense of reform. The dignity and freedom of the individual formed the basis for the gospel message, and anything that prevented an individual from experiencing this dignity and freedom must be abolished. Any form of racism, sexism, and discrimination based on color, social condition or sexual orientation should never be present in the Catholic Church.

In 1976 a group of American Catholics gathered in Detroit to discuss the issues facing the American Catholic Church. The proponents and leaders of the meeting named the conference Call to Action. At this meeting 1,340 delegates from throughout the United States brought with them over 800,000 comments and proposals coming from parish discussions in at least half of the dioceses of the country. The ordination of women, optional celibacy for priests, reincorporating the divorced and remarried into full sacramental communion, just wages for all in the Church, along with a Catholic Bill of Rights (including the right to participate in accord with each person's gift in the life and ministry of the Church) supported the democratic and voluntaristic character of American culture and religion. The conference called for action on the part of the Church to develop structures to fit these proposals. The American bishops had sponsored the conference but then, precisely because of the tone of many of the proposals, withdrew their support. The issues, however, have not gone away. They are discussed not only in the United States but throughout the world, especially in developed countries.

## The Present Faces the Future

Pope John Paul II, depending on one's viewpoint, has either restored the true spirit of Vatican Council II or betrayed it. No one, however, can deny that the Catholic Church as it exists today is not the Church that existed prior to the council. Women may not be ordained, but they function in increasingly important governing roles in the Church. Laypeople have moved into responsible positions in ministry. The Church has expressed a preferential option for the poor, and without fear takes on political regimes and economic policies. Diversity in the Church has increased. Latino, Hispanic, Asian and African American Catholics take their place alongside the European American Catholics with equal dignity. The present American Catholic Church includes the most literate, affluent and ethnically diverse generation of young people in its history. What will they be? What will they do? How can the Church hold on to its beliefs and traditions while responding to the demands of congregations never before seen in the history of the Church? How will the Church continue the ministry, described in the Gospel of Matthew, of bringing from its storeroom both the new and the old (Matt 13:52)?

American Catholics love their Church, even if they are not sure how this Church will function in the next millennium. In the words of Augustine, quoted in the Vatican Council documents, "...one possesses the Holy Spirit in the measure that one loves the Church." American Catholics are not blind to the faults of the Church, nor to their own need for self-reform. In a series of texts within the council's documents the bishops insisted that the Church must continuously pursue the path of penance and reform, (*Lumen Gentium,* nos. 8 and 15; *Unitatis Redintegratio,* no. 6). In *Gaudium et Spes* the bishops noted: "...it does not escape the Church how great a distance lies between the message she offers and the human failings of those who offer it (no. 43). In history the Church has many times concealed rather than revealed the authentic face of Jesus (*Gaudium et Spes,* no. 19)." American Catholics know all the failures well. This, however, does not denigrate the powerful force for good that the Catholic Church has offered to millions of Americans over the past two hundred years. The exalted goals of the Church expressed in the documents of the Vatican Council challenge all of the members of the Church to live what they are. American Catholics, whatever their positions regarding the Church, will continue to accept Catholic values, beliefs and traditions. They will make them their own, and in so doing will give them an American flavor. The rest lies in the unknown chronicles of the future.

# Works Consulted

Carlin, David. R. "Why Catholic Liberals Should Settle for Half a Loaf." *America* 176, no. 2 (1987): 11–14.

Dulles, Avery. "The Four Faces of American Catholicism." *Louvain Studies* 18 (1993): 99–109.

Fogarty, Gerald P. "The American Catholic Tradition of Dialogue." *America* 175, no. 12 (1996): 9–14.

Johnson, Mary, Dean Hoge, William Dinges, and Juan Gonzalez. "Young Adult Catholics." *America* 180, no. 10 (1999): 9–13.

Rausch, Thomas P. "The Church and the Council." *Contemporary Catholic Theology*. Trowbridge, U.K.: Cromwell Press, 1998, 259–78.

———. "Divisions, Dialogue and the Catholicity of the Church." *America* 180 (January 31, 1998): 20–29.

Sullivan, Francis. "Evaluation and Interpretation of the Documents of Vatican II." *Contemporary Catholic Theology*. Trowbridge, U.K.: Crowell Press, 1998, 335–48.

Tripole, Martin R. "The American Church in Jeopardy." *America* 175, no. 8 (1996): 9–15.

# NOTES

1. Dom Helder Pessoa Camera, quoted in *People's Tribune* 26, no. 10 (Oct. 1999).

2. Albert Camus, *The Plague* (New York: Modern Library, 1957), 230.

3. From the Fourth Lateran Council, cited in *The Teaching of the Catholic Church* (New York: Alba House, 1967), 116.

4. Vatican I, Dogmatic Constitution on the Catholic Faith, cited in *The Teaching of the Catholic Church* (New York: Alba House, 1967), 153–54.

5. Thomas Aquinas, *Summa Theologica,* Pt. III, Q. 1, art. 3 (New York: Benziger, 1947).

6. Gerard Manley Hopkins, "Inversnaid," *Gerard Manley Hopkins: Poems and Prose,* selected and edited by W. H. Gardner (Middlesex, U.K. and New York: Penguin, 1978), 50–51.

7. Gerard Manley Hopkins, "God's Grandeur," *The New Oxford Book of English Verse* (New York: Oxford University Press, 1972), 724.

8. Yevgeny Yevtushenko, "Talk," *Selected Poems* (New York: Penguin, 1962), 81.

9. Robert Bellarmine, *De Controversiis,* tom 2, liber 3, *De Ecclesiae militante,* cap 2, *De Definitione ecclesiae* (Naples: Giuliano, 1857), v.2, 75.

10. Leo I, Sermon, quoted in W. Ullmann, "Leo I and the Theme of Papal Primacy." Journal of *Theological Studies* 2 (1960): 34.

11. William Shakespeare, *The Merchant of Venice,* act IV, scene 1, in *The Complete Works of William Shakespeare.* (Hertfordshire, U.K.: Wordsworth Editions Ltd., 1996), 408–9.

12. Rite of Penance, in *The Rites of the Catholic Church as Revised by Decree of the Second Vatican Council and Published by Authority of Pope Paul VI,* English translation prepared by the International Commission on English in the Liturgy (New York: Pueblo Publishing Co., 1976), 361.

13. Ibid., 362–63.

14. Ibid., 363.

15. *Roman Missal (Missale Romanum)* (New York: Catholic Book Publishing Co., 1964), 227.

16. Pius X, cited in E. O'Connor, *Marian Apparitions Today– Why So Many?* (Santa Barbara, Calif.: Queenship Publications, 1996), 92–93.

17. Author's composition.

18. Author's composition.

19. Augustine of Hippo, *Confessions of St. Augustine* (New York: Colliers, 1961), X, xxvii. For a contemporary translation of this passage, see *Augustine of Hippo: Selected Writings,* translation and introduction by Mary T. Clark. Classics of Western Spirituality (Mahwah, N.J.: Paulist Press, 1984), 144.

20. Dag Hammarskjöld, *Markings* (New York: Knopf, 1966), 160.

21. George Santayana, *The Idea of Christ in the Gospels or God in Man* (New York: Scribners, 1946), 129.

22. Henry W. Longfellow, "Morituri Salutamus," *The Complete Works* (Boston: Houghton, Mifflin and Co., 1866).

23. Dylan Thomas, "Do Not Go Gentle," *The Premier Book of Major Poets: An Anthology,* Anita Dore, ed. (Greenwich, Conn.: Fawcett Publications, Inc., 1970), 144.

24. Martin Luther King, *Strive Toward Freedom: A Testament of Hope.* James W. Washington, ed. (San Francisco: Harper, 1986), 480.

25. Ernesto Cardenal, *The Gospel of Solitaname,* vol. 2 (Mary-knoll, N.Y.: Orbis, 1978), 2.

26. Paul VI, cited in *Catholic Mind* 73 (March 1975): 6.

27. Ibid.

# BIBLIOGRAPHY

Abbott, Walter M., ed. The *Documents of Vatican II*. New York: America Press, 1966.

Adam, Adolf. *Foundations of Liturgy: An Introduction to Its History and Practice*. Collegeville, Minn.: Liturgical Press, 1992.

Alszeghy, Zoltan. "What Did Trent Define about Original Sin?" *Gregorianum* 52 (1971): 57–65. *Theology Digest* 5 (1967): 197ff.

Armstrong, Karen. *A History of God*. New York: Knopf, 1994.

Aune, D. E. "Eschatology (Early Christian)." *Anchor Dictionary of the Bible*. New York: Doubleday, 1992, vol. 2, 594–609.

Barton, John. *People of the Book: The Authority of the Bible in Christianity*. Philadelphia: Westminster, 1989.

Baum, Gregory. *Theology and Society*. Mahwah, N.J.: Paulist Press, 1988.

Bausch, William J. *A New Look at the Sacraments*. Mystic, Conn.: Twenty-Third Publications, 1998.

Beguerie, Philippe and Claude Duchesneau. "The Sacraments in the History of the Church." In *Contemporary Catholic Theology*. Trowbridge, U.K.: Cromwell Press, 1998, 484–99.

Behm, Johannes. "Kardia (heart)." *Theological Dictionary of the New Testament*. Grand Rapids: Eerdmans, 1964, vol. 3, 605–14.

Bellah, Robert. "Religion and the Shape of National Culture." *America* 181, no. 3 (1999): 9–14.

Bermejo, Luis M. *Infallibility on Trial: The Church, Conciliatory and Communion*. Westminster, Md.: Christian Classics, 1992.

Blenkinsopp, Joseph. *The Pentateuch*. New York: Doubleday, 1992.

Bonsor, Jack. "Homosexual Orientation and Anthropology: Reflections on the Category 'Objective Disorder.'" *Theological Studies* 59 (1998): 60–83.

Borg, Marcus. *Jesus in Contemporary Scholarship*. Valley Forge, Pa.: Trinity Press, 1994.

Boris, Ladislaus. *The Mystery of Death*. New York: Herder and Herder, 1965.

Brown, Raymond. *An Introduction to New Testament Christology*. Mahwah, N.J.: Paulist Press, 1994.

———. *Biblical Exegesis and Church Doctrine*. Mahwah, N.J.: Paulist Press, 1985.

———. *Biblical Reflections on Crises Facing the Church*. Mahwah, N.J.: Paulist Press, 1975.

———. *The Birth of the Messiah*. New York: Doubleday, 1993.

———. *The Churches the Apostles Left Behind*. Mahwah, N.J.: Paulist Press, 1984.

———. *The Critical Meaning of the Bible*. Mahwah, N.J.: Paulist Press, 1981.

———. *Priest and Bishop*. Mahwah, N.J.: Paulist Press, 1970.

———. *Responses to 101 Questions on the Bible*. Mahwah, N.J.: Paulist Press, 1990.

———, ed. *Mary in the New Testament*. Philadelphia: Fortress, 1978.

Brown, Raymond, and John Meier. *Antioch and Rome*. Mahwah, N.J.: Paulist Press, 1983.

Cahill, Lisa. *Between the Sexes*. Philadelphia: Fortress, 1985.

Carlin, David. R. "Why Catholic Liberals Should Settle for Half a Loaf." *America* 176, no. 2 (1987): 11–14.

Coffey, David. "The Theandric Nature of Grace." *Theological Studies* 60 (1999): 405–31.

Coleman, Gerald. "The Vatican Statement on Homosexuality." *Theological Studies* 48 (1987): 727–34.

Collins, John J., and John Dominic Crossan. *The Biblical Heritage in Modern Catholic Scholarship.* Wilmington, Del.: Michael Glazier, 1986.

Collins, Raymond. *Christian Morality, Biblical Foundations.* Notre Dame, Ind.: Notre Dame University Press, 1986.

———. Letters *That Paul Did Not Write.* Wilmington, Del.: Michael Glazier, 1988.

Connery, John. *Abortion: The Development of the Roman Catholic Perspective.* Chicago: Loyola University Press, 1977.

Connor, James, "Original Sin: Contemporary Approaches." *Theological Studies* 29 (1968): 215–40.

Cook, Michael L. *Responses to 101 Questions about Jesus.* Mahwah, N.J.: Paulist Press, 1993.

Cooke, Bernard J. *God's Beloved.* Philadelphia: Trinity Press, 1992.

———. *Ministry to Word and Sacraments.* Philadelphia: Fortress, 1980.

Cunningham, Lawrence. "A Decade of Research on the Saints: 1980–1990." Theological Studies 53(1992): 517–33.

———. *The Meaning of Saints.* New York: Harper and Row, 1980.

———. "Saints and Martyrs." *Theological Studies* 60 (1999): 529–37.

Curran, Charles E. *The Catholic Moral Tradition Today.* Washington, D.C.: Georgetown University Press, 1999.

Davis, Charles. *God's Grace in History.* London: Fontana, 1967.

Dedek, John. *Contemporary Sexual Morality.* New York: Sheed and Ward, 1971.

Dionne, J. Robert. *The Papacy and the Church: A Study of Praxis and Reception in Ecumenical Perspective.* New York: Philosophical Library, 1987.

Dorr, Donal. *Option for the Poor: A Hundred Years of Vatican Social Teaching.* Maryknoll, N.Y.: Orbis, 1983.

Doss, Richard. *The Last Enemy: A Christian Understanding of Death.* New York: Harper and Row, 1974.

Downey, Michael. *The New Dictionary of Catholic Spirituality.* Wilmington, Del.: Michael Glazier, 1993.

Duffy, Stephen. "Our Hearts of Darkness: Original Sin Revisited." *Theological Studies* 49 (1988): 597–622.

Dulles, Avery. "The Four Faces of American Catholicism." *Louvain Studies* 18 (1993): 99–109.

———. *Models of the Church.* New York: Doubleday, 1974.

———. *The Resilient Church.* New York: Doubleday, 1977.

Duquoc, C. "New Approaches to Original Sin." *Cross Currents* 28 (1978): 189–200.

Dwyer, Judith. *The New Dictionary of Catholic Social Thought.* Wilmington, Del.: Michael Glazier, 1993.

Eliade, Mircea. *Images and Symbols.* New York: Sheed and Ward, 1969.

Ellis, John Tracy. *American Catholics and the Intellectual Life.* Chicago: Heritage Foundation, 1956.

Fabry, H. J. "Leb (heart)." *Theological Dictionary of the Old Testament.* Grand Rapids: Eerdmans, 1964, vol. 4, 399–437.

Fantino, Jacques. "Whence the Teaching Creation ex nihilo?" *Theology Digest* 46 (1999): 133–40.

Fink, Peter. The *New Dictionary of Sacramental Worship.* Wilmington, Del.: Michael Glazier, 1994.

Fischer, Heribert. "Mysticism." *Sacramentum Mundi.* New York: Herder and Herder, 1967–69, vol. 4, 136–52.

Fogarty, Gerald P. "The American Catholic Tradition of Dialogue." *America* 175, no. 12 (1996):9–14.

Fortman, Edmund. *Everlasting Life after Death.* New York: Alba, 1976.

———. *The Triune God.* Philadelphia: Westminster, 1972.

Fransen Peter. "Augustine, Pelagius and the Controversy on the Doctrine of Grace." *Louvain Studies* 12 (1987): 172–81.

————. *Divine Grace and Man.* New York: Mentor Omega, 1965.

Freedman, Noel, ed. *The Anchor Bible Dictionary.* New York: Doubleday, 1992.

Fries, H., and J. Finsterholzl. "Infallibility." *Sacramentum Mundi.* New York: Herder and Herder, 1967–69, vol. 3, 132–38.

Genovesi, Vincent J. *In Pursuit of Love: Catholic Morality and Human Sexuality.* Wilmington, Del.: Michael Glazier, 1987.

Gleason, Philip. *The Search for God.* New York: Sheed and Ward, 1964.

Gnuse, Robert. *The Authority of the Bible.* Mahwah, N.J.: Paulist Press, 1985.

Grabner-Haider, Anton. "God-Talk in a Multireligious Society." *Theology Digest* 45 (1998): 51–58.

Granfield, Patrick. *The Papacy in Transition.* New York: Doubleday, 1980.

Grant, Robert M. *Gods and the One God.* Philadelphia: Westminster, 1986.

Greeley, Andrew. "Sex and the Single Catholic." *Sex: The Catholic Experience.* Chicago: Thomas More, 1994.

Grisez G., and F. Sullivan. "The Ordinary Magisterium's Infallibility." *Theological Studies* 55 (1994): 720–38.

Gulley, Norman R. "Death." *Anchor Dictionary of the Bible.* New York: Doubleday, 1992, vol. 2, 108–11.

Guzie, Tad. "From Symbol to Sacrament." *Contemporary Catholic Theology.* Trowbridge, U.K.: Cromwell Press, 1998, 434–44.

Haag, C. *Is Original Sin in Scripture?* New York: Sheed and Ward, 1969.

Haight, Roger. "The Mission of the Church in the Theology of the Social Gospel." *Theological Studies* 49 (1988): 477–97.

Happel, Stephen, and David Tracy. *A Catholic Vision.* Philadelphia: Fortress, 1984.

Hayes, Michael and Liam Gearon, eds. *Contemporary Catholic Theology.* Trowbridge, U.K.: Cromwell Press, 1998.

Himes, Kenneth, and James Coriden. "Pastoral Care of the Divorced and Remarried." *Theological Studies* 57 (1996): 97–123.

Hofmann, Rudolf. "Conscience." *Sacramentum Mundi.* New York: Herder and Herder, 1967–69, vol 1, 411–14.

Houlden, J. L. "Lord's Prayer." *Anchor Bible Dictionary.* New York: Doubleday, 1992, vol. 4, 356–62.

John Paul II. *Centesimus Annus.* May 1, 1991.

———. "Day of Pardon" *Homily.* March 12, 2000.

———. *Evangelium Vitae.* March 25,1995.

———. *Fides et Ratio.* October 15, 1998.

———. *Laborem Exercens.* September 14, 1981.

———. *Ut Unum Sint.* October 30, 1995.

———. *Veritas Splendor.* August 6,1993.

Johnson, Elizabeth. "A Community of Holy People in a Sacred World." *New Theology Review* 12 (1999): 17–26.

———. *Friends of God and Prophets: A Feminist Theological Reading of the Communion of Saints.* New York: Continuum, 1998.

———. "Mary and the Female Face of God." *Theological Studies* 50 (1989): 500–26.

Johnson, Mary, Dean Hoge, William Dinges, and Juan Gonzalez. "Young Adult Catholics." *America* 180, no. 10 (1999): 9–13.

Kavanagh, Aidan. "Liturgy *(Sacrosanctum Concilium)."* In *Contemporary Catholic Theology.* Trowbridge, U.K.: Cromwell Press, 1998, 445–51.

Kilmartin, Edward. *Christian Liturgy.* New York: Sheed and Ward, 1988.

———. "Sacraments as Liturgy of the Church." *Theological Studies* 50 (1989): 527–47.

Kittel, G. *Theological Dictionary of the New Testament.* Grand Rapids: Eerdmans, 1964.

Klausnitzer, Wolfgang. "Roman Catholicism and the Papal Office." *Theology Digest* 45 (1998): 233–37.

Klinger, Elmar. "Purgatory." *Sacramentum Mundi.* New York: Herder and Herder 1967–69, vol. 5, 166–68.

Komanchak, Joseph, Mary Collins, and Dermot Lane, eds. *The New Dictionary of Theology.* Wilmington, Del.: Michael Glazier, 1987.

Kreeft, Pete. *Everything You Wanted to Know about Heaven...But Never Dreamed of Asking.* San Francisco: Ignatius Press, 1990.

Küng, Hans. *The Church.* New York: Doubleday, 1967.

———. *Does God Exist?* New York: Random House, 1981.

———. *Eternal Life? Life After Death as a Medical, Philosophical and Theological Problem.* New York: Doubleday, 1984.

Lachenschmid, Robert. "Hell." *Sacramentum Mundi.* New York: Herder and Herder, 1967–69, vol. 3, 7–10.

Lawler, Michael G. *Secular Marriage, Christian Sacrament.* Mystic, Conn.: Twenty-Third Publications, 1985.

Lawler, Ronald, Joseph Boyle, and William May. *Catholic Sexual Ethics.* Huntington, Ind.: Our Sunday Visitor Press, 1985.

Lewis, Theodore J. "Abode of the Dead." *Anchor Dictionary of the Bible.* New York: Doubleday, 1992, vol. 2, 101–5.

Mackin, Theodore. *What Is Marriage?* Mahwah, N.J.: Paulist Press, 1982.

Mac Namara, Vincent. "Approaching Christian Morality." *Contemporary Catholic Theology.* Trowbridge, U.K.: Cromwell Press, 1998, 374–88.

Martos, Joseph. "The Development of the Catholic Sacraments." *Contemporary Catholic Theology.* Trowbridge, U.K.: Cromwell Press, 1998, 453–83.

Mason, Herbert, et al. *Myth, Symbol and Reality.* Notre Dame, Ind.: University of Notre Dame Press, 1980.

Maurer, Christian. "Sundoida, suneidaesis (Conscience)." *Theological Dictionary of the New Testament.* Grand Rapids: Eerdmans, 1964, vol. 7, 889–919.

McBrien, Richard. *The Encyclopedia of Catholicism.* San Francisco: Harper, 1995.

McCarthy, Timothy G. *The Catholic Tradition: Before and After Vatican II.* Chicago: Loyola University Press, 1994.

McCormick, Richard. "Notes on Moral Theology." *Theological Studies* 30 (1969): 635–44.

McDermott, Brian. "The Theology of Original Sin: Recent Developments." *Theological Studies* 38 (1977): 511–24.

———. *Word Become Flesh.* Collegeville, Minn.: Liturgical Press, 1993.

McGoldrick, Terence. "Episcopal Conferences Worldwide on Catholic Social Teaching." *Theological Studies* 59 (1998): 22–50.

Meier, John. *A Marginal Jew.* Vols.1, 2. New York: Doubleday, 1991, 1994.

Mertens, Herman-Emiel. "Nature and Grace in Twentieth-Century Catholic Theology." *Louvain Studies* 16 (1991): 242–62.

Miller, M. *What Are They Saying about Papal Authority?* Mahwah, N.J.: Paulist Press, 1983.

Montague, George T. *Understanding the Bible.* Mahwah, N.J.: Paulist Press, 1997.

Nickelsberg, George W. E. "Eschatology (Early Jewish)." *Anchor Dictionary of the Bible.* New York: Doubleday, 1992, vol. 2, 579–94.

O'Callaghan, Denis F. "What's Special about Christian Morality?" *Contemporary Catholic Theology.* Trowbridge, U.K.: Cromwell Press, 1998, 369–73.

O'Collins, Gerald. "Did Apostolic Continuity Ever Exist? Origins of Apostolic Community in the New Testament." *Louvain Studies* 21(1996): 138–52.

———. *Jesus Risen.* Mahwah, N.J.: Paulist Press, 1987.

O'Collins, Gerald, and Daniel Kendall. *The Bible for Theology.* Mahwah, N.J.: Paulist Press, 1997.

O'Connell, Timothy. "The History of Moral Theology." *Contemporary Catholic Theology.* Trowbridge, U.K.: Cromwell Press, 1998, 389–402.

——. *Principles for a Catholic Morality*. San Francisco: Harper and Row, 1990.

O'Grady, John F. *According to John*. Mahwah, N.J.: Paulist Press, 1999.

——. *Christian Anthropology*. Mahwah, N.J.: Paulist Press, 1976.

——. *Disciples and Leaders*. Mahwah, N.J.: Paulist Press, 1991.

——. *The Four Gospels and the Jesus Tradition*. Mahwah, N.J.: Paulist Press, 1989.

——. *Models of Jesus Revisited*. Mahwah, N.J.: Paulist Press, 1994.

——. *Pillars of Paul's Gospel: Galatians and Romans*. Mahwah, N.J.: Paulist Press, 1992.

——. *The Roman Catholic Church: Its Origin and Nature*. Mahwah, N.J.: Paulist Press, 1997.

Orsy, Ladislas. "Magisterium: Assent and Dissent." *Theological Studies* 48 (1987): 473–97.

——. "Marriage Annulments: An Interview with Ladislas Orsy." *America* 177 (1997): 10–18.

Otten, Willemien. "Augustine on Marriage, Monasticism and the Community of the Church." *Theological Studies* 59 (1998): 385–405.

Padovano, Anthony. "Original Sin and Christian Anthropology." *Catholic Theological Society of America Proceedings* 22 (1967): 93–133.

Paul VI. *Ecclesiam Suam,* August 6,1964.

Pelikan, Jarislav. *Mary through the Centuries*. New Haven: Yale University Press, 1996.

Petersen, David L. "Eschatology (OT)." *Anchor Dictionary of the Bible*. New York: Doubleday, 1992, vol. 2, 575–79.

Phan, Peter C. *Eternity in Time: A Study of Karl Rahner's Eschatology*. Selinsgrove, Pa.: Susquehanna University Press, 1988.

——. *Responses to 101 Questions on Death and Eternal Life*. Mahwah, N.J.: Paulist Press, 1997.

Pope, Stephen J. "The Order of Love and Recent Catholic Ethics: A Constructive Proposal." *Theological Studies* 52 (1991): 255–88.

Prusak, Bernard. "Bodily Resurrection in Catholic Perspectives." *Theological Studies* 61 (2000): 64–105.

Purcell, Michael. "Gloria Dei, Homo Vigilans: Waking Up to Grace in Rahner and Levinas." *Louvain Studies* 21(1996): 229–60.

Quinn, John. The Reform of the Papacy. New York: Crossroad, 1999.

Rahner, Karl. *The Church and the Sacraments*. New York: Herder and Herder, 1963.

———. "The Church's Commission to Bring Salvation and the Humanization of the World." *Theological Investigations*. New York: Seabury, 1976, vol. 14, 295–313.

———. "Concerning the Relationship between Nature and Grace." *Theological Investigations*. London: Darton, Longman and Todd, 1961, vol. 1, 297–318.

———. *The Dynamic Element in the Church*. New York: Herder and Herder, 1964.

———. *Foundations of Christian Faith*. New York: Crossroad, 1978, 111–15.

———. et al. "Grace." *Sacramentum Mundi*. New York: Herder and Herder, vol. 2, 1967–69, 409–27.

———. *Hominization*. New York: Herder and Herder, 1965.

———. "Original Sin." *Sacramentum Mundi*. New York: Herder and Herder, 1967–69, vol.

———, ed. *The Teaching of The Catholic Church*. Cork: Mercier, 1966.

———. *On the Theology of Death*. New York: Herder and Herder, 1961.

———. "The Theology of the Symbol." *Theological Investigations*. London: Darton, Longman and Todd, 1961, vol. 4, 221–52.

Rausch, Thomas. "The Church and the Council." *Contemporary Catholic Theology.* Trowbridge, U.K.: Cromwell Press, 1998, 259–78.

———. "Divisions, Dialogue and the Catholicity of the Church." *America* 180 (January 31, 1998): 20–29.

———. "Sexual Morality and Social Justice." *Contemporary Catholic Theology.* Trowbridge, U.K.: Cromwell Press, 1998, 403–33.

Rebeiro, M. "The Ongoing Debate on Infallibility." *Louvain Studies* 19 (1994): 307–31.

Reddish, Mitchell G. "Heaven." *Anchor Dictionary of the Bible.* New York: Doubleday, 1992, vol. 3, 90–91.

Reese, Thomas. *Inside the Vatican.* Cambridge: Harvard University Press, 1996.

Ricca, Paolo. "New Possibilities for the Papacy." *Theology Digest* 46 (1999): 48–52.

Robinson, John A. T. *Honest to God.* Philadelphia: Westminster, 1963.

Rondet, Henri. "Pelagianism." *Sacramentum Mundi.* New York: Herder and Herder, 1967–69, vol. 4, 383–85.

Roy, Louis, and W. Meissner. "Toward a Psychology of Grace." *Theological Studies* 57 (1996): 322–37.

Sabourin, Leopold. "Original Sin and Freudian Myths." *Biblical Theology Bulletin* 4 (1974): 323–31.

———. "Original Sin Reappraised." *Biblical Theology Bulletin,* 3 (1973): 51–81.

Sachs, John. "Apocatastasis in Patristic Theology." *Theological Studies* 54 (1993): 617–40.

———. "Current Eschatology: Universal Salvation and the Problem of Hell." *Theological Studies* 52 (1991): 227–54.

Schillebeeckx, Edward. *The Church with the Human Face.* New York: Crossroad, 1987.

———. *Jesus: An Experiment in Christology.* New York: Seabury, 1979.

————. *Mary Mother of the Redeemer.* New York: Sheed and Ward, 1964.

Schoonenberg, Piet. *The Christ.* New York: Herder and Herder, 1971.

————. *Man and Sin.* Notre Dame, Ind.: University of Notre Dame Press, 1965.

Schussler-Fiorenza, Francis. *Foundational Theology.* New York: Crossroad, 1985.

Segundo, Juan. *Grace: The Human Condition.* New York: Orbis, 1973.

Shelley, Thomas. "Lessons from Early Maryland Catholics." *America* 174, no. 20 (1996): 9–16.

Shogren, Gary. "Grace." *Anchor Dictionary of the Bible.* New York: Doubleday, 1992, vol. 2, 1086–88.

Smith, C. W. F. "Prayer." *Interpreter's Dictionary of the Bible.* New York: Abingdon, 1962, vol. 3, 857–67.

Strathman, H., and R. Meyer. "Leitourgeo, leitourgia, leitourgos, leitourgikos." *Theological Dictionary of the New Testament.* Grand Rapids: Eerdmans, 1964, vol. 4, 215–31.

Sudbrack, Josef. "Prayer." *Sacramentum Mundi.* New York: Herder and Herder, 1967–69, vol. 5, 74–81.

Sullivan, Francis. "Evaluation and Interpretation of the Documents of Vatican II." *Contemporary Catholic Theology.* Trowbridge, U.K.: Crowell Press, 1998, 335–48.

Tavard, George. *Images of the Christ.* Washington, D.C.: University of America Press, 1982.

Tripole, Martin R. "The American Church in Jeopardy." *America* 175, no. 8 (1996):9–15.

Ullmann, W. "Leo I and the Theme of Papal Primacy." *Journal of Theological Studies* 2 (1960): 32–41.

United States Bishops. *The American Catholic Heritage.* Washington, D.C.: United States Catholic Conference, 1992.

————. *The Catechism of the Catholic Church.* Mahwah, N.J.: Paulist Press, 1994.

Vandervelde, George. "The Grammar of Grace: Karl Rahner as a Watershed in Contemporary Theology." *Theological Studies* 49 (1988): 445–59.

Vogels, Walter. "The Human Person in the Image of God." *Theology Digest* 43 (1996):3–7.

Vorgrimler, Herbert. *Sacramental Theology*. Collegeville, Minn.: Liturgical Press, 1992.

Wall, Robert W. "Conscience." *Anchor Dictionary of the Bible*. New York: Doubleday, 1992, vol.1, 1128–30.

Willis, John R., ed. *The Teachings of the Church Fathers*. New York: Herder and Herder, 1966.

# INDEX

8005

**DATE DUE**